Tradition and Culture in the Millennium

Tribal Colleges and Universities

A volume in
Educational Policy in the 21st Century: Opportunities, Challenges, and Solutions
Bruce Anthony Jones, *Series Editor*

Tradition and Culture in the Millennium

Tribal Colleges and Universities

Edited by

Linda Sue Warner
Haskell Indian Nations University

Gerald E. Gipp
American Indian Higher Education Consortium

INFORMATION AGE PUBLISHING, INC.
Charlotte, NC • www.infoagepub.com

Library of Congress Cataloging-in-Publication Data

Tradition and culture in the millennium : tribal colleges and universities /
edited by Linda Sue Warner, Gerald E. Gipp.
    p. cm. – (Educational policy in the 21st century: oportunities,
challenges, and solutions)
  Includes bibliographical references.
  ISBN 978-1-60752-000-9 (pbk.) – ISBN 978-1-60752-001-6 (hardcover)
1. Indian universities and colleges–United States. 2. Indians of North
America–Education (Higher) I. Warner, Linda Sue, 1948- II. Gipp, Gerald E.

E97.55.T73 2008
378.73089'97–dc22

2008037766

Printed in the United States of America

CONTENTS

PART I

OUR HISTORY

PART II
CULTURE AND TRADITION

PART III
LEADERSHIP

PART IV
OUR FUTURE

LIST OF CONTRIBUTORS

Marjane Ambler   Former Editor, *Tribal College Journal*
　　　　　　　　　　　　of American Indian Higher Education
　　　　　　　　　　　Atlantic City, WY
　　　　　　　　　　　970-946-6133
　　　　　　　　　　　marjane@tribalcollegejournal.org

Phil Baird   Academic Dean
　　　　　　　　　United Tribes Technical College
　　　　　　　　　Bismarck, ND
　　　　　　　　　701-255-3285/701-530-0605
　　　　　　　　　pbaird@uttc.edu

Bay Barnhardt   Center for Cross-Cultural Studies
　　　　　　　　　　University of Alaska–Fairbanks
　　　　　　　　　　907-474-1902/907-474-1957
　　　　　　　　　　ffrjb@uaf.edu

Carrie Billy   Executive Director, AIHEC
　　　　　　　　　Alexandria, VA
　　　　　　　　　703-838-0400/703-838-0388
　　　　　　　　　cbilly@aihec.org

Paul Boyer   President, Boyer & Associates
　　　　　　　　Barto, PA
　　　　　　　　610-845-0686
　　　　　　　　boyerassociates@dejazzd.com

Rosemary Ackley Christensen   Humanistic Studies (First Nations Studies)
　　　　　　　　　　　　　　　University of Wisconsin–Green Bay
　　　　　　　　　　　　　　　920-46502158
　　　　　　　　　　　　　　　christer@uwgb.educ

Tradition and Culture in the Millennium: Tribal Colleges and Universities, pages ix–xi
Copyright © 2009 by Information Age Publishing
ix

Douglas Clement

fedgazette
Federal Reserve Bank of Minneapolis
Minneapolis, MN
612-204-5000
doug.clement@mpls.frs.org

Cheryl Crazybull

President, Northwest Indian College
Bellingham, WA
360-676-2772/360-738-0136

David Gipp

President, United Tribes College
Bismarck, ND
701-255-3285/701-530-0605
dgipp@uttc.edu

Gerald Gipp

Former Executive Director, AIHEC
Alexandria, VA
703-838-0400/703-838-0388
gippg@yahoo.com

Kathryn Harris-Tijerina

External Affairs Representative
University of Phoenix, Santa Fe
Santa Fe, NM
505-474-9680
kathryn.tijerina@phoenix.edu

Al Kuslikis

AIHEC
Alexandria, VA
703-838-0400/703-838-0388
akuslikis@aihec.org

Richard Littlebear

President, Chief Dull Knife College
Lame Deer, MT
406-477-6215/406-477-6219

Cornel Pewewardy

Educational Consultant
Fresno, CA
580-647-0742
cpewewardy@comcast.net

Jim Shanley

President, Fort Peck Community College
Poplar, MT
406-768-6300/406-768-6301
jshanley@fpcc.edu

Wayne Stein

Native American Studies/Higher Education
  Native American Studies
Montana State University
Bozeman, MT
406-994-3883
wstein@montana.educ

John W. Tippeconnic, III

Pennsylvania State University
University Park, PA
814-863-1626/814-865-1480
jwt7@psu.edu

Linda Sue Warner

President, Haskell Indian Nations University
Lawrence, KS
785-749-8497/785-749-8411
lwarner@haskell.edu

Robin Williams

Multicultural Student Center Coordinator
Oklahoma State University
Stillwater, OK
405-744-500
robin.starr.williams@okstate.edu

SERIES FOREWORD

Bruce A. Jones

This volume represents one of the most important contributions to the series. It is groundbreaking in its own right because of the stellar line-up of scholars, including our volume editors, Dr. Linda Sue Warner and Dr. Gerald E. Gipp, who serve as contributors. It is also unique in its own right because there are no comparable volumes in existence.

American Indian history is integral to American history. Yet it is a history that remains largely untold, and what has been told is too often a gross distortion of the truth. In a recent issue of *Diverse: Issues in Higher Education Journal,* Dr. Alyssa Mt. Pleasant, who is an assistant professor of history at Yale University, reported (Diverse, 2007):

> We cannot understand how we got to where we are as a nation without an understanding of American Indian history...Our school system has done a disservice to American citizens by not sharing more information about American Indian history. (p. 8)

Tribal Colleges and Universities play a critical role in the advancement of our understanding of the vital role of American Indian history and culture in the United States as well as American Indian culture and tradition from academic, social and policy advocacy standpoints. Since the establishment of the first Tribal College (Diné College) in 1968, these institutions have served as the model for community-based learning, or what Williams (2007) refers to as a "whole community approach to lifelong learning"

Tradition and Culture in the Millennium: Tribal Colleges and Universities, pages xiii–xiv
Copyright © 2009 by Information Age Publishing
All rights of reproduction in any form reserved.

(p. 41). These approaches to higher education and learning serve to reduce alienation among university community members, such as faculty,
students and staff, and provide the sense of connectedness and cultural
relevancy between people that is sorely missing on other types of campuses
(Braun, 2008). The failure of other campuses to provide this kind of "whole
community approach" may explain, in part, the existence of deplorable
retention and graduation rates among historically disenfranchised groups
(i.e., African American and Latino/a American students) on college campuses across America.

Tribal Colleges and Universities have played an integral role in the growing numbers of students who attain the bachelor's degree. According to
Ward (2002), these colleges and universities experienced a five-fold increase
in student enrollment between 1982 and 1996. As it stands today, approximately 142,800 American Indians and Alaska Natives who are 25 and older
hold a graduate or professional degree (Diverse, 2007), and Tribal Colleges
and Universities have been integral to this graduate level attainment.

With this edited volume, Dr. Linda Sue Warner and Dr. Gerald E. Gipp,
and the invited scholarly contributors, have provided a comprehensive ex-
plication of the phenomenal history of Tribal Colleges and Universities in
the United States and the policy issues and concerns that these colleges and
universities face. I am deeply grateful to Dr. Warner and Dr. Gipp for the
production of the volume and their decision to publish the volume in the
educational policy series.

REFERENCES

Braun, J. (2008). What's in a name? Tribal colleges cultivate students' cultural
identity. *TCJ, Tribal College Journal of American Indian Higher Education, 19*(3),
14–19.

Diverse (2007). Spectrum: Getting to know Alyssa Mt. Pleasant. *Diverse Issues in Higher Education Journal, 24*(21), 8.

Ward, K. (2002). *Tribal colleges.* In J. Forest & K. Kinser (Eds.), *Higher education in the
United States: An encyclopedia* (Vol. 2, M-Z, pp. 680–682). Santa Barbara, CA:
ABC-CLIO, Inc.

Williams, R. B. (2007). Tribal colleges: The model for cultural and community-based
education reform. *Diverse Issues in Higher Education Journal, 24*(21), 41.

CHAPTER 1

INTRODUCTION

Linda Sue Warner
Gerald E. Gipp

This volume of The David C. Anchin Research Center Series on Educational Policy in the 21st century: Opportunities, Challenges, and Solutions focuses on tribal colleges and universities. As a recent member of higher education community, tribal colleges and universities provide a unique perspective on higher education policy. Policies and structures rely increasingly on native culture and traditions and yet provide the framework for academic rigor, collaboration, and relevance.

When we proposed this edition, we worked on the fringes of higher education academe; both of us were program officers at The National Science Foundation. Both of us worked with tribal colleges throughout the United States in the Rural Systemic Initiatives in Alaska, Utah-Colorado-Arizona-New Mexico (UCAN), the Navajo Nation and the High Plains. Since that time, we both have moved into positions which provide a closer perspective; Dr. Gipp is the recent Executive Director of the American Indian Higher Education Consortium (AIHEC). AIHEC serves as the professional organization for the tribal colleges and universities. Dr. Warner currently serves as one of the Council Leaders to the newly approved Comanche Nation College in Oklahoma. We proposed an outline which would allow multiple voices.

Tradition and Culture in the Millennium: Tribal Colleges and Universities, pages 1–3
Copyright © 2009 by Information Age Publishing

We acknowledge the help of writers and researchers with expertise in academic scholarship from mainstream universities and we are particularly pleased to be able to provide perspectives from seven scholars who currently are serving as academic administrators in tribal colleges and universities. The perspectives are divided into four sections: Our History, Culture and Tradition, Leadership, and Our Future.

In the section on *Our History*, David M. Gipp, President of United Technical College retells the history of the tribal college development with emphasis on the organization and growth of the American Indian Higher Education Consosrtium. Having lived the early years as a critical advocate for the legislation, his perspective adds to our understanding of the commitment, energy, and resiliency of our colleagues. Wayne J. Stein began working with tribal colleges while a doctoral student at The Pennsylvania State University. His dissertation on the development of tribal colleges remains a critical piece of scholarship on the movement. Jim Shanley is currently the President of Fort Peck Community College in Montana and his chapter deals with all Montana tribal colleges. Dr. Shanley served as President of AIHEC from 2000 to 2003. As a writer and researcher for the *fedgazette*, a publication of the Federal Reserve Bank of Minneapolis, Douglas Clement adds an outsider's perspective on the economic impact of the tribal colleges. Professor Ray Barnhardt's work with the World Indigenous People's Organization: Education and World Indigenous Higher Education Consortium links both organizations with tribal colleges through native ways of knowing.

In the section on *Culture and Tradition*, Richard Little Bear, current President of Chief Dull Knife College defines culture and indigenous pedagogy as a preface to Rosemary Ackley Christensen's chapter on revitalization of culture in Indian Country. Linda Sue Warner and Kathryn Harris Tijerina examine indigenous governance using examples from The Institute of American Indian Arts in Santa Fe, New Mexico and the Comanche Nation College in Lawton, Oklahoma. John W. Tippeconnic, III traces the development of the first tribal college in Oklahoma, a state with thirty-eight federally recognized tribes and one of the largest Indian populations in the nation. Cornell Pewewardy and Robin Williams provide insight on student achievement in tribal colleges.

In the section on *Leadership*, Gerald E. Gipp sets the philosophical framework for the discussion of indigenous leadership. Phil Baird, academic dean at United Tribes Technical Institute discusses tribal college succession using his work with the W.W. Kellogg Foundation leadership initiative. Marjane Ambler and Paul Boyer highlight the critical role of the *Tribal College Journal* in the history of the tribal college movement.

Carrie Billy, AIHEC Executive Director and Al Kuslikis, AIHEC STEM Development Coordinator examine how the tribal colleges have emerged as technology leaders in Indian Country. The colleges are creating the infrastructure and setting the stage for tribal communities to come online in the global economy as providers of goods and services, not imply consumers, and the colleges are important generators of intellectual capital, not simply its beneficiaries.

In the final section, *Our Future*, Cheryl Crazy Bull, the current President of AIHEC and President of Northwest Community College, provides insights into the strategic directions for the organization. Each chapter is intended to provide future scholars with a broad view of an impressive legacy and it is our honor to share these with you.

PART I

OUR HISTORY

The ground on which we stand is sacred ground.
It is the blood of our ancestors
—Chief Plenty Coups, Crow

CHAPTER 2

THE STORY OF AIHEC

David M. Gipp

IN THE BEGINNING

The history of tribal college and university development is inextricably tied to the American Indian Higher Education Consortium (AIHEC). This history is, like many tribal enterprises, a story. It is a story that links the personal histories of hundreds of individuals.[1] This history of AIHEC is a story of dedication, persistence, and collaboration. The idea of tribal higher education existed before AIHEC, but AIHEC proved to be the catalyst to a dynamic process that has continued to expand these past thirty years.

The American Indian Higher Education Consortium (AIHEC) was officially founded in June 1973. Its beginnings originate from a number of documented meetings held throughout 1972. there are accounts which predate even these meetings. According to Wayne Stein's Tribally Controlled Colleges—Making Good Medicine, delegates from the then established Indian postsecondary schools met in Washington, DC in October 1972. "Institutions represented at the meeting were Hehaka Sapa College/D-Q University, Davis California; Navajo Community College, Many Farms, AZ; Oglala Sioux Community College, Pine Ridge, SD; Sinte Gleska College, Rosebud, SD; Standing Rock Community College, Fort Yates, ND; Turtle Mountain Community College, Belcourt, ND; and three Bureau of Indian affairs institutions: Haskell Junior College, Lawrence, KS; Institute of Amer-

Tradition and Culture in the Millennium: Tribal Colleges and Universities, pages 7–15
Copyright © 2009 by Information Age Publishing

ican Indian Arts, Santa Fe, NM; and Southwest Indian Polytechnic Institute, Albuquerque, NM" (Stein, p. 109).

Stein says the following five common traits found founding member schools together:

1. They were located on or near Indian reservations which were isolated geographically and culturally.
2. The institutions had Indian boards of regents or directors and a majority of the administrators and faculty were Indian.
3. Indian student bodies were small, ranging in numbers from seventy-five to eight hundred.
4. All institutions suffered from chronic underfinancing and funding unpredictability.
5. Student bodies and the Indian communities surrounding the institutions were from the lowest income areas in the United States (One Feather, 1974, p. 72) (Stein, pp. 109–110).

Because of a decision to seek federal funds for a new organization called the American Indian Higher Education Consortium (AIHEC), the already federally funded Indian schools would be initially excluded as members. These were Haskell Indian Junior College, and the Southwest Indian Polytechnic Institute. Of course, these schools were to later become non-voting associate members.

Thus, the first founding members were DQ University, Navajo Community College, Oglala Sioux community College, Sinte Gleska College, Standing Rock Community College, and Turtle Mountain Community College.

NAVAJO COMMUNITY COLLEGE

AIHEC surely would not exist had it not been for the original Navajo community College (NCC) commitment and sponsorship for Title III, Higher Education Act Funds (1973–1975) among the six colleges. Under the authorization of the NCC Board of Regents and the direction of past NCC President Thomas Atcitty, AIHEC received an initial $350,000 in funds to operate and provide services on October 1, 1973. An additional $125,000 was granted for the cooperative education programs among the six colleges (1973–1975). NCC and its Navajo Community College Act of 1968 served as an initial model and legal precedent for the development of the Tribally Controlled community College Act of 1978.

In 1973 the only two schools which were candidates with their respective regional accrediting associations were DQ University and Navajo Community College. In order for consortia to receive funds, a sponsor institution was required which was either accredited or a candidate for accreditation. Thus, NCC was one of the two logical sponsors of the six member colleges.

Atcitty provided a critical link in leadership for AIHEC and future tribal colleges. He served as an executive officer and a president of AIHEC, as well. Atcitty carried the difficult task of enabling cooperation and advocacy for tribal colleges, while at the same time assuring protection and advocacy of the Navajo Community College and the NCC Law. Later, the Navajo Community College Act would become Title II under the Tribally Controlled Community College Act of 1978.

Atcitty, who left NCC in 1976, continued as a leader in education, business and ranching, and as an elected member of the New Mexico State House of Representatives. Current AIHEC presidents and representatives acknowledge the vision and leadership of Thomas Atcitty in the 1970s.

EARLY AIHEC LEADERSHIP

Leadership among the founding members was critical. It remains critical as some of the original challenges remain. The stories of AIHEC's leadership includes individuals who provide a legacy for current leaders. Helen Schierbeck (Lumbee), David Risling (Hoopa) and Gerald One Feather (Oglala Lakota) are among those who made a call for the initial 1972 meetings. Patricia Lock (Standing Rock Sioux) was among the first to be involved with AIHEC developments. Leroy Clifford (Oglala Lakota) and Rose Buffalo-head (Ponca) were among those who discussed concept meetings which led to AIHEC, according to David Risling. Clifford served as an organizational consultant (along with Francis Killer) to develop AIHEC operating policies and later served as executive director beginning in September 1977.

The first six charter member colleges all had strong leaders. Frequently mentioned original representatives of the AIHEC board from the 1972–1973 era include: David Risling, Chairman of the DQ University board; Gerlad One Feather, chair of the Oglala Sioux Community College; Lionel Bordeaux, president of Sinte Gleska College and Board Chair Stanley Red Bird; Thomas Atcitty, then president of Navajo community College, and Guy Gorman, board chair at the time. James Hena frequently represented NCC at early AIHEC meetings as well. Initially, Glen Eagle, Chair of the Board, and Menard White, the first president, presented Standing Rock Community College.

Carol Davis, chair of the Turtle Mountain Community College Board, was an advocate of equity among the colleges; Twila Martin was the first director/president of the Turtle Mountain Community College in 1973. The late Stanley Red Bird (Sicangu Lakota) from Rosebud served as a spiritual leader to the AIHEC delegates. During spirited discussions among AIHEC representatives, Red Bird's wisdom, patience and quiet humor served as a focus for unity. Later—in the mid-1970s—his soft-spoken Lakota words served as the speech which convinced the Black Caucus in the U.S. House of Representatives to support sorely needed legislation for tribal colleges. Red Bird made his presentation in a small ante room of the U.S. Capitol before then New York Congresswoman Shirley Chisholm and members of the Caucus. After listening to the English interpretation, Mrs. Chisholm turned to her peers and gave an eloquent responsorial—a commitment to support AIHEC member college legislation.

Gerald One Feather, the first elected AIHEC board president in 1972 and 1973 was a past chair of his own tribe, the Oglala Lakota Tribe. His experience as an educator and writer, a strong believer in the Lakota traditions and values, and his vision were part of the origins of AIHEC. One Feather continued his work in 1993, lending his skills toward the development of a Lakota language-based university which will include all the dialects from this tribal nation in the United States and Canada.

David Risling was frequently called on as the AIHEC parliamentarian and Indian education historian at early 1970s meetings. Risling was a retied professor form the University of California-Davis. A retrospective of the first twenty years of AIHEC's story includes many other talented, energetic and insightful leaders.[2]

LEGISLATIVE HISTORY

A major culmination of the 1970's era of AIHEC—aside from the growth in numbers—was the passage of the Tribally controlled community College Act of 1978, signed into law by President Jimmy Carter. There were many tasks at hand to see successful passage. Helen Schierbeck wrote the first several paragraphs which represented the first draft college legislation in 1974. The colleges had no recourse, and no support from the various states. Their own tribes, for the most part, provided land or existing facilities and authorized local support for the collection of schools. But, most tribes had no money to support the operating costs for classes or administration.

The first version of the Tribally Controlled community College Act was introduced as Senate Bill 1017. Senator James Abourezek (D, SD); Senators Quentin Burdick (D, ND) and Milton Young (R, ND); Scoop Jackson (D, WA) were among the first sponsors. Other sponsors on the House side included freshman Congressman Mike Bluon (D, IA) and Al Qui (R, MN). The effort was clearly bipartisan. The first hearings were conducted in the Fall, 1975, by the U.S. Senate when Senator James Abourezek introduced the first round of bills to authorize a law for the colleges. This hearing was a milestone for the AIHEC schools. Now there was a record and history before the U.S. Congress.

The hearing was held at the Senate Dirksen Office Building. Among those who testified were Lionel Bordeaux, Phyllis Howard, and Thomas Atcitty. Testifying against the need for a tribal/Indian college law was acting Bureau of Indian Affairs Director David Warren and officials representing the higher education offices from the Department of Health, Education, and Welfare (now Department of Education).

The key justification for the law was:

1. geographic isolation of the tribes;
2. lack of access to mainstream higher education opportunities for tribal populations;
3. cultural disparities with mainstream or non-Indian society;
4. student success was more likely when education is offered locally and in a community setting;
5. local control was an important element in providing higher education to tribal members;
6. there was no available local tax or other state funding to the schools.

Prior to passage, the support of many organizations and individuals, congressmen and others were a requisite. It took some five years to assure successful passage. Organizations such as the National Indian Education Association and the National Congress of American Indians, and individual tribes supported AIHEC and proposed legislation. Debates, pleas, and research were required of those who chose to support the tribal college movement. The Association of American Community and Junior Colleges lent their skills and support to the initial passage.

Congressman Lloyd Meeds, (D, WA) was an initial sponsor of the first versions on the House side. He changed his mind, however, and withdrew his sponsorship when anti-Indian forces in his home state threatened his chances at reelection. The legislation was ready for passage in 1976, but had been delayed due to personal, political vendettas and until major debate as to whether tribal colleges would enhance or take away from tribal governmental authority. This debate culminated at the 1977 annual fall conference of the National Congress of American Indians (NCAI) in Dallas, Texas. The debate was led by AIHEC president Lionel Bordeaux. Patricia Locke (Standing Rock Sioux/White Earth Chippewa) presented views which challenged the colleges and their relationship to tribes. Phillip "Sam" Deloria was asked by NCAI leadership to mediate the debate held at the NCAI education committee. The results included changing the wording from "Indian Controlled Community Colleges" to "Tribally Controlled Community Colleges." In addition, since tribal colleges (and later universities) were to be either chartered or endorsed by prescription of the future law, it was agreed (by the committee) that funding could be made directly to the schools as opposed to requiring that funding had to first be made through the respective sponsor tribal government. In the end, Mr. Deloria declared, as did the National Congress of American Indians, that the colleges enhanced tribal sovereignty.

Later, following this debate in 1977 Forrest Gerard who worked for Senator Jackson (D, WA) convened a meeting at which AIHEC representatives agreed to the terminology and the final drafts on the senate version. There were numerous congressmen, house and senate staff and other individuals who worked diligently in finalizing the version that would ultimately become law in 1978. AACJC's Jack Terrell provided invaluable assistance and advice to AIHEC in securing support for ultimate passage. There are others, as well. It was not until December 1978, however, that the legislation was signed into law by President Jimmy Carter.

Jim Shanley, former president at Standing Rock College and president of Fort Peck Community College was an active proponent of the first passage in 1978. Additionally, he and Gerald Gipp were among those who formed the initial guidelines for what is now the American Indian College Fund. Lionel Bordeaux was perennial with his own personal and professional time and efforts through what is now Sinte Gleska University. He is the longest standing AIHEC college president. He trekked the halls of Congress, many times returning home empty handed—but for a promise to be heard the next time. He continues to return to see the power brokers in Washington, DC.

LEADERSHIP DEVELOPMENT

Ford, Carnegie, and Donner Foundations agreed to provide initial start-up funds in the Spring of 1973 to establish an AIHEC office and for organizational development. The office was housed in Denver, CO. Interim director Gerald Brown was appointed. The Rockefeller Foundation provided AIHEC's first leadership grant through the American Association of Colleges and Junior Colleges which in turn provided interns at Sinte Gleska and Navajo Community College.

The Story

The story of AIHEC and the Tribal Colleges and Universities movement goes on. It does not end. The service, role, and reexamination of purpose, mission, and opportunities for rebuilding and re-empowering tribal nations is constant. Despite funding shortages for Title I colleges under the TCU ACT, there have been other key funding and resources developed along the way. These included:

- The American Indian College Fund created and controlled by the colleges and universities along with private partners in 1987 and which has generated millions of dollars and other resources from the private sector. This includes the largest gift to American Indians for facility development at some $31.0 million from the Eli Lily Corp. and other funders. In addition, the W.K. Kellogg Foundation Higher Education Initiative which resulted in some $27 million granted represented a major inroad to the foundation world in the mid-1990s for the TCUs.
- The White House Initiative on Tribal Colleges and Universities, a Presidential Executive Order which was initially signed by President Bill Clinton and President George W. Bush. This order has resulted in millions of federal dollars being made available from federal agencies to the TCU's along with access to other resources—this despite the difficulty sometimes to garner enough attention from some of the agencies. Currently, it is the only American Indian executive order signed by President Bush (not true now).

Opportunities for special funding have opened up at the Department of Education's Title III Higher Education office, the National Science Foundation, the Department of Commerce, CASA, the Center for Disease Control and other federal agencies.

In 1994 Congress included the U.S. Agricultural legislation the initial Land Grant status for the designated tribal colleges and universities. This authorization opened the doors at the U.S. Department of Agriculture for Equity funding, as well as access to research and extension programs and other infrastructure grants and loans offered by such agencies as Rural Development. There are numerous accounts of this development, which first began when Senator Tom Daschle (D, SD) and Senator Bingaman (D, NM) introduced the first versions in 1991.

DEDICATION AND UNITY

It took a high degree of dedication and unity to create AIHEC by the six original member colleges, as well as the same—and more—to see the successful enactment of the first Tribally Controlled Community College Assistance Act of 1978. Indeed, there are numerous accounts of events and names of individuals who played important roles in the first and later successive revisions and legislative amendments to the law. The law is currently an amendment tied to the Higher Education Act. The law remains an authorization for the schools under the Department of Interior, Bureau of Indian Affairs. It continues the same comprise titles—one for all the qualifying colleges with a formula, and the other title (II) for Diné College which submits a needs-based Diné budget and receives a commensurate budget.

Overall it remains evident that the respective presidents, their local tribal college boards and the tribal governments which were attuned to the schools gave an unlimited amount of time and commitment to passage. Indeed, at least one president paid the price of too much good will toward other schools, resulting in untimely and detrimental criticism from his own tribe and elements of his college and board. In addition, the work—research, advocacy, and lobbying—was done through volunteerism and came almost exclusively from the presidents, community members and other tribal and local leaders. No high paid consultants or lobbying firms did the work. AIHEC and its member schools did not have the money to do so, and thus, had to do the work themselves.

Long days, late nights, intense debates, frequent visits on the Hill by the tribal college leadership were the normal duty of AIHEC advocates. It resulted in a unique law that followed and supports Self-Determination and reinforces tribal sovereignty. This is just the beginning of the story.

NOTES

1. Many individuals contributed time and energy to the early development activities. If an individual has been omitted from this essay, please contact David. Gipp@nttc.edu or ggipp@aihec.org for inclusion in future editions. Please accept the regrets of the editors.
2. Phyllis Howard, Will Wasson, Sarah Hutchison, Robert Harcharek, Steve Baldy, Dwight Billeceaux, John Tippeconnic, Tom Short bull, Larry Belgarde, Charles Foote, Keith Jewett, Carol Juneau, Wilbur Red Tomahawk, Tom LeBlanc, Schuyler Houser, Gwenn Hill, Meril Berg, Peggy Nagel, Margaret Perez, Jim Shanley, Joe Mcdonald and his wife Sherri, Menard White, Gerald Gipp, Dean Jackson, Louis LaRose, Thelma Thomas, Bob Martin, Art McDonald, Janine Pease Windy Boy, Carol Murray, Elgin Bad Wound, Jim Jaum, Ray Howe, Joy Hanley, Carlos Cordero, Lowell Amiotte, Robert Lorence, Jasjit Minhas, David L. Archambault, Ron McNeil, L. Jack Briggs, Jack Terrell, Frances Kelly, A. Gay Kingman, Ernest Boyer, Barbara Bratone, Anne Sward Hanson, Forrest Gerald, Alan Lovesee, Sherman Broadhead, Ella Mae Horse, Robert Sullivan, Tommy Lewis, Jim Tutt, Paul Jones, Carolyn Elgin, Vine Deloria, Jr., Kurt Kicking Bird, Kathryn Harris Tijerina, Walter Mondale, Paul Boyer, John Forkenbrock, Georgianna Tiger, Franklin Williams, Deborah Demarais, Perry G. Horse, W "Buddine" Steward, Larry Dennison, Cletus Satepauhoodle, Barbara Walking Stick, Patricia Grayson, Lilly Saume, Richard Nichols, John Em-

hoolah, Roberta Wilson, Yvonne Choate, Toni Snow, Kathy Nagel, David Lee, Mary Rose Moran, Paige Baker, Jr. Scott Little, John Waubaunsee, Kurt Blue Dog, Jack Barden, Robert Gipp, Margaret Teachout, Roger Condon, Melvin White Eagel, Paul McLaughlin, Marie Marule, Tom Katus. A list such as this is not all inclusive, but is intended to be representational.

REFERENCES

One Feather, Gerald. (1974). See http://www.aihec.org/about/historyMission.cfm. Accessed September 13, 2008.

Stein, W. J. (1992). Tribal coleges: 1968–1998. In K. G. Swisher & J. W. Tippeconnic, (Eds.), *Next steps*. Charleston, WY: ERIC.

CHAPTER 3

TRIBAL COLLEGES AND UNIVERSITITES

Supporting the Revitalization in Indian Country

Wayne J. Stein

INTRODUCTION

In today's modern world not much is taught or remembered about the world of the many American Indian and Alaskan Native (American Indian) tribes before the coming of Europeans, and later the Euro-Americans, to their homelands. Most often overlooked in our modern educational systems are their diverse cultures, languages, and institutions, and the subsequent destruction or near destruction of those same cultures, languages, and institutions. American Indian tribal institutional structures have come under tremendous pressure from east to west and north to south for over a 500-year period after contact with the outsiders that came to their homelands. Their political structures would be eroded until they crumbled, economic structures would be seriously altered, stressed, and ultimately destroyed, the health and spiritual belief systems of the tribes would be challenged, belittled, and suppressed,

Tradition and Culture in the Millennium: Tribal Colleges and Universities, pages 17–34
Copyright © 2009 by Information Age Publishing
17

and ultimately, the education of American Indian children would be taken from the tribes once their other institutions had collapsed.

By 1890, in the United States of America (U.S.), all of the remaining and surviving free American Indian tribes had finally succumbed to total subjugation to the U.S. government. Their institutions such as economics, whether based on farming or hunting, had been seriously compromised or outright destroyed by the United States. Their land bases had been greatly reduced to reservation lands, which they were able to retain through treaty negotiations. The loss of control over their tribal destines has led to a continuous struggle as American Indians endeavor to regain some semblance of control over their world. It was the priority struggle to regain control over the lives and education of their children that American Indians have made some of their most important and early gains. And, it was within the tribal college movements that a number of tribes charted a new and independent way for tribes to truly regain control of the post- secondary education of their people.

Tribal Colleges and Universities (TCUs) founders recognized that they couldn't just prepare tribal students to be proficient in their own cultures but must also prepare them to be proficient in the non-Indian world that surrounds the tribal communities. They had to prepare their students to live productively in two very different worlds. It had to be that way if their peoples were to survive with some semblance of whom they really were and are, and were to protect what they had retained of their homelands and sovereign rights into the twenty-first century (Stein, Shanley, & Sanchez, 2002, pp. 2–3).

The founders of the TCU movement undertook the challenge of entering a system of education in which American Indian people had been denied input and had seen a concentrated effort by the U.S. government to eradicate all things American Indian. To counteract the U.S. government's philosophy, a small group of American Indian educators (and their non-Indian colleagues) chose the relatively new higher education community college model on which to pattern their efforts at regaining control of education for their tribal communities. The founders developed a philosophy in the late 1960s and early 1970s that would support a dual mission, protecting and enhancing their own cultures and at the same time embracing many of the tools of standard post-secondary education. Tribally controlled colleges continue their nearly four-decade effort of exploration, initiative, and development that began in the summer of 1968 with the founding of Navajo Community College in Tsaile, Arizona. TCUs can best be described as small, tenacious institutions of higher education, which serve the smallest and poorest minority group in the United States (American Indians) under difficult and challenging circumstances. TCUs are chronically underfunded, with overworked administrators, faculties, and staffs, and are viewed by the rest of American higher education with some wonder at their ability not only to survive, but also to survive with panache (Stein, 1999, p. 259).

The initiative and development work done by the TCU presidents, Boards of Trustees, and the Native American Higher Education consortium (AIHEC), the national organization of TCUs, has led to many innovative and productive outcomes. Two of these are: (1) The passage of PL. 103-32, the Equity in Education Land Grant Status Act of 1994, which grants land grant status to the TCUs. This important piece of legislation now helps to preserve and expand a solid agriculture, programmatic, and financial base for all TCUs (AIHEC Senate Agricultural-Development Testimony, May 31, 1995); and (2) Executive Orders signed by Presidents Clinton and Bush which are an important reminder that the TCUs are constituents of the entire federal government and are part of a larger federal mandate to American Indian education. President Clinton signed Executive Order No. 13021 on October 19, 1996 which promoted TCUs access to all federal programs and instructed those same agencies to explore ways in which they might assist TCUs carry forward their mandate to serve American Indian communities (Robbins, 2002, p. 88). On July 3, 2002, President Bush signed an executive order creating two powerful new advocacy tools for TCUs, which are the President's Board of Advisers on Tribal Colleges and Universities and the White House Initiative on Tribal Colleges and Universities (Morgan, *The Chronicle of Higher Education Daily News*, 07/08/02). However, to truly understand the nature of the TCU movement one must review its history, which includes the American Indian Higher Education Consortium (AIHEC), key participants within the TCUs, its structures, and its impact on tribal communities.

TCU HISTORY

The movement toward American Indian self-determination in the late 1960s was hastened by many earlier events such as World War II, the Civil Rights Movement, and the political policies and leadership of presidents Kennedy, Johnson, and Nixon. It should however be noted that since the beginning of the 20th century some Americans such as August Breuninger, an American Indian, believed that American Indians should control their own educational institutions and he went on to propose in 1911 to the Bureau of Indian Affairs (BIA) that they have their own university. In the mid-1950s Tribal Chairman Robert Burnette of the Rosebud Sioux (Sicangu Lakota) proposed total tribal control of education on the Rosebud Sioux reservation and the development of a college. In the early 1960s educator Dr. Jack Forbes, an American Indian, pulled together a small but well known group of American Indian leaders and put forward to the U.S. federal government a well-thought out plan to develop and found an American Indian university (Stein et al., 2002, p. 30).

Each of the afore mentioned efforts didn't come to fruition, yet each illustrates the ongoing and continuous desire of American Indian people to regain control of the education of their people.

Nowhere in Indian country were events moving more quickly concerning American Indian control of Indian education than in the Navajo Nation. Political leaders such as Navajo Nation Chairman Raymond Nakai, councilmen Guy Gorman and Allen Yazzie, and educators such as Dr. Ned Hatathli, Dr. Robert Roessel, and Ruth Roessel formed Diné, Inc. in the early 1960s with the intention of taking control of the education of Navajo students. One area of Indian education that the founders of Diné, Inc. desired to impact immediately was that of higher education. The attrition rate of 90% or more experienced by Navajo students attending colleges off the reservation seemed to demand innovative solutions. The participants in Diné, Inc. began exploring the possibility of a community college for the Navajo people. This wasn't a totally new topic of discussion as noted earlier but never before had it been approached with such seriousness. A new era was about to be born in Indian education (G. Gorman, Personal Interview, November 22, 1986).

The 1960s were an era of exciting expansion in higher education with community colleges playing a major role. Toward the end of the decade, a new community college opened its doors each week somewhere in the United States. TCUs were to make their appearance on the United States higher education scene within this historical movement (Ramirez, 1987).

Though there is a visible separation between non-Indian community colleges and tribally controlled colleges, their functions are much more similar than different. Both strive to serve their communities as comprehensive institutions providing programs that respond to community and student needs. Their differences lie in funding sources, jurisdiction, and cultural factors, not educational goals. The founders of the TCUs deliberately chose the community college model of higher education as most appropriate to meet their need. Today, the TCUs and their sister non-Indian institutions generally remain separate in the political and fiscal arenas, but not in spirit. An atmosphere of educational exchange, mutual trust, and mutual appreciation does exist between the two systems (Stein, 1992).

The individuals forming Diné, Inc. during the mid-1960s developed a plan for a Navajo controlled community college and they were able to gain the support of the Navajo Nation, which led to the Navajo Nation founding and chartering Navajo Community College in July of 1968. Though underfunded and forging a completely new path in higher education, Navajo Community College (now called Diné College) survived and succeeded, encouraging more than thirty other tribes to found and charter their own institutions during the '70s, '80s, and '90s of the twentieth century and now into the twenty-first century.

TCUs have made significant progress and gained much sophistication as institutions of higher education since 1968 in their effort to improve the educational opportunities of American Indian people. This was illustrated at a February 1996 gathering of higher education administrators convened in Albuquerque by the W. K. Kellogg Foundation's Native American Higher Education Initiative (NAHEI) Project, where the consensus of the attendees was that everyone in higher education had much to learn from these newest members of the higher education community. The non-TCU administrators of higher education present especially agreed that the TCUs ability to serve students and communities under very difficult circumstances holds many lessons for other higher education institutions. This change in attitude is significant when it is remembered that many non-TCU administrators believed that the TCU movement was just a "flash-in-the-pan" of higher education and was doomed to fail because of the harsh economic status of the American Indian reservations of the early '70s.

TCUs, tribal governments, tribal institutions such as tribal schools and tribal businesses, and local privately owned reservation-based businesses have done much work together to improve the economies of their reservations. The relationships formed among all the above entities are a natural outgrowth of the TCUs, Tribal government's, and privately owned business's desire to facilitate in the prosperity of their community. Most TCU's have as a part of their overall mission statement a statement that says in some form that they will do what they can to promote the economic well being of their community. To carry out this aspect of their mission statement TCUs have over the years done economic assessment studies to determine the needs of the community, designed and implemented specific training programs to meet the job skill requirements of employers of the community, and developed specific programs and/or institutes to explore and develop certain aspects of the community's resources, whether natural or human.

Harsh economic realities such as a 60–80% unemployment rate during the winter months (especially among the northern plains American Indian tribes) illustrate the challenges facing the TCUs on their home reservations. It is because the economic realities on Indian reservations are grounded in endemic poverty that it should be noted just how important TCUs have become to the economic revitalization of their reservations. It becomes even clearer when American Indian reservations with TCUs are compared to those without a TCU. A 1997 study done by David D. Harris of Cornell University asking the question, "Do Colleges Promote Local Economic Development" found statistically important data that reinforces the contention that TCUs have become a significant part of economic development on their reservations when compared to other nearby reservations without TCUs. Mr. Harris's study was done using data between 1980–1990, before any reservation in the study had a hugely successful gaming operation. American

Indian women's income of those living on a reservation with a TCU saw an increase of 4.9% per year, or a 49% increase over a 10-year period; a sizable sum in a small economy such as exists on an Indian reservation. A similar gain in income was noted among Indian males living on a reservation with a TCU. And, overall the poverty rate for families went down on reservations with TCUs; it was noted that families living on a reservation without a TCU were 20% worse-off then their neighbors living on reservations with TCUs. Mr. Harris's study states that TCUs have a significant and positive impact on workers' income and significantly lower poverty levels, both for the individual and families where American Indians live on a reservation that also has a TCU (Harris, 1997, pp. 19–25).

Figure 3.1 outlines the geographic locations of the 33 institutions that are part of the AIHEC.

Figure 3.1 Tribally controlled community colleges.

Today there are thirty-nine TCUs reaching from the State of Washington to the State of Michigan and from the provinces of Saskatchewan and Alberta to the state of Arizona. These colleges serve numerous American Indian tribes, but all adhere to several basic principles in their mission statements. Each has stated that the needs to preserve, enhance, and promote the language and culture of its tribe is central to its existence. The colleges serve their communities as resources to do research on economic development, human resource development, and community organization. Each provides quality academic programs for students seeking two-year degrees for transfer to senior institutions. Wherever possible, each college provides vocational and technical programs that help assure that students can find decent jobs in their communities upon completion of their studies (Boyer, 1989).

In 1972, leaders of the fledgling TCU movement recognized that unity among the small number of TCUs was essential to promoting the TCUs as a viable option for Indian people in higher education and in stifling those who would use tribal differences to create havoc within this unique movement. Thus the American Indian Higher Education Consortium (AIHEC) was born of political necessity (D. Risling, Personal Interview, November 23, 1986).

AMERICAN INDIAN HIGHER EDUCATION CONSORTIUM (AIHEC)

In 1972, the American Indian Higher Education Consortium (AIHEC) was born of political necessity. Leaders of the Tribally Controlled Community College Movement (TCUs) recognized that unity among the small number of TCUs was imperative in promoting TCUs as a viable option for Indian people in higher education and in stifling those who would use tribal differences to create havoc within this unique movement. Gerald One Feather of the Oglala Sioux Community College, David Risling of D-Q University, Pat Locke of the Western Interstate Commission for Higher Education (WICHE) and Helen Schierbeck of the United States Office of Education organized a meeting and convened all those interested in such a national organization (Risling Interview, 1986). At an October 1972 meeting held in Helen Schierbeck's Washington, DC office the decision was reached that the colleges could agree on several principles by which to form a national organization (Risling Interview, 1986; One Feather, 1974). The colleges found they had many unique traits in common that bonded them:

1. They were located on or near Indian reservations that were isolated geographically and culturally.

2. The institutions had Indian Boards of Regents or directors with a majority of Indian administrators and faculty.
3. Indian student bodies were small, serving a student population ranging from seventy-five to eight hundred.
4. They suffered from chronic underfinancing and funding unpredictability, affecting their institutions.
5. Student bodies and the Indian communities surrounding the institutions were demonstrably from the lowest income areas in the United States (One Feather, 1974, p. 72).

Two other important decisions were also reached. First, the colleges called their organization the American Indian Higher Education Consortium. Second, with the encouragement of Helen Schierbeck, the newly founded organization would pursue higher education Title III funds from the federal government to finance its operation. The decision to pursue federal funds from USOE set into motion the rules, which excluded federally controlled institutions from being a part of AIHEC. Shortly after the meeting, it was found that one federal program could not benefit financially from another. The finding excluded Haskell, Southwest Indian Polytechnic Institute, and the Institute of American Indian Art, which are all federally funded postsecondary Indian institutions. Each however remained a part of AIHEC as an associate member until AIHEC no longer had to rely on Title III funds for its survival. Each is now a full member of AIHEC.

AIHEC has continued to fulfill multiple roles as the national representative of the TCUs over the past thirty-plus years of its existence with one subsuming priority over all others. Its most important role has been that of advocates in Washington, DC on behalf of the TCUs, charged with securing and maintaining the principal funding source of the colleges. The TCUs interact with the federal government much as state-supported institutions do with their state governments. AIHEC was able to convince Congress and President Carter in 1978 that funding the TCUs was part of the trust responsibility that the federal government had with American Indian peoples through its treaty agreements and obligations. The Tribally Controlled Community College Act of 1978 has had a stabilizing influence on the tribal college movement. Implementation of the act came at a time in the movement's history when it meant the difference between life and death for a number of the fiscally stressed TCUs. Having said that, it must also be stated that the TCUs have never been fully funded through the Congressional appropriation process at the level ratified by the Act.

Funding of the TCUs

Title I of The Tribal College Act, in F/Y 2000, authorized $6000 per American Indian FTE (full-time equivalent student). Based on the Consumer Price Index over the past several decades, the authorization should now be $8,450 per FTE to have kept pace with inflation. Either figure is considerably higher than the actual amount of $4,447 per FTE appropriated in the 2005 federal budget for funding Title I the Tribal College Act. In addition the several TCUs that aren't covered by Title I had their funding reinstated by Congress after the President's budget had eliminated their funding in his budget (Voorhees, 2003, p.4; Goetz, 2005). To keep the funding of tribal colleges in perspective, these figures need to be compared to the national average for mainstream nonresident community colleges without dormitories. Non-TCU community colleges received approximately $7,000 per FTE from states and local non-Indian communities during the nineteen-nineties according to the National Association of Colleges and Business Officers. TCUs are still $3–4,000 per student and a decade behind in funding then their non-Indian state-supported sister institutions.

The tribal colleges do seek funding vigorously from a number of other sources such as federal agencies (other than the Bureau of Indian Affairs and the Tribally Controlled College Act), philanthropic organizations such as the W. K. Kellogg Foundation and the Bush Foundation, corporate foundations such as U.S. West, and the establishment of their own foundation, the Tribal College Fund. These additional funds are targeted to specific high priority tasks by the individual TCUs as they are identified and funds are secured. Upon occasion AIHEC will also seek grants from these sources to carry out membership wide projects needed by all the TCUs or by the central office of AIHEC itself to improve its infrastructure. The recently completed "Capture the Dream Project," the W. K. Kellogg Foundation's twenty-five million dollar American Indian Higher Education Initiative (NA-HEI), focused on (a) strengthening the faculties and internal programs of TCUs, (b) Cultural, Languages, and Sovereignty Issues of tribal communities, and (c) improving the relationships between TCUs and mainstream institutions of higher education. Often the TCUs must compete on an equal basis against non-TCUs for these funds (Stein, 1999, p. 263).

Students of the TCUs

TCUs continue to focus on their students and the special abilities and needs these students bring to their colleges. Diné College and all subsequent TCUs recognized that mainline institutions of higher education were not adequately serving American Indian students, especially those from geographically isolated reservations. The reasons were many: the social isolation of Indian students on off-reservation campuses, culture shock, and poverty were some of the main contributors to the near 90% attrition rate experienced by Indian students in mainstream colleges and universities for much of the twentieth century.

TCUs students are generally older students; often female single heads of households; many speak English as a second language; have families; are poor; and, prior to their tribal college experience, have found formal educational settings to be a hostile environment for them (Figures 3.2 and 3.3). TCU personnel work closely with each student to help that student design a program that will fit his or her individual needs and abilities.

This concern for the individual student has played an important role in the high retention rates of first-generation American Indian students within the TCUs. Retention rates for the TCUs can be measured in two ways: (1) the conventional fashion which counts as a dropout any student who leaves college before completion of a degree program, in which case

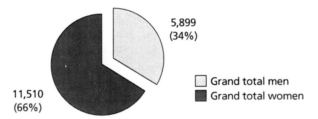

Figure 3.2   Enrollment at TCUs by gender, all undergraduate students.

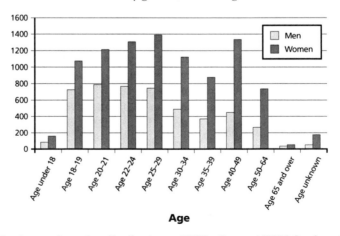

Figure 3.3   Age and gender distribution at TCUs. *Source:* AIHES Student Count (2004).

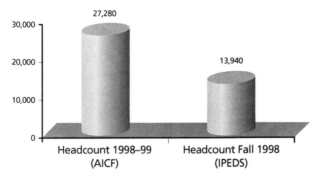

Figure 3.4 Contrasting views of TCU headcount enrollment. *Source:* IPEDS Peer Analysis System and AICF Staff Survey (Voorhees, p. 7, 2003).

TCUs have a retention rate of approximately 45%; (2) or a more accurate method begun by the TCUs which labels as "stop-outs" those who leave and then return within a quarter to continue their studies. By measuring in this fashion, the colleges' retention rate is approximately 75–80%. Students who stop-out generally do so because of financial difficulties or because they have been put on academic probation (A. Three Irons, Personal Interview, December 5, 1991).

In an early AIHEC study conducted in 1990, researchers from the AIHEC gathered data from six of AIHEC's members with large enough enrollments and long enough track records to accurately assess the effectiveness of TCUs in educating their students. The colleges generating the statistically significant data were Oglala Lakota College, Sinte Gleska University (both located in South Dakota), Standing Rock College (now called Sitting Bull College), Turtle Mountain Community College (both in North Dakota), Salish Kootenai College, and Blackfeet Community College (both in Montana). The data collected for the period 1983–1989 revealed that the six colleges graduated 1,575 students with 210 earning one-year vocational certificates, 1,198 earning associate degrees, 158 earning bachelor's degrees, and 9 earning master's degrees (Houser, 1992).

The numbers of Associate and Bachelor degrees earned at TCUs is becoming truly impressive as the TCUs further mature as intuitions of higher education as is illuminated by this data commissioned by the American Indian College Fund (Figures 3.5 and 3.6).

An earlier AIHEC survey taken in 1982 found that Indian students who completed a course of study at a TCU went on to complete a four-year degree program at a senior institution with a 75% greater success rate than Indian students who bypassed TCUs and went directly to four-year institutions. Another interesting set of data from the survey found that about 85% of TCU graduates who stayed on the reservation were employed—this on

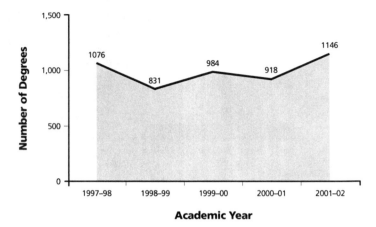

Figure 3.5   Associate degrees awarded at TCUs (1997–98 to 2001–02). *Source:* IPEDS Peer Anaylsis System (Voorhees, p. 9, 2003).

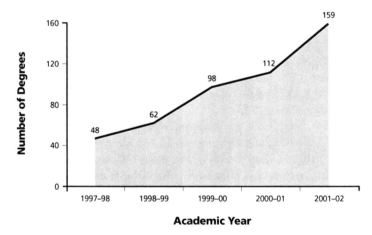

Figure 3.6   Bachelor degrees awarded at TCUs (1997–98 to 2001–02). *Source:* IPEDS Peer Anaylsis System (Voorhees, p. 9, 2003).

American Indian reservations that annually have a 45 to 80% unemployment rate (Stein, 1992).

Governing Boards and Personnel of TCUs

TCUs are a reflection of their communities at the board of trustees level. Boards of trustees that are nearly 100% local American Indian community members control all TCUs. Boards of trustees for TCUs play the important role of buffers between tribal politics and the colleges. They also often act as mediators among policy makers, personnel selections committees, and are the local watchdogs of and for the TCUs. These important responsibilities make TCU boards of trustees unique in Indian country because of the autonomous nature of their authority as granted by the tribal charters founding the TCUs. Most American Indian decision-making entities (including tribal governing councils) must seek the approval of the Secretary of the Interior for their important decisions. Not so the boards of trustees of TCUs. However, board members do keep in mind how their decisions will impact their communities and their long-term relations with their chartering tribal governments.

Administrators and faculty of tribal colleges are a mixture of American Indians and non-Indians with most administrators being American Indian, however, many TCU faculty members are non-Indian. Whatever the race of a TCU administrator or faculty member, the strongest characteristic of members of both groups is dedication to their students and to the missions of their colleges. The accreditation associations evaluating the tribal colleges in almost every report made over the past thirty years have written about the importance of the dedication of TCU administrators and faculty.

Faculty problems experienced by TCUs generally fall into three main areas. First is the difficulty in finding and keeping science and mathematics instructors. Second is the high turnover among faculty who find life on Indian reservations too isolated and culturally different. And third and toughest to solve is the fact that, as the colleges mature and their student populations grow, salaries generally remain low among TCU faculty. The issue of under-funding facing the TCUs is a serious one, but nowhere is it more serious than in recruiting, hiring, and keeping good faculty, administrators, and support staff (Stein, 1999, pp. 262–265).

Curricula of the TCUs

Areas of special concern to TCUs are those of curricula and programs that have been developed in response to tribal community needs. A typical academic and teaching curriculum offered today at a TCU would be two-year Associate of Applied Science degrees, Associate of Arts degrees, and Associate of Science degrees, and one-year certification programs.

Associate of Applied Science degrees combine practical course work and general education designed to prepare students for immediate entry into the world of work the day after graduation. Typical disciplines for Associate of Applied Science degrees would be human services, computer science and information systems, tribal language arts, office technology, tribal administrative practices, and dental assisting technology.

Associate of Arts degrees are academic programs designed to prepare students intending to transfer to a four-year higher education institution to further their education. Typical areas of study include general and/or liberal arts studies, business administration, tribal or Native American studies, psychology, and the social sciences.

Associate of Science degrees are also designed to prepare students wishing to transfer to four-year colleges or universities upon completion of their education at a tribal college. Typical courses of study are business administration, health sciences, environmental science, elementary education, information technology, nursing, and pre-engineering.

One Year Certificate programs are designed by the tribal colleges to respond to local community employment opportunities. Students are prepared within a sharply focused vocational program with much hands-on practical experience. Such programs are as wide-ranging and diverse as the communities and tribal colleges that create them. General office skills, health sciences, hospitality, automotive trade skills, medical office clerk, digital arts and design, and manufacturing assembly are examples of certificate programs from just one tribal college (Bay Mills Community College Catalog, 1994–96; Salish Kootenai College Web Catalog, 2006).

Four tribal colleges, Sinte Gleska University, Oglala Lakota College, Haskell Indian Nations University, and Salish Kootenai College, have instituted targeted four-year baccalaureate programs in human resources, social sciences, business/entrepreneurship, nursing, information technology, environmental science, tribal management, and education (details can be found on each home web site). Sinte Gleska University then led the way for TCUs beyond the baccalaureate by developing and receiving accreditation for the first ever master's degree program in education at a TCU. This achievement marks a major stride by the TCUs in curriculum development, considering the financial hardships and isolation they have endured. This growth is illustrated by the fact that in 1972, Sinte Gleska University, then Sinte Gleska College, offered twenty-two undergraduate and one year certificate courses in a scattering of disciplines from psychology to math with thirteen part-time administrators and faculty making up the college staff (Stein, 1992).

The TCUs have made receiving full accreditation for every tribal college from their respective sanctioning agencies an AIHEC goal. Each college has had to travel the accreditation path alone, but morale and expertise have been liberally shared among AIHEC members to the benefit of all TCUs. This accreditation effort has so far resulted in thirty-four of the thirty-six TCUs gaining full accreditation as institutions of higher education. The two remaining TCUs that have not gained full accreditation are new colleges and are diligently working on gaining candidacy status and full accreditation.

Development Among TCUs

An important effort by the tribal colleges to build a diversified funding base was in began 1989 with the founding of the American Indian College Fund (AICF). AICF has an independent board of directors, yet is answerable to AIHEC as its chartering agent. It has raised significant amounts of funding over the past decade and has allowed the college fund to award each tribal college, from the interest earned on its endowment, a sum for scholarships to benefit their students. Also a major capital fund-raising effort by the Tribal College Fund has committed building funds to be distributed to the TCUs for much needed facilities at each TCU (Robbins, 2002, p. 87). Fitting these additional funding sources into the tribal colleges' fiscal designs allows the colleges to begin examining new programs, new curricula, new forums, new buildings, and additional and advanced degrees for their students and communities.

Another important achievement of the TCUs and AIHEC is the development and publishing of the "The Tribal College Journal." The Journal has led the way in informing the world about the TCU movement, has played a vital role in spreading the news among the TCUs of innovative programs they can share, and has begun an important research agenda on behalf of the TCUs (Robbins, 2002, p. 84).

Sinte Gleska University, Oglala Lakota College, and Salish Kootenai College and Haskell have demonstrated that advanced degrees are possible. Many of the TCUs are now researching advanced curriculum options for their students and are seriously studying the move to become four-year institutions (Stein, 1999, p 266). This latest focus of TCUs, expanding to become four-year colleges, is a strong indication of how optimistic these institutions are about their future growth and development.

The need for bigger and better TCUs is borne out by an important statistic in Indian country: fifty-six percent of the American Indian population of the United States is twenty-four years old or younger. This contrasts with the figure of 36% of the general U.S. population being twenty-four years old or younger (AIHEC testimony to the House Veterans Affairs Committee, April 5, 1995).

TCUs have also reached out to their non-Indian sister institutions of higher education, and have been doing so since the founding of the TCU movement. In the early days of the movement to found TCUs, non-Indian institutions would act as funding conduits to the TCUs who hadn't yet earned accreditation candidacy. Non-Indian institutions also participated in cross-registration of students and lent faculty to the TCUs when requested. This tradition has blossomed into full partnerships between TCUs and four-year mainstream institutions, partnerships which provide to both kinds of institutions innovative science and mathematics opportunities, two-plus-two teacher training programs, distance learning and other tele-communications programs, and effective articulation and course transfer agreements. The land-grant status bestowed on tribally controlled colleges in 1994 by the U.S. federal government has enhanced the opportunities for TCUs and non-Indian institutions to continue their development of mutually beneficial partnerships.

Even with all the positives that have transpired over the past nearly four decades of the TCU movement, there are still major obstacles facing American Indian tribes who desire to develop and found a new TCU. The two major obstacles to such developments are funding for such efforts and maintaining the community will to persevere in the face of all the difficulties that appear when trying to start such institutions. There are only thirty-five (and several in western Canada) TCUs serving their tribes on geographically isolated reservations scattered across the western half of the United States, but there are approximately three hundred tribal nations of American Indians in the United States. This means that only 10%, or so, of all reservations are being served by TCUs. Leaders of the TCU movement believe that there is much room for growth in their movement, if adequate resources and leadership can be further developed in Indian Country.

TCUs and AIHEC have also embarked on an aggressive new outreach program and are now communicating regularly with their sister indigenous-controlled institutions from around the world such as the Maori's Te Wanangaes of New Zealand, and the Saami's college of Norway. At the 2002 World Indigenous Peoples Conference on Education (WIPCE) held on the Nakoda Reserve west of Calgary, Alberta, Canada, the World Indigenous Higher Education consortium (WIHEC) was founded among the indigenous peoples of the world to regain control of the post-secondary education of their peoples. AIHEC is at the forefront of the development of this worldwide organization that will bring the international indigenous institutions together as a research entity, program development entity, and political force in the international affairs of the world.

CONCLUSION

TCU presidents and AIHEC staff are asked frequently by indigenous people from across the country and the world, "How can we start our own college?" This question and the willingness of TCU and AIHEC personnel, friends, and supporters of the TCU movement to help others start their own TCU is the hallmark of a truly serious social and educational movement. The period from 1968 to 2006 has seen the number of tribally controlled colleges and Universities grow from one to nearly forty, a remarkable movement in the history of higher education that has spread to indigenous communities well beyond the borders of United States. The positive impact of TCUs on the American Indian people and communities they serve is phenomenal, particularly as represented by the successes of their students in the workplace and in the mainstream institutions to which they transfer. The impact is even more powerful when one considers the pride and hope the TCUs have spread throughout Indian Country.

The "can do" attitude exhibited by those associated with the TCU movement is an example that many in the United States and around the world can look to for inspiration and encouragement and as a worthy model to emulate. TCUs still have a ways to travel in reaching fiscal security, but relative to that most important higher education goal—staying true to their missions—TCUs have succeeded in abundance (Stein, 1999, p. 268).

REFERENCES

American Indian Higher Education Consortium (AIHEC). (1994, March 8). *Testimony to the Appropriations Subcommittee on Interior.* Washington, DC: U.S. House of Representatives.

American Indian Higher Education Consortium (AIHEC). (1995, May 31). *Testimony to the Senate Agricultural, Rural Development, and Related Agencies Appropriations Sub-Committee.* Washington, DC: U.S. Senate.

American Indian Higher Education Consortium (AIHEC). (1995, April 5). *Testimony to the House Subcommittee on Veterans' Affairs, Housing and Urban Development, and Independent Agencies Appropriations.* Washington, DC: U.S. House of Representatives.

American Indian Higher Education Consortium (AIHEC). (1995). *Tribal colleges* [Informational handout]. Arlington, VA: AIHEC.

American Indian Higher Education Consortium (AIHEC). (2006). *Map of tribal college locations and addresses.* AIHEC Home Page. AIHEC. Alexandria, VA.

Bay Mills Community College. 1994). *1994–1996 Catalog.* Bay Mills, MI.

Boyer, P. (1989). *Tribal colleges.* The Carnegie Foundation. Princeton, NJ: Princeton University Press.

Butler, M. E. (1995, Winter/1996, Spring). Tribally controlled colleges can start a technical career. *Diversity/Careers, 3*(7). Publication for Technical Workforce Diversity. Springfield, NJ: Renaud Communication, Inc.

Goetz, M. (2005, Spring). AIHEC's efforts pay off with 05 funding. *Tribal College Journal, 16*(3). [Mancos, Co.]

Harris, D. D. (1997). *Do colleges promote local economic development?* Ithaca, NY: Cornell University.

Houser, S. (1992). Underfunded miracles: Tribal colleges. *Indian Nations at Risk.* [Paper number 8]. Washington, DC: U.S. Department of Education.

One Feather, G. (1974). American Indian community colleges. In V. Deloria Jr. (Ed.), *Indian education confronts the seventies.* Vol. 5: *Future concerns.* Oglala, SD: American Indian Resource Associates. (ERIC Document Reproduction Service, ED 113 092.)

Ramirez-Shkweqnaabi, B. (1987). *Roles of tribally controlled community college trustees: A comparison of trustees' and presidents' perceptions of trustees' role.* Unpublished dissertation. Madison, WI: University of Wisconsin-Madison.

Robbins, R. L. (2002). *Tribal colleges and universities profiles.* Pablo, MT: Salish Kootenia College.

Salish Kootenai College. (2006). *Web catalog.* http://www.skc.edu/.

Stein, W. J. (1992). *Tribally controlled colleges: Making good medicine.* Vol. 3, *American Indian Studies.* New York: Peter Lang Publishing.

Stein, W. J. (1999). Tribal colleges: 1968–1998. In K. C. Swisher & J. W. Tippeconnic (Eds.), *Next steps.* Charlston, WV: ERIC.

Stein, W. J., Shanley, J., & Sanchez, T. (2002). Founding and governance of TCUs. In M. Benham & W. J. Stein (Eds.), *Renaissance of American Indian higher education.* Mahwah, NJ: Lawrence Erlbaum.

Tiger, G. (1995, March __). *Testimony to Ralph Regula, Chairman of the Subcommittee on Appropriations for Interior and Related Agencies.* Washington, DC: U.S. House of Representatives.

U.S. Department of Education. (1993). *Trends in higher education by racial/ethnic involvement.* Washington, DC: National Center for Educational Statistics.

Voorhees, R. (2003). *Characteristics of tribal college and university faculty.* Littleton, CO: Voorhees Group.

CHAPTER 4

MONTANA TRIBAL COLLEGES

James Shanley

INTRODUCTION

Higher Education in Montana is an important proposition. It is directly connected to the type of life that we hope our children and grandchildren will have in this "Last Best Place." There is common agreement that education of the diverse populations within the State is an important part of that proposition. In Montana, American Indians are the major minority group, making up some 6.2% (62,662 people) of the state's population. American Indians live primarily on seven reservations around the state and represent nine Montana-based tribes. The seven reservations consist of some 8,365,995 acres of land. If natural resources and agriculture are considered, the reservation economies generate around a billion dollars a year, which flow into the general economy of Montana.

Thirty years ago, Montana Indians did not have much success within the state higher education system (or within the K–12 system either). Indian students who attended college found themselves surrounded by strangers who did not understand them, and they often confronted racism, both of the subtle institutional kind and the more overt, "in your face" kind. Montana was not unusual in this regard. This situation for American Indian students was common across the United States. As a result, very few American Indians completed college.

Tradition and Culture in the Millennium: Tribal Colleges and Universities, pages 35–47

In 1968, as a response to this crisis, the tribal college movement started with the development of Navajo Community College. The Navajo (or Diné) Tribe was able to convince the U.S. Congress to pass the Navajo Community College Act. Other Indian tribes became interested in this model and decided to start their own colleges. In 1972, the American Indian Higher Education Consortium was formed. It was made up of five fledging tribal colleges. This central organization allowed the tribal colleges to grow and develop. In 1978, the Tribal College Assistance Act was passed by the US Congress, and in 1994 the tribal colleges were made Land Grant Institutions.

During those early years, the tribal colleges had very little except for the idea and a lot of enthusiasm. Many of the colleges formed extension relationships with nearby mainstream institutions, primarily community colleges. As the colleges developed, they sought accreditation on their own and eventually became self-standing. Now there are 35 tribal colleges and universities across the United States serving more than 30,000 students. There are also several new colleges in the early stages of development.

The development of tribal colleges was often greeted with skepticism from mainstream higher education professionals despite the fact that American Indians were not succeeding in the mainstream colleges and universities. Many people did not understand why American Indians needed their own institutions. There was also a standing belief that colleges needed to be large in order to offer a quality higher-education experience. And many people did not understand the American Indian desire to teach and preserve the history, language and culture of their particular tribal peoples. As the colleges became more successful, these misunderstandings began to disappear and many people became aware of some of the remarkable achievements taking place at tribal institutions.

In Montana, the tribal colleges have been particularly successful. Each of the seven reservations has established and chartered a tribal college and all of these colleges are accredited by the Northwest Commission on Colleges and Universities at the Associate level. Salish Kootenai College is accredited at the four-year level.

It is interesting actually to examine the contributions that Montana Tribal Colleges are making to higher education in the state. During the school year 2003 and 2004, the following is an unduplicated twelve-month head count of Indian students in the state for the 2003–2004 academic year.

	Montana University System	Tribal Colleges	Private Colleges	Total
Head count	1,298	4,972	143	6,413

This means that in 2003–2004, out of the total of 6,413 American Indian university or college students in the state, 77.5% were attending Tribal Colleges. However, this might be slightly misleading, because it is based on headcount rather than FTE and most students in the university system are probably full-time. If the FTE numbers for Tribal Colleges (estimated at 2,119) are used instead of head count, it would still mean that at least 59.5% of all American Indians in the state attended tribal colleges. Although transfers have not been reported by ethnicity, some estimate that up to 50% of all Indians attending Montana private colleges and the MUS institutions have transferred from a tribal college.

In short, the tribal colleges have a tremendous impact on the state in terms of the education of American Indians. In addition, the colleges are not closed institutions. Many non-Indian students who live on or near the reservations attend Montana Tribal Colleges. In 2003–2004, 609 non-Indian students attended tribal colleges.

Above and beyond enrollment statistics, tribal colleges are incredible places to learn and work. Across Montana, the tribal colleges have succeeded in constructing bright new campus buildings. The colleges have developed innovative student services programs, language programs, distance education programs and community service programs. The colleges are connected to and represent both their unique tribal communities, and the region of Montana in which they are located.

Tribal colleges are not funded in the same way that state or private colleges are funded. The majority of land on an Indian Reservation is held in trust by the federal government. This means that a property tax cannot be applied to the trust property. Tribal governments do not have a property tax to use as a revenue base to support government or education projects. Likewise, the tribal governments have never applied an income tax on tribal citizens. The primary reason has been that much of the income for tribal members in the past was generated from trust property and therefore not taxable. The tribal colleges receive the major parts of their general operating budgets from tuition and fees and the Tribal Controlled Colleges and Universities Act (TCCU) which is section IX of the U.S. Higher Education Act. Funding is routed through the Department of Interior and the Bureau of Indian Affairs which distributes the money by formula which provides approximately $4200 for each full-time Indian student. The colleges charge relatively low tuition and fees compared to the Montana University System. Tuition for the seven tribal colleges averages $2410 per student with 87% of all tribal college students receiving financial aid.

The tribal colleges also receive funds on a continuous basis from other areas of the federal government such as the Department of Agriculture through the 1994 Land Grant Colleges Act. In some instances, the colleges have also received financial support from their tribal governments. During the last legislature, the State of Montana provided $1500 a year for each non-Indian student attending tribal colleges. Tribal college students are fairly representative of the communities that the colleges serve. As with other community colleges, the students tend to be older (their average is somewhere in the late 20s). There are more female than male students and many students are married parents or single parents. The tribal colleges have open enrollment policies and try to help anyone that comes through their doors. This means that many students enter with low basic skill levels, particularly in math and writing. The colleges focus on these problems with learning centers and pre-college curriculums. Most of the colleges also serve the reservations as Adult Basic Education and GED Centers as well.

The tribal colleges collectively have no direct relationship to the Montana State University System although all of the tribal colleges have coordinated arrangements and articulation agreements with state (and private) institutions. Montana State University, Bozeman for example, as the Land Grant University for Montana, has coordinated efforts with all of the tribal colleges. Other colleges have other distinct arrangements. For example Salish Kootenai College collaborates with Western Montana College in an Elementary Education program; Fort Peck Community College has education and business degree programs with Rocky Mountain College and Montana State University Northern. The University of Montana works with the colleges in the areas of Pharmacy and Psychology.

The tribal colleges are governed by Boards of Directors, which are selected in different manners as specified in the establishment charters of each college. Some of the Boards are elected; some are appointed by tribal governments. The Boards have typical institutional governance roles. The staff and faculty are hired by the Boards and selected to meet the mission defined for the college. In general, the missions are very similar to mainstream community colleges and offer a blend of general education courses and a variety of vocational/technical courses of study. Qualifications for staff are also similar to mainstream schools with the Master's degree viewed as the minimum requirement for teaching most courses of study. Vocational courses vary in terms of qualifications required. There have not been any comparative studies done looking at staff qualifications between mainstream community colleges and tribal colleges but it appears that tribal colleges have a proportionate number of Ph.D.'s to public institutions (particularly community colleges). Although pay levels tend to be a little lower in some instances, there are some distinct advantages to teaching at tribal colleges. Classes are smaller. There is a lot of individual contract with students. The cost of living in rural areas is lower and reservation areas are multicultural. The reservations also have the beautiful outside environment of rural Montana.

Faculty at other institutions often question "academic standards" at tribal colleges in comparison to mainstream colleges. Although comprehensive studies have never been conducted, anecdotal evidence indicates that standards are equivalent between tribal colleges and mainstream institutions. Fort Peck Community College, for example, has maintained a distance education relationship with Rocky Mountain College in Billings for more than fifteen years. Between 1998 and 2004, 43 students transferred and graduated in Applied Business Management, 40 students graduated in Economics and two in Psychology. Between 2002–2005, 13 students graduated from MSU-N in Elementary Education, one in Biology and two students in Business Technology. Transfer students from FPCC generally compete well with upper division students from those institutions with collective grade point averages more than three points.

The tribal colleges all have a mission to maintain the language, history, culture and world view of their individual tribes. In today's changing world this is perhaps the most challenging part of the mission of tribal colleges. And the colleges have to develop and maintain community involvement in order to be successful in these areas. Tribal colleges therefore work more closely with their governments and their communities than typical mainstream institutions. The tribal colleges often become the focal point for activity for the entire reservation.

In summary, tribal colleges began as unique experiments and have developed into stable, productive institutions that greatly increase the capacity of Montana to provide higher education opportunities for its tribal citizens. The colleges struggle with budgets, staffing and rural locations but are producing students that are empowering their communities. This in turn strengthens the entire state.

Following are descriptions of the Montana tribal colleges that have been compiled by the American Indian Higher Education Consortium.

BLACKFEET COMMUNITY COLLEGE

Blackfeet Community College is located in Browning, Montana on the Blackfeet Indian Reservation, on the eastern side of the Rocky Mountains, where terrain flows from rugged mountaintops to rolling hills of grasslands, to farmland plains. The reservation occupies an area of 1,525,712 acres adjacent to Glacier National Park, Lewis and Clark National Forest, and the province of Alberta, Canada. Browning, the largest community on the reservation, is the trade/service center for the reservation. Smaller communities include Babb, St. Mary, Heart Butte, Blackfoot, Starr School, East Glacier Park, and Seville.

In October 1974, the Blackfeet Tribal Business Council chartered the Blackfeet Community College to provide post-secondary and higher educational services to the residents of the Blackfeet Indian Reservation and Surrounding communities. The impetus for this action grew from early tribal efforts to provide educational opportunities to residents in a physical, climatically and culturally isolated area. In December 1976, extension courses were offered through Flathead Valley Community College. In 1979, BCC became an independent institution. In December 1985, BCC received full accreditation from the Northwest Commission on Schools and Colleges. The college's accreditation was reaffirmed most recently in 2000 after an extensive self-study review process.

Blackfeet Community College has developed objectives and purposes based on goals identified by the Blackfeet Tribe: promote educational opportunities, increase the educational level, advance the knowledge and pride in Blackfeet heritage; improve tribal management; provide community facilities for advancement in education and other tribal institutions; and provide cultural and recreational opportunities for the residents.

Blackfeet Community College enrolls an average of 650 students annually. Students range in age from 18 to 75 and come from Browning and surrounding communities on and off the reservation. Through the website, the college has the potential to reach many more individuals outside of their program area.

The Blackfeet Community College campus is located on the south end of Browning, just off Highway 2 and 89. Thirteen buildings house the administration, Student Services, Academic Affairs, and Vocational Education Departments, as well as the library, classrooms, and various programs.

The Blackfeet Community College staff and faculty employees are approximately 90% Blackfeet enrolled tribal members or descendants.

Degrees Offered

Associate of Arts: Blackfeet Studies, Blackfeet Language Studies, Early Childhood Education, Elementary Education, General Studies: Library Studies, and Human Services.

Associate of Science: Business Management, Computer Information Systems, General Studies: Math and Science, and Pre-Nursing/Allied Health.

Associate of Applied Science: Construction Technology, Hospitality Operations Management, Natural Resource Management, Network Technician Support, Office Administration, and Small Business Management.

Certificates: Building Trades, Heavy Equipment Operations, and Hospitality Operations Management.

CHIEF DULL KNIFE COLLEGE (CDKC)

Chartered in 1975 by the northern Cheyenne Tribal Council, Chief Dull Knife (CDKC) is located on the Northern Cheyenne Indian Reservation in Southeastern Montana. CDKC enjoys full transfer agreements with the colleges and universities of the Montana University System, other Tribal Colleges within Montana, and colleges and universities in both North and South Dakota.

Formerly called Dull Knife Memorial College, CDKC was renamed in 2001 to honor one of the Northern Cheyenne's most respected historical leaders, Chief Dull Knife, also known as Chief Morning Star. Chief Dull Knife, fighting with great courage and against overwhelming odds, led his band of Northern Cheyenne back to their homeland to maintain the sovereignty of the Northern Cheyenne tribe. Reflecting Chief Dull Knife's determination, the College's primary mission is to provide educational and cultural leadership to its constituents.

Accredited by the Northwest Commission on Colleges and Universities, the original curriculum was designed to train students for mining jobs near the reservation. The college eventually expanded its vocational classes and in 1978, broadened its curriculum to include post-secondary academic offerings. In the future, the CDKC would like to expand its degree programs to include information technology, paralegal and cultural studies. In academic year 2003–2004, CDKC awarded 30 associate degrees and three certificates.

The campus' most interesting structure, the John Woodenlegs Memorial Library, is a state-of-the-art library named after the college's founder. In 2003, CDKC renovated their maintenance facility to expand the college's extension programs and classes. In addition, the college completed a straw bale house to accommodate their GED/Adult Literacy program

Degrees Offered

Associate of Arts: General Studies: Agriculture, Allied Health, Biology/Pre-med, Business, Information Systems, Early Childhood Education, Native American Studies and Special Education Program.

Associate of Applied Sciences: Business Management and Office Management.

Certificate: Police Science and Pre-Apprenticeship Carpentry.

FORT BELKNAP COLLEGE (FBC)

Located on the sparsely populated plains of north-central Montana, Fort Belknap College (FBC) provides a center of excellence in higher education for the Assiniboine and Gros Ventre people. The college provides high quality, post-secondary education for community members who would otherwise have to travel long distances to pursue higher learning. In 1984, the Fort Belknap Indian Community Council chartered FBC as a long-term educational strategy to fight against generations of economic depression. The college received accreditation as an institution of higher education in 1993.

FBC's mission is to provide quality post-secondary education for residents of the Fort Belknap Indian Reservation and surrounding communities. The college offers learning opportunities to maintain the cultural integrity of the Gros Ventre and Assiniboine Tribes as well as to succeed in today's technological society. Students can choose from 14 degree programs: two associate of science 12 associate of arts. The academic programs are business, entrepreneurship, health administration, business technology, early childhood education, elementary education, human services, liberal arts, American Indian studies, computer information systems, pre-psychology, allied health, natural resources, and hazardous materials technology.

Fort Belknap College offers a wide range of community programs and services. The college operates a public radio station (KGVA) that serves as audience of approximately 25,000 people spread out over thousands of square miles of north-central Montana. Listeners represent four American Indian tribes, five Hutterite colonies, local ranchers and farmers, and small town residents.

FBC is the home of the White Clay (Gros Ventre) Immersion School, located in the college's new Sitting High Cultural Center. Second- and third-grade students at the immersion school receive instruction in the Gros Ventre language while learning a full range of academic subjects.

FBC's Extension Program works to reduce the incidence of diet-related illnesses such as diabetes, obesity, and other chronic health problems through healthy lifestyle education. In 2003, more than 225 adults and children participated in tours of the college's community greenhouse and demonstration garden. Participants taste-tested fresh garden produce and learned how to grow and cook vegetables for their own household meals.

The college engages in scientific research that addresses identified community needs. Current faculty-student research projects are studying questions related to: (1) the impacts of mining activities on soil microbes, (2) the incidence of West Nile Virus in the area's mosquito population, and (3) the development of cropping systems to improve forage crop yields and increase farm/ranch income.

FORT PECK COMMUNITY COLLEGE (FPCC)

Fort Peck Community College (FPCC) is located in the northeast corner of Montana on the Fort Peck Indian Reservation, which encompasses more than two million acres. Chartered by the Fort Peck Assiniboine and Sioux Tribes in 1978, its mission, in part, is to serve the people of the Fort Peck Indian reservation through educational opportunities and community service. The philosophy of FPCC is based on the belief that the opportunity for higher education must be provided locally on the reservation. Many of the tribal members choose not to leave their home communities; thus, it is essential post-secondary education opportunities are made readily accessible to them. One of the primary roles of FPCC is to preserve the Assiniboine and Sioux cultures, languages, histories, and beliefs and to perpetuate them between its students and community members.

FPCC provides a variety of programs to meet the career goals of its students and the training needs of the reservation. As a two-year degree granting community college, it offers associate degrees and certificates in 38 fields of study such as automotive technology, building trades, hazardous materials waste technology, business administration, teacher education, Native American studies, surveying, and science-biomedical. In collaboration with A&S Industries, a new degree program in machine technology was established. Moreover, FPCC has several memorandums of agreement with four-year degree granting institutions that allow students to earn bachelor degrees in elementary education, business education, and applied management.

FPCC recently built a campus in Wolf Point to address the higher education needs of the western part of the reservation. The College's student services department operates a student daycare center near the Poplar campus. Student services include financial aid, assessment and placement testing, orientation, retention services, admission/placement, student organizations and activities, alumni relations and athletics.

FPCC has a strong and innovative community focus that has identified the institution as an economic and social community development center for the Fort Peck Indian Reservation and northeastern Montana. Within the Department of Community Services there are five divisions: Agriculture, Health and Wellness, K–12 Outreach, Youth Leadership and Economic and Social Development. The agriculture division is a leader in Global Agriculture: it has made strong international connections with India through international staff exchanges, participates in regional pulse crop farming, oversees an 800-cow/calf operation, and a 47,000 acre Tribal Ranch. FPCC's wellness division has two community wellness centers in Wolf Point and the main campus in Poplar. Community Health issues such as diabetes, obesity, and prevention are major concerns for the college. FPCC has as one of its goals the strengthening of local public schools through the development of K–12 programming. K–12 outreach programs include Gear Up, Rural Systemic Initiative, Diabetes Education in Tribal Schools, college preparation for high school juniors and seniors, Even Start Family Literacy. Youth Leadership has been an area of emphasis through the development of 4-H groups, violence prevention, and community beautification. Economic and Social development is strengthened through grant writing seminars, economic development summits, a Community Business Assistance Center, a micro-loan, Americorp and the administration of an Enterprise Community.

FPCC is accredited by the Northwest Commission on Schools and Colleges and has an average enrollment of 430 students.

LITTLE BIG HORN COLLEGE (LBHC)

Little Big Horn College is a public two-year community college chartered by the Crow Tribe of Indians in 1980. The college is located in the town of Crow Agency, Montana, the heart of the Crow Indian Reservation in south central Montana. Little Big Horn College was granted accreditation status in 1990 by The Northwest Association of Schools and of Colleges and Universities. Accreditation was reaffirmed in 2001 by the Northwest Commission on Colleges and Universities. In 1994, Little Big Horn College was granted Land-Grant College status.

Eight associate of arts degrees and two associate of science degrees are offered. The courses of study are directed to the economic and job opportunities in the Crow Indian Reservation area. The student body comprises Crow tribal members (95%), members of American Indian tribes from around the Intermountain west (3%), and residents of the Big Horn County area (2%). Little Big Horn College has an open admission policy and as a public institution welcomes enrollment from any adult 18 years of age with a high school diploma or GED.

LBHC students commute to campus and are responsible to family, especially as parents. Three-fourths of the students speak the Crow Language as their first language. As a result, the college student services and business office functions are conducted in the Crow Language. College Board of Trustee meetings are also conducted in the Crow Language. The College campus is located in the town of Crow Agency on the banks of the Little Big Horn River, adjacent to the Crow Indian Agency of the Bureau of Indian Affairs and Crow Tribal Housing Authority headquarters. The college facility has 35,000 square feet of educational space situated on two acres of wooded river valley.

Little Big Horn College has recently built and moved into two new campus buildings. The first building to be completed was The Cultural Learning Lodge, which is utilized for academic and public activities. In 2004 Little Big Horn College also saw the completion of the Seven Stars Learning Center, which is a two-story classroom and office building with 22,870 square feet.

SALISH KOOTENAI COLLEGE (SKC)

Salish Kootenai College is a tribally controlled college charted in 1977 under the sovereign governmental authority of the Confederated Salish and Kootenai Tribes. It is accredited as a four-year institution of higher education by the Northwest Commission on Colleges and Universities. Since its inception, under the leadership of founding President Dr. Joseph McDonald, the College has conferred 2,370 bachelors and associate degrees and certificates of completion.

The College started in 1977 in an abandoned public school building in Pablo. The campus was moved several times prior to locating to its present site east of Pablo, 10 miles south of the magnificent Flathead Lake. Today, SKC is blessed with 22 major modern buildings occupying nearly 150,000 square feet, situated on 128 contiguous acres. The value of the property exceeds $17 million. The College is always proud to point out that its Building Trades students contributed substantially to the construction of many of these beautiful, environmentally harmonious buildings, earning course and certificate credit while gaining practical experience.

During Fall Quarter 2004, 1,150 students were enrolled at SKC, 60% of whom were female and 40% were male. Native American students comprised 76% of the student body, representing 68 tribes from 19 states. During 2004–05, the College employed 56 full-time and 28 part-time instructors, and graduated 192 students with the class of 2005.

Degrees Offered

Bachelors Degrees: Business/Entrepreneurship, Environmental Science, Forestry, Information Technology, Nursing and Social Work.

Associate Degrees: Business Management, Dental Assisting Technology, Early Childhood Education, Environmental Science, Environmental Science/Forestry, General Studies: Elementary Education Emphasis, General Science Emphasis, Liberal Arts, Pre-engineering Emphasis and Psychology Emphasis, Information Technology, Native American Studies, Nursing and Office Professions.

Certificates of Completion: Dental Assisting Technology, Digital Arts and Design, Highway Construction Training, Medical Office Clerk, Native American Studies, Nursing and Office Professions.

Students Services: Salish Kootenai College offers comprehensive support services, including recruitment, financial aid, personal and career counseling and job placement, academic skills labs, tutoring, cafeteria, housing, and a new fitness center.

Job Placement and Beginning Wages: The College's annual placement rate (postsecondary transfers and job) averages 84%. The job placement rate alone averages 77%. During the five-year period 1999–2003:

- 441 graduates were placed in jobs with an average salary of $26,461.32, or combined beginning wages totaling $11,669,446, or an annual average of $2,333,889.
- An economic turnover of four times this combined amount totals $46,677,784, while a turnover of seven times totals $81,686,122.
- Beginning wages of Native American students during this period totaled $6,947,066. A turnover of four times this amount totals $27,788,264, while a turnover of seven times totals $48,629,462.
- These salaries and wages and local area turnover contributes significantly to tribal, local and state economics, including federal, state, and local tax coffers.

STONE CHILD COLLEGE (SCC)

Stone Child College is a tribally controlled community college of the Chippewa-Cree Tribe. Chartered in 1984 by the Chippewa Cree Business Committee, Stone Child College (SCC) was established to preserve and maintain and Chippewa Cree culture and to better educate its tribal members.

Accredited by the Commission of the Northwest Association of Schools and Colleges, SCC offers programs of study that lead to Associate of Arts and Associate of Science Degrees and certificates of completion. These courses are listed in the Accredited Institutions of Higher Education, published by the American Council on Education for the Council on Post-secondary Accreditation.

SCC enrolls predominantly American Indian Students with the current enrollment reflecting 98% American Indian descent. Based upon the U.S. Department of Education's definitions of special population, 90% of the College's student population is considered low income, 81% are first generation College students, 77% are of limited English proficiency, and 2% are disabled.

The Chippewa-Cree families of the Rocky Boy Reservation in north-central Montana have had to learn to help themselves. With a high unemployment rate and low per capita annual income and accelerating student enrollment numbers and a tribal population expected to double by the year 2005, SCC completed a new campus consisting of three brand-new buildings: the Cultural Archives Building; Sitting Old Woman Center (the community/library building), and Kennewash Hall (the academic building). The campus held its Grand Opening and Dedication on July 31, 2003. In addition, SCC offers community outreach programs, which include cooking for diabetes, food safety, community gardening, animal and range management, youth development, home based enterprises and agricultural marketing.[1]

NOTE

1. The statistical information in the article has been obtained from the American Indian Measures For Success (AIMS) Data Collection Project conducted by the American Indian Higher Education Consortium and funded by the Lumina Foundation. Montana University System information was obtained from the 2005 Montana University System Diversity Reports.

CHAPTER 5

GROWTH BY DEGREES

Douglas Clement

INTRODUCTION

In American Indian cultures, few things are revered as highly as land. Land's value has deep historic and religious roots; its significance is impossible to overstate. But as important as land is, most researchers would suggest that education is even more crucial to the economic future of Indian Country.

"Economic history tells us that land as the source of wealth and growth was important in the 19th century, but it's really human capital, not land capital, that's the source of growth and wealth today," said Ralph J. Brown, an economist at the University of South Dakota, Vermillion, who has studied the economic development of Indian reservations in his state. "More investment is needed in the area of human capital, and we see recognition of that in those reservations with colleges."

Indeed, the growth of tribal colleges and universities over recent decades has been nearly as phenomenal—if far less heralded—than the growth of Indian casinos. The first tribal college, now called Diné College, was formed in 1968 by the Navajo Nation in Arizona. Now there are 35 tribal colleges in the United States, one in Canada, and 22 of them are located in the Ninth District of the Federal Reserve System—seven in Montana, five in North Dakota, four in South Dakota, three in Minnesota, one in Wisconsin and another two in the Upper Peninsula of Michigan. Nationwide as of Fall

Tradition and Culture in the Millennium: Tribal Colleges and Universities, pages 49–60
Copyright © 2009 by Information Age Publishing
49

2002, they had an enrollment of nearly 16,000 students (more than 10,000 in district colleges).

From the start, these schools have operated on shoestring budgets. "The typical campus is a hodgepodge of renovated buildings and doublewide trailers," according to a 2004 article in *Native Peoples* magazine. While some schools are beginning to build well-equipped facilities, most rely on rehabbed structures. The main building of Bay Mills Community College in Brimley, Michigan, for instance, is an old fish-processing facility. For many years, Little Big Horn College's chemistry lab in Crow Agency, Montana, was a defunct sewage treatment plant. Still, for many Indian students, tribal colleges provide an essential bridge from high school to a four-year college.

While the primary mission of tribal colleges is education and cultural preservation, tribal college officials and researchers in the field contend that tribal colleges also make significant contributions to the economic development of their reservations and local communities. At the same time, however, these colleges face chronic funding shortages, which exacerbate ongoing problems in retaining students and faculty.

Still, the commitment of both Indian and non-Indian leadership to their existence suggests that tribal colleges will continue to grow, and even thrive, in coming years. "These colleges are underfunded [and] overworked," wrote Wayne Stein, professor of American Indian Studies at Montana State University, Bozeman, a few years ago. But, he added, they are also "viewed by the rest of American higher education with some wonder at their ability not only to survive, but to survive with panache."

ECONOMIC ENGINES

Tribal colleges were begun in response to the poor educational outcomes experienced by many Indians attending mainstream colleges and also in recognition of the importance of sustaining traditional cultural values. But in addition, tribal colleges have been looked to as economic engines, a means of generating improved living standards for individual Indians and their communities, in both the short and long term.

That they do so for individuals are confirmed by research showing better employment outcomes among tribal college graduates than nongraduates, in line with research on economic returns to higher education among the general population. A 1997 survey of graduates from Stone Child College on the Rocky Boy Reservation in Montana found that 15% of graduates were unemployed, compared to an overall unemployment rate of 72% on the reservation. A similar study of Turtle Mountain Community College

(ND) graduates in 1995 found an unemployment rate of 13% for graduates, less than a third of that reservation's 45% unemployment rate.

While hard data on the broader economic impact of tribal colleges is scarce, evidence suggests a positive effect, both directly through expenditures and indirectly through support of business infrastructure and development of workforce quality—the hard-to-measure "human capital" to which Brown refers.

"Tribal colleges are becoming a vital tool for promoting Native entrepreneurship," wrote Brad Bly, in a 2005 issue of the Minneapolis Fed's *Community Dividend,* "through their curricula, community services and business development initiatives." In addition, tribal colleges increase skill levels and foster employment in local economies, according to a 2000 report by the American Indian Higher Education Consortium (AIHEC) and the Institute for Higher Education Policy, which argued that "tribal Colleges are vital components of the process of building a foundation for future growth on Indian reservations and are strongly contributing to the economies of this nation's most disadvantaged areas."

As detailed by Bly, many tribal colleges sponsor chapters of American Indian Business Leaders, a national student group that serves as a support network for young business students. Almost all campuses offer business programs with specific training for entrepreneurs, and business is the most popular major among students at the nation's 35 tribal colleges.

JOBS ON THE RESERVATION

Moreover, almost all tribal colleges are located on reservations and are often the largest local employer, with all that entails. While jobs would be created wherever such expenditures were made—on Indian reservations or Madison Avenue—it's undeniable that the reservations themselves benefit from the boost tribal colleges give to their local economies, and the boost can be considerable in areas so burdened by poverty.

"We are one of the primary economic anchors of the region," noted William LoneFight, in an e-mail. LoneFight, the president of Sisseton Wahpeton College, located on Lake Traverse Reservation, near Sisseton, SD, estimated that his school has "a direct impact of [approximately] 5 million dollars annually." Other college administrators emphasized their local employment effect. "We've been referred to as the hub of the community," said Carole Falcon-Chandler, president of Fort Belknap Community College in Harlem, Montana, "because we employ tribal members mostly."

Many tribal college programs are geared toward meeting needs in their local and regional economy. FBCC has responded to community economic needs by starting a small business center that offers entrepreneur and computer skills training for local citizens. "We've gone into the community and asked them what they think is needed," said Falcon-Chandler. "That's where we learned that they want these programs."

Steve Goulding, business manager at Lac Courte Oreilles Ojibwa Community College in Hayward, Wisconsin, said the school conducts surveys "on a regular basis to see what kind of training is needed. We go out and talk to local employers, and we try to find out what kind of training they need for their employees. And then we try to see what we can do with our curriculum." The school has started a nurse's aide program in response to employer needs surveys, in addition to programs in tourism and hospitality. "Those are big industries in our area."

Fort Peck Community College in Poplar, Montana, has also surveyed local businesses to learn employer needs and design curricula accordingly. Salish Kootenai College in Pablo, Montana, on the Flathead Reservation, was one of the first in the state to develop forestry courses to train students for jobs in that local industry. A few years after the Oglala Lakota College began graduating students from its nursing program, 50% of the nurses at the local Indian Health Services clinic were American Indian, up from a small fraction before the program began.

Other tribal schools have begun their own businesses. Sitting Bull College in Fort Yates, N.D., started the SBC Construction company in 1997 "to provide employment experience opportunities for graduates of the Building Trades Program," according to the college Web site. To date, SBC Construction has built 21 houses and eight office buildings—a slow pace by commercial standards—but the firm plans to build 18 residential units per year over the next few years as the college expands to a new campus. With experience under their belts, says the college Web site, the SBC Construction employees will have "better job opportunities than they would have as program graduates with no experience."

STOPPING OUT

But how many will actually graduate? Tribal colleges were created because of the difficulty Indian students were having in mainstream colleges. Underprepared, culturally disoriented, far from family, Indian students in traditional colleges often dropped out before completing four-year degrees.

"When you look at the history of mainstream institutions, they were retaining about 10% of Native American students in the 1960s," said Iris PrettyPaint, co-director of Research Opportunities in Science for Native Americans, at the University of Montana, Missoula. While retention rates have improved somewhat at conventional four-year colleges, she said, the prevalence of dropping out motivated Indian educators to try a different path. "One of the reasons tribal colleges originated is because of frustration with such low retention."

Tribal colleges are close to home and provide culturally sensitive environments (offering courses in Indian languages and culture, for example), factors that should improve graduation rates. But retention of students has remained a challenge, even at tribal schools. "We have all struggled with retention, and we're still struggling," observed Fort Belknap's Falcon-Chandler. To some degree, it's a question of poor student preparation prior to attending tribal college. Recent research by AIHEC indicates that 70% of tribal college students need remedial math, for example. But Falcon-Chandler suggests that broader issues play a part. "There's all kinds of problems. Transportation. Young people who have babies. We've been addressing drug and alcohol problems. All of it has an impact."

"Retention rates are problematic for most tribal colleges," concurred Betty Red Leaf, academic dean at Little Priest Tribal College in Winnebago, Nebraska. The most common factors for attrition, said Red Leaf, who has studied college persistence among American Indians at tribal colleges, are family obligations, lack of financial support and employment. "It's because of the makeup of our student population," she said. "A lot of them are single head of households with child care, work and family responsibilities, so it takes them longer to get through. Sometimes they have to stop out."

"Stopping out" is not a euphemism for dropping out, but rather a term to describe what many Indian students see as a necessary phase in attending college. If family needs arise, if financial burdens are too great, then college will have to wait until the immediate situation is resolved. The student may well return to college, but degree completion will often be substantially delayed while the student stops out to attend to other pressing concerns.

FAMILY EDUCATION

While no one has discovered exactly how to ensure high rates of completion at tribal colleges, research by PrettyPaint and others suggests that emphasis on strong college support systems that resemble families in their cohesiveness can increase successful outcomes.

"A close examination of the retention factors for Indian students reveals that replicating the extended family structure within the college culture enhances the student's sense of belonging and leads to higher retention rates," wrote PrettyPaint in a 2002 article in the *Journal of American Indian Education,* coauthored with Richard DeCelles. "Establishing and maintaining a sense of 'family,' both at home and at college, fortifies American Indian students' academic persistence."

PrettyPaint's research on student/family support programs at four trib-al colleges in Montana—Fort Peck, Salish Kootenai, Blackfeet and Stone Child—found that such programs significantly improve college comple-tion. At Fork Peck, for example, "we were able to track an increase in stu-dent retention from 54% to 81%" between 1997 and 2001, she said.

Falcon-Chandler speaks of a similar initiative at Fort Belknap. Last year, says Falcon-Chandler, the college graduated only 15 students, the smallest number in recent history. "We really had a bad year, and we don't know why," she said. This year, with a special grant, the school hired a retention counselor who has organized a committee to meet monthly with students to review progress and deal with problems. "We have 30 potential graduates, so we're [trying] to make sure that they do graduate," explained Falcon-Chandler. The counselor and his committee members are "checking in on these students every month to make sure that they're in the right place. So we're gearing up for this year. We're watching them [carefully]. They don't get this in the mainstream [colleges]; they don't get that monitoring."

TURNOVER

Retention isn't a problem only among students. Tribal colleges have also had periodic bouts of difficulty in retaining faculty and administration. Part of it is politics; though the colleges are nominally independent of tribal gov-ernment, they can't help but be influenced by it. A recent editorial in the Grand Forks Herald headlined "Tribal Colleges Must Rise Above Politics" noted that in North Dakota, "a number of college presidents and adminis-trators . . . made institutions out of nothing but were not supported by their tribal councils."

But economics also plays a powerful role. Tribal college pay scales are well below those at four-year colleges and even two-year community col-leges to which they're often compared. According to the National Center for Education Statistics, the average 2003–04 salaries of full-time faculty on 9/10-month contracts were $36,434 at tribal colleges, but $52,819 at associ-ate's colleges (schools, like community colleges, which confer associate's degrees rather than baccalaureates) and $61,560 at liberal arts colleges.

"There are seven tribal colleges right now that are looking for a college president, and right now we're operating without a college president," said Goulding, of Lac Courte Oreilles Ojibwa Community College. "It's quite a pain." They've had several good candidates apply for the position, he said, but can't afford them. "We've had problems adjusting our budget to pay what these people are actually worth. . . . That's been a stopping block for us."

Pay is an issue for staff and faculty as well as top leadership, says Gould-ing. "Well, for example, I've been the business manager here for six years, and yesterday I interviewed for a job, a county job, that would pay about $20,000 a year more," he said. "So that's what we have, a problem with funding ... to retain some of the experienced and good people."

Faculty instability has clear implications for students: If faculty members leave, the "family-like atmosphere" is broken, exacerbating the tendency of students to stop out. Falcon-Chandler expects to retain most of her faculty in coming years due to her efforts to improve compensation. "We changed our salary scale, which is still not adequate, but it's better than it used to be," she said. "And then we offer benefits; some places don't, but we have health insurance and retirement [plans], 401(k)s. We never had that before. We weren't able to afford it."

"UNDERFUNDED MIRACLES"

Asked about the adequacy of his school's federal funding, LoneFight of Sisseton Wahpeton College wrote in an e-mail that total funding per full-time student is approximately two-thirds that of a mainstream institution. "You can think of [the] difference between receiving adequate nutrition and receiving two-thirds of necessary calories. One is health, and the other is chronic malnourishment and eventual starvation." A colleague, Schuyler Houser, former president of Lac Courte Oreilles Ojibwa Community College in Wisconsin, has described tribal colleges simply as "underfunded miracles."

Insufficient funding in higher education is a common complaint at all levels and schools. But for tribal schools, the grievance seems particularly well founded. The Tribally Controlled College and University Assistance Act of 1978 mandates Congress to provide federal funding for tribal colleges, and the schools have relied on these allocations for core operational funding. Because they're on reservation land, tribal colleges can't depend on state or local taxes for supplemental funding, as two-year and four-year colleges do. Federal dollars, then, are crucial.

In fiscal year 1981, Congress appropriated $2,831 per Indian student. In FY 2005, it brought appropriation up to $4,448. But factor in inflation, noted Meg Goetz, AIHEC's director of congressional relations, and tribal colleges are actually losing buying power. In 1981 dollars, the 2005 appropriation is just $2,078, a 27% drop.

Moreover, federal funding is allotted to schools on the basis of Indian students only, but many tribal colleges enroll significant numbers of non-Indian students—about 20% on average. Joseph McDonald, president of Salish Kootenai College, has taken a strong stand on the issue because of the financial impact on his school's bottom line. In 2003, he petitioned the Montana Board of Regents for state funding for non-Indian students attending SKC—termed "nonbeneficiaries" since they don't benefit from federal funding—estimated at 26% of the student body for the five-year period 1998 to 2002.

"This is a tremendous burden for a small college to shoulder," he argued. "Twenty-six percent of SKC's annual costs are properly attributable to nonbeneficiary Montana resident students. These costs continue to have a huge impact on SKC's budget, which is stretched thin since the college receives little or no government support to offset these costs." His initial pleas went unheeded, but in 2005, the Montana Legislature passed into law a bill appropriating funding for non-Indian students at all the state's tribal colleges.

INCOMING

The recent Montana law is an exception to the rule that state legislatures generally provide little funding to tribal colleges. As Leonard Dauphinais, comptroller of Turtle Mountain Community College, put it, TMCC "receives no funding from the coffers of the State of North Dakota." Kyle Erickson, development director at Leech Lake Tribal College in Minnesota said that "we're kind of kept out of the loop for the state money...which puts us at a bit of a disadvantage" relative to two-year community colleges in Minnesota that can receive federal and state monies. In fact, the only tribal college in Minnesota which does receive state funding is Fond du Lac, which has a majority non-Indian enrollment. (In most states, according to a November 2000 report by the Education Commission of the States, community colleges receive about two-thirds of their funding from state and local sources.)

Tribal schools therefore seek additional federal funding, through their newly granted status as land-grant schools and a variety of other federal programs. They also rely heavily on corporate donations and private foundations. From 1989 and 2002, according to the Harvard Project on American Indian Economic Development, five tribal colleges or tribal college organizations were among the leading recipients of grants for Native American concerns. The American Indian College Fund received nearly $62 million in grants, Sinte Gleska University received $11 million, Salish Kootenai College got $9.4 million, AIHEC received $6.5 million and Oglala Lakota College was granted $5.7 million (all in 2002 dollars). Sounds like a fair amount of money, but if it were divided on a per capita basis—16,000 students enrolled in 2002—it barely covers books.

Some tribal colleges have struggled unsuccessfully to make ends meet. California's only tribal college lost its accreditation in 2005 after not remedying fiscal problems. Southwestern Indian Polytechnic Institute in New

Mexico laid off 29 employees and required unpaid leave of other staff this past spring after facing a $1 million budget deficit. And in South Dakota, Si Tanka University declared bankruptcy and closed its off-reservation campus last year, while maintaining its on-reservation campus.

Of course, tribal colleges also depend on their students, but according to a 2003 study by the U.S. Commission on Civil Rights, "because tribal colleges do not receive sufficient federal funds, tuitions are typically so high that many Native American students cannot afford them." Even at comparatively inexpensive schools, going to school is an expensive endeavor. Annual full-time tuition at Turtle Mountain, for instance, is $1,776, significantly less than tuition at North Dakota's state-run community colleges. But tuition is only the tip of the financial iceberg for students. Turtle Mountain estimates total student costs, including room and board, transportation, books and so on can add up to almost $22,000 per year. That isn't much compared to Harvard, but for students from a reservation where the median household income in 2000 was $23,642, it's a lot of money.

The American Indian College Fund provides scholarships for many students, more than 6,000 in 2003, but the reality is that there's not enough for everyone. Other financial aid is available, but the Civil Rights Commission concluded that "bureaucratic hurdles and increasingly complex application procedures, coupled with unrealistic earning requirements, often mean that students do not have enough financial resources to cover costs." A 2005 NCES report showed that American Indian college students received less financial aid in 1999–2000 than students of other racial groups, but the same as Hispanic students. And so, inevitably, some Indian students stop out to earn more money for college—or perhaps for the more pressing financial needs of other family members.

RETAKING THE COMMONS

Despite the problems that tribal colleges face, most of them are likely to survive. Some will even prosper. Tribal officials are committed to them— if not always to their administrators. Students and families support them, as demonstrated by their growing enrollment. Local communities depend upon them more than ever as one of the reservation's most stable institutions. Even politicians are beginning to recognize the importance of tribal colleges.

At the June 2005 graduation ceremony at Salish Kootenai College, Montana's largest tribal college, nearly 180 students took their diplomas. Among the new graduates stood a white man wearing blue jeans and a beaded vest, a man granted an honorary degree that day in Native American Studies: Gov. Brian Schweitzer of Montana. "We will invest in tribal colleges," promised Schweitzer in his commencement speech. And he urged the new graduates to travel off-reservation in the coming year, to be ambassadors, to let the world know about their home community. And then, he said, "Come home. We need you. You are the brightest and the best. Please come home and help us to grow."

Schweitzer's presence at the ceremony implies a sincere support of tribal colleges. But it also suggests a shrewd calculation that Indians hold significant political power in Montana and other district states, a potency that will grow as their numbers begin to dominate in rural counties and as educated Indian leaders provide political voice. With high birth rates and migration from urban centers, Indian populations are growing in counties on or near many reservations while non-Indian populations are shrinking. And as tribal colleges add to their economic and educational clout, Indians will, in many areas, become an ever more serious political force. The plains of the Upper Midwest may never again be populated by buffalo—but Indians, by degrees, are making a comeback.

ACKNOWLEDGMENT

This chapter is a reprint from the March 2006 issue of the *fedgazette*, a publication of the Federal Reserve Bank of Minneapolis.

APPENDIX Tribal Colleges in the Ninth District of the Federal Reserve System

College	Location	Chartering Tribe	Year established	Enrollment Fall 1997	Enrollment Fall 2002	Enrollment Change 1997 to 2002	Percent American Indian
Bay Mills Community College	Brimley, MI	Bay Mills Indian Community	1984	453	430	-5%	55%
Blackfeet Community College	Browning, MT	Blackfeet Tribal Business Council	1974	411	418	2%	96%
Cankdeska Cikana Community College	Fort Totten, ND	Spirit Lake Sioux Tribal Council	1974	142	160	13%	98%
Chief Dull Knife College[a]	Lame Deer, MT	Northern Cheyenne Tribal Council	1975	508	268	-47%	77%
Fond du Lac Tribal and Community College	Cloquet, MN	Fond du Lac Band of Lake Superior Chippewa	1987	704	1,315	87%	24%
Fort Belknap College	Harlem, MT	Gros Ventre and Assiniboine Tribes	1984	218	158	-27%	86%
Fort Berthold Community College	New Town, ND	Three Affiliated Tribes of the Arikara, Hidatsa and Mandan	1974	223	249	12%	94%
Fort Peck Community College	Poplar, MT	Assiniboine and Sioux Tribes	1978	360	443	23%	80%
Keweenaw Bay Ojibwa Community College	Baraga, MI	Keweenaw Bay Indian Community	1975	—	—	—	—
Lac Courte Oreilles Ojibwa Community College	Hayward, WI	Lac Courte Oreille Band of Lake Superior Chippewa	1982	493	550	12%	77%
Leech Lake Tribal College	Cass Lake, MN	Leech Lake Tribal Council	1990	135	244	81%	93%
Little Big Horn College	Crow Agency, MT	Crow Tribal Council	1980	243	275	13%	96%

(continued)

APPENDIX Tribal Colleges in the Ninth District of the Federal Reserve System (continued)

College	Location	Chartering Tribe	Year established	Enrollment Fall 1997	Enrollment Fall 2002	Enrollment Change 1997 to 2002	Percent American Indian
Oglala Lakota College	Kyle, SD	Oglala Sioux Tribal Council	1971	1,219	1,279	5%	88%
Salish Kootenai College	Pablo, MT	Confederated Salish and Kootenai Tribal Council	1977	967	1,109	15%	80%
Si Tanka College[b]	Eagle Butte, SD	Cheyenne River Sioux Tribal Council	1974	171	434	154%	71%
Sinte Gleska University	Rosebud, SD	Rosebud Sioux Tribal Council	1971	766	787	3%	100%
Sisseton Wahpeton Community College	Sisseton, SD	Sisseton Wahpeton Sioux Tribal Council	1979	199	285	43%	84%
Sitting Bull College	Fort Yates, ND	Standing Rock Sioux Tribe	1973	217	214	–1%	89%
Stone Child College	Box Elder, MT	Chippewa Cree Business Committee	1984	166	83	–50%	94%
Turtle Mountain Community College	Belcourt, ND	Turtle Mountain Band of Chippewa	1972	579	897	55%	92%
United Tribes Technical College	Bismarck, ND	North Dakota Development Corp (representing four tribes)	1969	263	463	76%	91%
White Earth Tribal and Community College	Mahnomen, MN	White Earth Reservation Tribal Council	1997	—	99	—	75%

— Not available.

a Previously named Dull Knife Memorial College

b Previously named Cheyenne River Community College

Source: U.S. Department of Education, National Center for Education Statistics; American Indian Higher Education Consortium

CHAPTER 6

THE IMPLEMENTATION OF A WORLD INDIGENOUS ACCREDITATION AUTHORITY

Ray Barnhardt

INTRODUCTION

In August of 2002, representatives of Indigenous higher education institutions from around the world, ranging from Maori Wananga in New Zealand to Tribal Colleges from across the United States, assembled in Kananaskis, Alberta and established the World Indigenous Nations Higher Education Consortium. WINHEC was created to provide an international forum and support for Indigenous Peoples to pursue common goals through higher education, including "creating an accreditation body for Indigenous education initiatives and systems that identify common criteria, practices and principles by which Indigenous Peoples live." A year later, after a series of extended planning meetings in Albuquerque, New Mexico and Otaki, New Zealand, the WINHEC Executive Board at its 2003 annual meeting in Honolulu brought this goal to reality with the formation of the WINHEC Accreditation Authority and the approval of a Handbook to guide Indigenous-serving institutions and programs as they prepared for a new form of accreditation self-study and review. This chapter will describe the

Tradition and Culture in the Millennium: Tribal Colleges and Universities, pages 61–85
Copyright © 2009 by Information Age Publishing

61

rationale for and implementation of the WINHEC accreditation system and its unfolding contribution to Indigenous self-determination in higher education.

WINHEC FOUNDING PRINCIPLES

This World Indigenous Higher Education Consortium was founded on the principles set out in the following Articles of the 1993 United Nations Draft Declaration on the Rights of Indigenous Peoples:

- Article #13.   Indigenous Peoples have the right to manifest, practice, develop and teach their spiritual and religious traditions, customs and ceremonies; the right to maintain, protect, and have access in privacy to their religious and cultural sites; the right to the use and control of ceremonial objects; and the right to the repatriation of human remains.
- Article #14.   Indigenous peoples have the right to revitalize, use, develop and transmit to future generations their histories, languages, oral traditions, philosophies, writing systems and literatures, and to designate and retain their own names for communities, places and persons.
- Article #15.   Indigenous peoples have the right to all levels and forms of education of the State. All Indigenous peoples also have this right and the right to establish and control their educational systems and institutions providing education in their own languages, in a manner appropriate to their cultural methods of teaching and learning. Indigenous children living outside their communities have the right to be provided access to education in their own culture and language. States shall take effective measures to provide appropriate resources for these purposes.
- Article #16.   Indigenous peoples have the right to have the dignity and diversity of their cultures, traditions, histories and aspirations appropriately reflected in all forms of education and public information. States shall take effective measures, in consultation with the Indigenous peoples concerned, to eliminate prejudice and discrimination and promote tolerance, understanding and good relations among Indigenous peoples and all segments of society.

Indigenous peoples throughout the world have been seeking to exercise the rights articulated above, as well as those outlined in the WIPCE Coolangatta Statement on Indigenous Rights in Education (1999), through the creation of educational institutions and programs that assert, as a basic form of self-determination, that Indigenous people have the right to be Indigenous. Diverse as they were in their own histories and cultural traditions, the representatives of the many Indigenous regions and institutions that assembled in Kananaskis took remarkably little time to articulate a common purpose for an international organization to pursue their interests, as reflected in the following adopted vision and goals.

WINHEC VISION

We gather as Indigenous Peoples of our respective nations recognizing and reaffirming the educational rights of all Indigenous Peoples. We share the vision of all Indigenous Peoples of the world united in the collective synergy of self-determination through control of higher education. Committed to building partnerships that restore and retain Indigenous spirituality, cultures and languages, homelands, social systems, economic systems and self determination.

WINHEC GOALS

The purpose of WINHEC is to provide an international forum and support for Indigenous Peoples to pursue common goals through higher education, including but not limited to:

1. Accelerating the articulation of Indigenous epistemologies (ways of knowing, education, philosophy, and research);
2. Protecting and enhancing Indigenous spiritual beliefs, culture and languages through higher education;
3. Advancing the social, economical, and political status of Indigenous Peoples that contribute to the well-being of Indigenous communities through higher education;
4. Creating an accreditation body for Indigenous education initiatives and systems that identify common criteria, practices and principles by which Indigenous Peoples live;
5. Recognizing the significance of Indigenous education;
6. Creating a global network for sharing knowledge through exchange forums and state of the art technology;
7. Recognizing the educational rights of Indigenous Peoples;
8. Protecting, preserving and advocating Indigenous cultural and intellectual property rights, in particular the reaffirming and observance of the U.N. Commission of Human Rights, Mataatua Declaration

on Cultural and Intellectual Property Rights of Indigenous Peoples (1994); and
9. Promoting the maintenance, retention and advancement of traditional Indigenous bodies of knowledge.

Once the purposes of the World Indigenous Nations Higher Education Consortium were established, a series of working groups were formed to address the various goals that had been adopted, including a Working Group on Accreditation (Goal 4). The accreditation working group convened a series of meetings at various venues over the next year to solicit input regarding what an Indigenous accreditation system might look like and how it could be implemented. The intent was not to replicate the many existing and varied national accreditation and quality assurance regimes to which Indigenous institutions and programs were already subject, but to address the unique features that distinguish such institutions and programs from their mainstream counterparts (Barnhardt, 1991). Drawing upon the sometimes frustrating experiences of Indigenous-serving institutions and programs that had been through an accreditation review under their respective national structures, as well as the limited but highly relevant experience of the First Nations Accreditation Board in Alberta, Canada, the Working Group on Accreditation began to piece together an Indigenous accreditation system for WINHEC implementation.

WINHEC ACCREDITATION

Accreditation is a process of recognizing educational institutions for performance, integrity, and quality that entitle them to the confidence of the cultural and educational community being served. In the case of the WINHEC Accreditation Authority, this recognition is extended to include significant participation by the Indigenous peoples to be served through the respective institution/program, including responsibility for establishing review criteria and participating in the self-study and review process. An underlying consideration in the implementation of this accreditation process is the inherent diversity of Indigenous cultural histories, traditions and world views, all of which must not only be acknowledged, but must be recognized and celebrated as a valued asset and serve as one of the fundamental premises on which the accreditation process rests (Kirkness & Barnhardt, 1991).

In postsecondary education, accreditation performs a number of important functions, including the validation of credibility on the part of the public being served, and encouragement of efforts toward maximizing educational effectiveness. The accrediting process requires institutions and programs to examine their own goals, operations, and achievements, and then provides the expert critiques and suggestions of an external review team, and the recommendations of the accrediting body. Since the accreditation is reviewed periodically, institutions are encouraged toward continued self-study and improvement.

Accreditation of institutions and specialized programs is granted by a number of national, regional and professional organizations, each representing a lens through which to examine the quality and integrity of the institutions/programs in question. Though each of these organizations has its distinctive definitions of eligibility, criteria for accreditation, and operating procedures, most of them undertake accreditation as one means of assuring the public constituencies about the quality and integrity of the services rendered. While the procedures of the various national and professional accrediting structures differ somewhat in detail, each is intended to fulfill the following purposes:

1. foster quality assurance in postsecondary education through the development of criteria and guidelines for assessing educational effectiveness in a context that values diversity and reflects locally defined definitions of what constitutes quality and effectiveness;
2. encourage institutional improvement of educational endeavors through continuous self-study and evaluation;
3. insure the educational community, the general public, and other agencies or organizations that an institution/program has clearly defined and appropriate educational objectives, has established conditions under which their achievement can reasonably be expected, appears in fact to be accomplishing them substantially, and is so organized, staffed, and supported that it can be expected to continue to do so; and
4. provide counsel and assistance to established and developing institutions (NWCCU, 2003).

Accreditation by the WINHEC Accreditation Authority strives to insure that an Indigenous-serving postsecondary institution/program's own goals are soundly conceived, that its educational and cultural programs have been intelligently devised, and that its purposes are being accomplished in a manner that should continue to merit confidence by the Indigenous constituencies being served. Thus, the WINHEC accreditation review process seeks to take into account and support the diversity that exists among Indigenous-serving postsecondary institutions/programs. This is accomplished through implementation of the following "Guiding Principles for WINHEC Accreditation Authority" (WINHEC, 2004).

1. The WINHEC Accreditation Authority will serve as a vehicle for strengthening and validating Indigenous higher education institutions and programs based on standards and procedures developed and implemented by WINHEC member institutions.
2. The criteria for accreditation review will be founded upon the diverse Indigenous language and cultural beliefs, protocols, laws and practices that provide the epistemological and pedagogical basis for the institutions and programs under review, and will be applied in a manner that is consistent with the principles outlined in the 1993 United Nations Draft Declaration on the Rights of Indigenous Peoples, the 1994 Mataatua Declaration on Cultural and Intellectual Property Rights of Indigenous Peoples, and the 1999 Coolangatta Statement on Indigenous Rights in Education.
3. The primary focus of the WINHEC Accreditation Authority will be the internal congruence and cultural integrity of the institutions/programs under review, with secondary consideration given to linkages with external/mainstream institutions and accreditation systems.
4. The WINHEC Accreditation Authority will provide a means for institution-level accreditation of Indigenous-controlled higher education institutions, as well as program-level accreditation of Indigenous-oriented programs within Indigenous and mainstream institutions (including teacher education programs).
5. The accreditation review process will include the role of locally respected Elders and recognized cultural practitioners, and the use of the heritage language(s) as reflected in the institution/program under review.
6. The WINHEC Accreditation Authority will promote Indigenous research that is respectful of cultural and intellectual property rights and closely integrated with the communities being served.
7. The WINHEC Accreditation Authority self-study process will be guided by local cultural standards that are developed by the respective Indigenous communities, and thus will provide international recognition and validation for educational initiatives grounded in Indigenous world views, knowledge systems and ways of knowing.
8. The WINHEC Accreditation Authority will provide accredited institutions and programs with access to the following WINHEC services:
   a. Each accredited institutional member shall receive formal acknowledgement and recognition of its accreditation status in the form of an official certificate from WINHEC, have one vote on the Accreditation Authority Board, and be invited to participate in program reviews of other applicants for accreditation.

b. Each accredited member shall be included in the planning and implementation of cooperative activities (e.g., conferences, scholar/student exchanges, shared programs/curricula, cooperative research initiatives) of WINHEC programs and institutions.

c. Each accredited member shall have opportunities to enroll students in and contribute to the offerings associated with articulated international baccalaureate and graduate degree programs focusing on Indigenous studies, including the acceptance of approved transfer credits among all member programs and institutions.

d. Accredited members shall have opportunities for faculty and students to form partnerships on joint research activities and to participate in faculty/student exchanges among member programs and institutions.

e. Accredited members shall be responsible for contributing to and have access to a database of Indigenous scholars for external review of research papers, theses, grant proposals, manuscripts, etc.

f. Accredited members shall be invited to participate in and contribute to international seminars, conferences, policy papers and comparable initiatives that pertain to the interests of the member programs and institutions.

Eligibility Requirements of Applicants for Accreditation

Applicants for accreditation are required to submit an application portfolio to the WINHEC Accreditation Authority and if accepted, prepare a self-study addressing the criteria for review outlined in the accreditation guidelines. Applicants may be either an Indigenous-serving institution (e.g., a Tribal College or Wananga), or an Indigenous-serving program contained within a mainstream institution, and the review process is adjusted accordingly. Programs are assessed with regard to their integrity and support in the context of the host institution.

The characteristics of an institution/program and the conditions required by the Accreditation Authority for consideration as an Applicant for Accreditation are outlined in the WINHEC Accreditation Handbook (2004). Each component of the eligibility requirements is a precondition that relates to the appropriate guidelines and criteria by which quality, integrity, effectiveness and accreditation are evaluated.

Overview of the Accreditation Review Process

The WINHEC Accreditation Authority appoints an accreditation review team made up of representatives from at least four member institutions/ programs, two of which are from the same national context as the applicant institution/program. The review team includes a minimum of one Elder who has been associated with a member program or institution.

The review team prepares a report based on a review of the self-study and an on-site visit to the candidate program/institution. This report (including the self-study) is submitted to the WINHEC Accreditation Authority for final consideration of membership approval.

The review process to be jointly conducted by the institution and the Accreditation Authority includes the following steps (Figure 6.1):

1. A representative of the Authority conducts a preliminary visit to the institution/program 6 to 12 months before a review team visit.
2. The institution/program analyzes itself through a self-study, as outlined below.
3. Review team members study the institutional self-study report, visit the institution/program and prepare a written report.
4. A draft report from the review team is prepared and sent to the institution/program chair. The chair is given an opportunity to respond to the review team's written report before the final report is prepared.
5. The team's final report is mailed to the chair and the Accreditation Authority board members four to six weeks before the next scheduled board meeting.
6. The WINHEC Accreditation Authority Board of Affirmation reviews the institution/program self-study and the review team's report, interviews the review team chair and if necessary, the person in charge of the institution/program, and takes action on the basis of information obtained. These actions may include, but are not limited to the following:
   a. The Authority may grant full accreditation with all rights and privileges thereof, which will be subject to renewal in 10 years.
   b. The Authority may grant a provisional accreditation, stipulating specific adjustments and modifications required and a time frame in which they must be addressed. If the modifications are met in the specified time, full accreditation will be granted. If the modifications are not met as specified, the Authority may

withdraw further recognition, or extend the provisional status until the modifications are met.

c. If at any time during the 10-year full accreditation period the Accreditation Authority is notified that an accredited institution/program no longer meets the minimal conditions under which it was originally accredited, the Authority will review the information to determine if it warrants investigation, if so, an investigation will be conducted and recommendations will be presented to the Accreditation Board for action. If deemed appropriate, the Authority reserves the right to rescind accreditation under its auspices. The institution/program involved may appeal such action to the WINHEC Executive Board for further consideration.

d. Institutions/programs that receive full accreditation are required to submit an Interim Report to the WINHEC Accreditation Authority at the 5-year mark of the 10-year period of full accreditation.

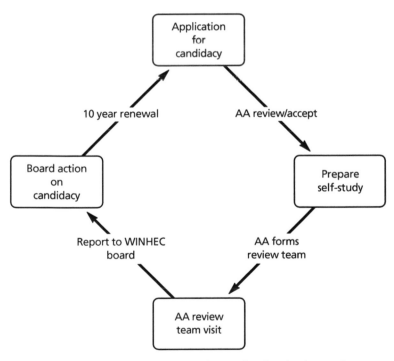

Figure 6.1 WINHEC accreditation authority application/review cycle.

The review process is a major undertaking, and a full academic year is considered to be the minimum working time needed. Preparation normally begins more than a year before the date of the site visit.

ACCREDITATION SELF STUDY

Role of Self-Study. The WINHEC Accreditation Authority, while requiring the submission of a self-study report in connection with a review for accreditation, recognizes that the self-study process is more beneficial to the institution/program when it is undertaken in response to significant needs felt by the Indigenous community being served. Accordingly, a variety of approaches to self-study are acceptable and an institution/program is permitted to propose some variation in the design of the self-study which it considers to be of intrinsic value as long as the overarching purposes of a comprehensive self-study are met and all Authority requirements are addressed.

Self-Study Steering Committee. It is important to have a steering committee broadly representative of the institution/program under review and the Indigenous communities being served so that a comprehensive assessment may be promoted. Also, others whose interests might be affected by the results of the study should in some way be involved. How the leadership and the participating personnel for the self-study are selected, whether by election, appointment, or some combination of both, should be resolved in accordance with the tradition and climate of the institution/program. Most institution/programs have multiple constituencies who have somewhat differing interests and values. An institution/program organizing for self-study is expected to have these various points of view in mind as it makes its plans and staffs its committees.

Development of the Report. The "Standards and Guidelines for Self-Study" which follow below provides a suggested framework of essential considerations for the self-study and for the external review team. An institution/program undergoing review is encouraged to design a narrative report best suited to its mission and supported by the necessary data presented in a concise and readable form (WINHEC, 2004).

CULTURAL STANDARDS AND THEIR USE
IN THE SELF STUDY

As indicated in Guiding Principles #5 and #7 above, one of the preconditions for a WINHEC Accreditation Authority review is the identification of a locally appropriate and accepted set of "Cultural Standards" against which the cultural integrity of the institution/program can be reviewed and assessed. "Cultural Standards" refers here to a locally defined set of guidelines, principles and/or values that reflect the cultural essence to which the goals of the particular program or institution are directed and under which it operates. The intent is to affirm the performance of Indigenous-serving institutions and programs in reference to standards appropriate to the Indigenous cultural contexts involved, rather than impose a single set of generic standards assumed to be equally applicable to all institutions/programs. These local Cultural Standards must be in place and submitted to the WINHEC Accreditation Authority for reference as a precondition for consideration of eligibility.

Cultural Standards Development. If such Cultural Standards do not yet exist in the Indigenous region under consideration, the candidate program or institution is urged to convene a broadly representative group of Indigenous people from across the region being served who can either develop and adopt an original set of cultural standards/guidelines applicable to the tribes/region/nation involved, or review, adapt and endorse an existing set of cultural standards, such as the Alaska version in Appendix A, or the Hawaii Guidelines for Culturally Healthy and Responsive Learning Environments (available at http://www.olelo.hawaii.edu/dual/nhmo/). Once adopted by the appropriate Indigenous authorities, the relevant cultural standards/guidelines are then submitted to the WINHEC Accreditation Authority to serve as the basis on which the educational and cultural integrity of the respective institution/program will be reviewed for accreditation.

In preparing the self-study, the institution/program under consideration is expected to demonstrate that it meets each element of the standards, and any applicable policy. The self-study document is expected to include an appraisal of the institution/program's strengths, weaknesses, and achievements relative to each standard.

CONCLUSION

In November 2004, a Maori Teacher Education program, a Maori Philosophy and Law program and a Maori Kaumatua/Elder program, each offered by one of the three Maori Wananga (Tribal Colleges) in New Zealand, underwent review and became the first programs to be accredited by the WINHEC Accreditation Authority. Two additional First Nations programs in Canada and two new Native Hawaiian institutions have each initiated the process to become candidates for WINHEC accreditation. In some cases, these programs and institutions are seeking WINHEC accreditation as the primary form of quality assurance and validation for their work, while others are seeking Indigenous validation in addition to existing regional or national accreditation. Either way, the WINHEC accreditation process reflects a new form of self-determination in which Indigenous peoples are asserting their rights to provide educational opportunities grounded in their own worldviews, knowledge systems and ways of knowing.

A copy of the WINHEC Accreditation Handbook, including sample "cultural standards" are available on the WINHEC web site at http://www.winhec.org, or on the Alaska Native Knowledge Network web site at http://www.ankn.uaf.edu/ihe.html.

REFERENCES

Barnhardt, R. (1991). Higher education in the fourth world: Indigenous people take control. *Tribal College Journal of American Indian Higher Education, 3*(2), 11–13.

Kirkness, V. J., & Barnhardt, R. (1991). First Nations and higher education: The four r's—respect, relevance, reciprocity, responsibility. *Journal of American Indian Education, 30*(3), 1–15.

NWCCU. (2003). *Accreditation overview.* Northwest Commission on Colleges and Universities, Redmond, WA. (http://www.nwccu.org/)

U.N. Commission on Human Rights. (1993). *United Nations Declaration on the Rights of Indigenous Peoples.* Working Group on Indigenous Populations, Geneva, Switzerland. (http://www.cwis.org/drft9329.html)

U.N. Commission on Human Rights. (1994). *Mataatua Declaration on Cultural and Intellectual Property Rights of Indigenous People,* First International Conference on the Cultural & Intellectual Property Rights of Indigenous Peoples, Whakatane, New Zealand. (http://www.ankn.uaf.edu/mataatua.html)

WINHEC. (2004). *WINHEC Accreditation handbook* (2nd ed.). World Indigenous Nations Higher Education Consortium, Honolulu, HI. (http://www.ankn.uaf.edu/ihe.html)

WIPCE. (1999). *Coolangatta statement on indigenous rights in education.* World Indigenous Peoples Conference on Education, Hilo, HI. (http://www.ankn.uaf.edu/IKS/cool.html)

SAMPLE CULTURAL STANDARDS

Attached is an example of the kind of culturally responsive accreditation review criteria and indicators that are proposed for WINHEC accreditation review, using a variation on the Alaska Cultural Standards as a vehicle to illustrate what locally appropriate standards might look like. These are included here to serve only as an illustrative example and are not intended as a prescribed model or format. Each program or institution seeking WINHEC accreditation is expected to develop and submit its own version of locally appropriate cultural standards/guidelines/principles/values/protocols to provide the basis on which it wishes to be assessed. In the end, the WINHEC accreditation process is an assessment of the consistency between what a candidate program/institution professes to be about and its actual practices in reference to the Indigenous peoples being served.

EXAMPLE OF CULTURALLY RESPONSIVE
ACCREDITATION STANDARDS

Based on Alaska Cultural Standards and Indicators for:
Program Graduates
Instructional Practice
Curriculum Design
Operational Characteristics
Community Involvement

PROGRAM GRADUATE INDICATORS

A. Program graduates are well grounded in the cultural heritage and traditions of their community.

Graduates who meet this standard are able to:

1. assume responsibility for their role in relation to the well-being of the cultural community and their life-long obligations as a community member;
2. recount their own genealogy and family history;
3. acquire and pass on the traditions of their community through oral and written history;
4. practice their traditional responsibilities to the surrounding environment;
5. reflect through their own actions the critical role that the local heritage language plays in fostering a sense of who they are and how they understand the world around them;
6. live a life in accordance with the cultural values and traditions of the local community and integrate them into their everyday behavior.
7. determine the place of their cultural community in the regional, state, national and international political and economic systems;

B. Program graduates are able to build on the knowledge and skills of the local cultural community as a foundation from which to achieve personal and academic success throughout life.

Graduates who meet this standard are able to:

1. acquire insights from other cultures without diminishing the integrity of their own;

2. make effective use of the knowledge, skills and ways of knowing from their own cultural traditions to learn about the larger world in which they live;
3. make appropriate choices regarding the long-term consequences of their actions;
4. identify appropriate forms of technology and anticipate the consequences of their use for improving the quality of life in the community.

C. Program graduates are able to actively participate in various cultural environments.

Graduates who meet this standard are able to:

1. perform subsistence activities in ways that are appropriate to local cultural traditions;
2. make constructive contributions to the governance of their community and the well-being of their family;
3. attain a healthy lifestyle through which they are able to maintain their own social, emotional, physical, intellectual and spiritual well-being;
4. enter into and function effectively in a variety of cultural settings.

D. Program graduates are able to engage effectively in learning activities that are based on traditional ways of knowing and learning.

Graduates who meet this standard are able to:

1. acquire in-depth cultural knowledge through active participation and meaningful interaction with Elders;
2. participate in and make constructive contributions to the learning activities associated with a traditional camp environment;
3. interact with Elders in a loving and respectful way that demonstrates an appreciation of their role as culture-bearers and educators in the community;
4. gather oral and written history information from the local community and provide an appropriate interpretation of its cultural meaning and significance;
5. identify and utilize appropriate sources of cultural knowledge to find solutions to everyday problems;
6. engage in a realistic self-assessment to identify strengths and needs and make appropriate decisions to enhance life skills.

E. Program graduates demonstrate an awareness and appreciation of the relationships and processes of interaction of all elements in the world around them.

Graduates who meet this standard are able to:

1. recognize and build upon the inter-relationships that exist among the spiritual, natural and human realms in the world around them, as reflected in their own cultural traditions and beliefs as well as those of others;
2. understand the ecology and geography of the bio-region they inhabit;
3. demonstrate an understanding of the relationship between world view and the way knowledge is formed and used;
4. determine how ideas and concepts from one knowledge system relate to those derived from other knowledge systems;
5. recognize how and why cultures change over time;
6. anticipate the changes that occur when different cultural systems come in contact with one another;
7. determine how cultural values and beliefs influence the interaction of people from different cultural backgrounds;
8. identify and appreciate who they are and their place in the world.

INSTRUCTIONAL PRACTICE INDICATORS

A. Instructors incorporate local ways of knowing and teaching in their work.

Faculty who meet this standard:

1. recognize the validity and integrity of the traditional knowledge system;
2. utilize Elders' expertise in multiple ways in their teaching;
3. provide opportunities and time for students to learn in settings where local cultural knowledge and skills are naturally relevant;
4. provide opportunities for students to learn through observation and hands-on demonstration of cultural knowledge and skills;
5. adhere to the cultural and intellectual property rights that pertain to all aspects of the local knowledge they are addressing;
6. continually involve themselves in learning about the local culture.

B. Instructors use the local environment and community resources on a regular basis to link what they are teaching to the everyday lives of the students.

Faculty who meet this standard:

1. regularly engage students in appropriate projects and experiential learning activities in the surrounding environment;
2. utilize traditional settings such as camps as learning environments for transmitting both cultural and academic knowledge and skills;
3. provide integrated learning activities organized around themes of local significance and across subject areas;
4. are knowledgeable in all the areas of local history and cultural tradition that may have bearing on their work as an instructor, including the appropriate times for certain knowledge to be taught;
5. seek to ground all teaching in a constructive process built on a local cultural foundation.

C. Instructors participate in community events and activities in an appropriate and supportive way.

Faculty who meet this standard:

1. become active members of the community in which they teach and make positive and culturally appropriate contributions to the well being of that community;
2. exercise professional responsibilities in the context of local cultural traditions and expectations;
3. maintain a close working relationship with and make appropriate use of the cultural and professional expertise of their co-workers from the local community.

D. Instructors work closely with parents to achieve a high level of complementary educational expectations between home and college.

Faculty who meet this standard:

1. promote extensive community and parental interaction and involvement in their student's education;
2. involve Elders, parents and local leaders in all aspects of instructional planning and implementation;

3. seek to continually learn about and build upon the cultural knowledge that students bring with them from their homes and community;
4. seek to learn the local heritage language and promote its use in their teaching.

E. Instructors recognize the full educational potential of each student and provide the challenges necessary for them to achieve that potential.

Faculty who meet this standard:

1. recognize cultural differences as positive attributes around which to build appropriate educational experiences;
2. provide learning opportunities that help students recognize the integrity of the knowledge they bring with them and use that knowledge as a springboard to new understandings;
3. reinforce the student's sense of cultural identity and place in the world;
4. acquaint students with the world beyond their home community in ways that expand their horizons while strengthening their own identities;
5. recognize the need for all people to understand the importance of learning about other cultures and appreciating what each has to offer.

CURRICULUM DESIGN INDICATORS

A. An Indigenous oriented curriculum reinforces the integrity of the cultural knowledge that students bring with them.

A curriculum that meets this standard:

1. recognizes that all knowledge is imbedded in a larger system of cultural beliefs, values and practices, each with its own integrity and interconnectedness;
2. insures that students acquire not only the surface knowledge of their culture, but are also well grounded in the deeper aspects of the associated beliefs and practices;
3. incorporates contemporary adaptations along with the historical and traditional aspects of the local culture;

4. respects and validates knowledge that has been derived from a variety of cultural traditions;
5. provides opportunities for students to study all subjects starting from a base in their own knowledge system.

B. An Indigenous oriented curriculum recognizes cultural knowledge as part of a living and constantly adapting system that is grounded in the past, but continues to grow through the present and into the future.

A curriculum that meets this standard:

1. recognizes the contemporary validity of much of the traditional cultural knowledge, values and beliefs, and grounds students learning in the principles and practices associated with that knowledge;
2. provides students with an understanding of the dynamics of cultural systems as they change over time, and as they are impacted by external forces;
3. incorporates the in-depth study of unique elements of contemporary life in Indigenous communities, such as the protection of land rights, subsistence, sovereignty and self-determination.

C. An Indigenous oriented curriculum uses the local language and cultural knowledge as a foundation for the rest of the curriculum.

A curriculum that meets this standard:

1. utilizes the local language as a base from which to learn the deeper meanings of the local cultural knowledge, values, beliefs and practices;
2. recognizes the depth of knowledge that is associated with the long inhabitation of a particular place and utilizes the study of "place" as a basis for the comparative analysis of contemporary social, political and economic systems;
3. incorporates language and cultural immersion experiences wherever in-depth cultural understanding is necessary;
4. views all community members as potential teachers and all events in the community as potential learning opportunities;
5. treats local cultural knowledge as a means to acquire the conventional curriculum content as outlined in state standards, as well as an end in itself;

6. makes appropriate use of modern tools and technology to help document and transmit traditional cultural knowledge;
7. is sensitive to traditional cultural protocol, including role of spirituality, as it relates to appropriate uses of local knowledge.

D. An Indigenous oriented curriculum fosters a complementary relationship across knowledge derived from diverse knowledge systems.

A curriculum that meets this standard:

1. draws parallels between knowledge derived from oral tradition and that derived from books;
2. engages students in the construction of new knowledge and understandings that contribute to an ever-expanding view of the world.

E. An Indigenous oriented curriculum situates local knowledge and actions in a global context.

A curriculum that meets this standard:

1. encourages students to consider the inter-relationship between their local circumstances and the global community;
2. conveys to students that every culture and community contributes to, at the same time that it receives from the global knowledge base;
3. incorporates the educational principles outlined in the Coolongatta Statement on Indigenous Rights in Education.

OPERATIONAL CHARACTERISTICS INDICATORS

A. An Indigenous oriented educational institution/ program fosters the on-going participation of Elders in all aspects of the education process.

A program that meets this standard:

1. maintains multiple avenues for Elders to interact formally and informally with students at all times;
2. provides opportunities for students to regularly engage in the documenting of Elders' cultural knowledge and produce appropriate print and multimedia materials that share this knowledge with others;

3. includes explicit statements regarding the cultural values that are fostered in the community and integrates those values in all aspects of the education program and operation;
4. utilizes educational models that are grounded in the traditional world view and ways of knowing associated with the cultural knowledge system reflected in the community.

B. An Indigenous oriented educational institution/ program provides multiple avenues for students to access the learning that is offered, as well as multiple forms of assessment for students to demonstrate what they have learned.

A program that meets this standard:

1. utilizes a broad range of culturally appropriate performance standards to assess student knowledge and skills;
2. encourages and supports experientially oriented approaches to education that makes extensive use of community-based resources and expertise;
3. provides cultural and language immersion programs in which student acquire in-depth understanding of the culture of which they are members;
4. helps students develop the capacity to assess their own strengths and weaknesses and make appropriate decisions based on such a self-assessment.

C. An Indigenous oriented educational institution/ program provides opportunities for students to learn in and/or about their heritage language.

A program that meets this standard:

1. provides language immersion opportunities for students who wish to learn in their heritage language;
2. offers courses that acquaint all students with the heritage language of the local community;
3. makes available reading materials and courses through which students can acquire literacy in the heritage language.

D. An Indigenous oriented educational institution/program has a high level of involvement of professional staff who are of the same cultural background as the students with whom they are working.

A program that meets this standard:

1. encourages and supports the professional development of local personnel to assume teaching and administrative roles in the program;
2. recruits and hires instructors whose background is similar to that of the students they will be teaching;
3. provides a cultural orientation and mentoring program for new personnel to learn about and adjust to the cultural expectations and practices of the surrounding community;
4. fosters and supports opportunities for staff to participate in professional activities and associations that help them expand their repertoire of cultural knowledge and pedagogical skills.

E. An Indigenous oriented educational institution/ program consists of facilities that are compatible with the community environment in which they are situated.

A program that meets this standard:

1. provides a physical environment that is inviting and readily accessible for local people to enter and utilize;
2. makes use of facilities throughout the community to demonstrate that education is a community-wide process involving everyone as teachers;
3. utilizes local expertise, including students, to provide culturally appropriate displays of arts, crafts and other forms of decoration and space design.

F. An Indigenous oriented educational institution/ program fosters extensive on-going participation, communication and interaction between program and community personnel.

A program that meets this standard:

1. holds regular formal and informal events bringing together students, parents, instructors and other program and community personnel

to review, evaluate and plan the educational program that is being offered;

2. provides regular opportunities for community participation in deliberations and decision-making on policy, curriculum and personnel issues related to the program;

3. sponsors on-going activities and events that celebrate and provide opportunities for students to put into practice and display their knowledge of local cultural traditions;

4. incorporates the participatory principles outlined in the Coolongatta Statement on Indigenous Rights in Education.

COMMUNITY INVOLVEMENT INDICATORS

A. A culturally supportive community incorporates the practice of local cultural traditions in its everyday affairs.

A community that meets this standard:

1. provides respected Elders with a place of honor in community functions;

2. models culturally appropriate behavior in the day-to-day life of the community;

3. utilizes traditional socialization practices that reinforce a sense of identity and belonging;

4. organizes and encourages participation of members from all ages in regular community-wide, family-oriented events;

5. incorporates and reinforces traditional cultural values and beliefs in all formal and informal community functions.

B. A culturally supportive community nurtures the use of the local heritage language.

A community that meets this standard:

1. recognizes the role that language plays in conveying the deeper aspects of cultural knowledge and traditions;

2. sponsors local heritage language immersion opportunities for young children when they are at the critical age for language learning;

3. encourages the use of the local heritage language whenever possible in the everyday affairs of the community, including meetings, cultural events, print materials and broadcast media;

4. assists in the preparation of curriculum resource material in the local heritage language for use in the education programs;
5. provides simultaneous translation services for public meetings where persons unfamiliar with the local heritage language are participants.

C. A culturally supportive community takes an active role in the education of all its members.

A community that meets this standard:

1. encourages broad-based support of families in all aspects of their member's education;
2. insures active participation by community members in reviewing all decision-making regarding initiatives that have bearing on the education of their members;
3. encourages and supports members of the local community who wish to pursue further education;
4. engages in subsistence activities, sponsors cultural camps and hosts local events that provide an opportunity for community members to actively participate in and learn appropriate cultural values and behavior;
5. provides opportunities for all community members to acquire and practice the appropriate knowledge and skills associated with local cultural traditions.

D. A culturally supportive community nurtures family responsibility, sense of belonging and cultural identity.

A community that meets this standard:

1. fosters cross-generational sharing of parenting and child-rearing practices;
2. creates a supportive environment for youth and adults to participate in local affairs and acquire the skills to be contributing members of the community;
3. adopts the adage, "It takes the whole village to raise a child."

E. A culturally supportive community assists new members in learning and utilizing local cultural traditions and practices.

A community that meets this standard:

1. sponsors a cultural orientation and community mentoring program for new personnel to learn about and adjust to the cultural expectations and practices of the community;
2. sponsors regular community potlucks to celebrate significant events and to promote on-going interaction and communication between all its members;
3. attempts to articulate the cultural knowledge, values and beliefs that it wishes to pass on to future generations;
4. establishes a program to insure the availability of Elders' expertise in all aspects of the life in the community, including the educational programs.

F. A culturally supportive community contributes to all aspects of curriculum design and implementation for local educational programs.

A community that meets this standard:

1. takes an active part in the development of the mission, goals and content of local educational programs;
2. promotes the active involvement of students with Elders in the documentation and preservation of traditional knowledge through a variety of print and multimedia formats;
3. facilitates student involvement in community activities and encourages the use of the local environment as a curricular resource;
4. promotes active community involvement in all aspects of educational programs and institutions impacting its members.

PART II

CULTURE AND TRADITION

It does not require many words to speak the truth.
—Chief Joseph, Nez Perce

CHAPTER 7

UNDERSTANDING AMERICAN INDIAN CULTURES

Richard Littlebear

INTRODUCTION

When asked, many white American people will say they have no culture and, for the most part, American Indians would tend to agree with them or that what culture they do have is nearly devoid of human values. However, if their automobiles, television set, laws, churches, sports, books, clothing, historical accounts were taken away, many of them would vociferously and adamantly refuse to relinquish them. "Culture" seems to be those artifacts, social phenomena, and ideas that one cherishes, that one builds belief systems and values. "Culture" seems to be those words, artifacts, social mores, and phenomena that people feel they must protect. When told this, white American people will quickly conclude that they too have a culture and that culture is not something relegated only to American Indians or to other indigenous people or to those people who are labeled 'tribal' people. There are many definitions of culture and although there is no standard definition of culture, most alternatives incorporate the Boasian postulates as in the case of Bates and Plog's offering, which we will accept as a working version:

Tradition and Culture in the Millennium: Tribal Colleges and Universities, pages 89–92
Copyright © 2009 by Information Age Publishing
89

> *Culture:* The system of shared beliefs, values, customs, behaviors, and artifacts that the members of society use to cope with their world and with one another, and that are transmitted from generation to generation through learning (7).

This definition is particularly apropos to this chapter since it ends with the word 'learning' which is what tribal colleges and universities (TCUs) are all about.

Then there are other issues, some purely of American Indians' own making:

> When American Indians started writing about their own cultures, the writings became a distinct genre and usually centered on conflict with European-based cultures that had superimposed (usually violently) themselves on the indigenous cultures of this hemisphere.

Later that emphasis changed to having conflicts with one's own culture. This seemingly occurred with intensity whenever American Indians view their own culture. Some segments of American Indian culture have become gate keepers of what they perceive should be their cultures; sometimes this is a blend of present day culture mixed with the values of pre-1830s cultures. Disputes arise about which is the right culture. They arise continuously within the bands and tribes. Sometimes these disputes are unforgiving and they pit relatives against relatives, societies and clans against other and can, therefore, last for generations.

THE INFLUENCE OF CULTURE

American Indian cultures have been in continual flux since 1492 because of the intentions of other governments. These intentions have included genocide and, when this hasn't succeeded, obliteration of cultures and languages has been the next step. In the present situation, it is up to individual tribal cultures to do their own recovery. The move to recover self-sufficiency must come from within and later from without. But it must be done. The mainstream United State government is not going to help recreate what it has spent millions of dollars trying to demolish and abolish. TCUs and the cultures they represent must look deeply within themselves and sometimes even compromise those beliefs and traditions that hold American Indians back.

In his book *The World Is Flat*, Thomas L. Friedman writes about cultures. He says,

In my own travels, two aspects of culture have struck me as particularly relevant in the flat world. One is how outward your culture is: To what degree is it open to foreign influences and ideas? How well does it "glocalize?" The other, more tangible, is how inward your culture is. By that I mean, to what degree is there a sense of national solidarity and a focus on development, to what degree is there trust within the society for strangers to collaborate together, and to what degree are the elites in the country concerned with the masses and ready to invest at home, or are they indifferent to their own poor and more interests in investing abroad?

This paragraph could be paraphrased to fit the current cultural situations of American Indians:

In my own travels, two aspects of American Indian tribal culture have struck me as particularly relevant in the contemporary world. One is how outward your tribal culture is: To what degree is it open to mainstream American influences and ideas? How well does it "glocalize?" [This word is a combination of 'globalize' and 'localize' and means the following: "glocalize"—that is, the more your culture easily absorbs American mainstream ideas and global best practices and melds those with its own tribal traditions—the greater advantage you will have in the contemporary world.] The other, more tangible, is how inward your tribal culture is. By that I mean, to what degree is there a sense of tribal solidarity and a focus on development, to what degree is there trust within the tribe for strangers to collaborate together, and to what degree are the tribal council in the reservation concerned with the issues of all the people and ready to invest efforts at job creation and other economic efforts, or are they indifferent to their own reservation issues and to their tribal population that is poor and more interested in perpetuating themselves in office?

THE IMPORTANCE OF CULTURE

Because of the make-up of American Indian societies, cultural concerns have always been of foremost importance to them. The role that tribal colleges and universities can and must contribute to American Indian tribes resides in helping their communities maintain traditional culture and values.

The communities in which tribal colleges and universities have influence or at the very least, an academic presence, have to realize that cultures are dynamic, vital, animate, living entities much like the beings they encompass. Cultures are not static. They are not momentary, like the bolt of lightning across the evening sky, but last as long as the people they encompass endure.

It is, therefore, the role of tribal colleges and universities to set the tone for which direction the whole tribe should take. This tone-setting is no easy charge because it often runs athwart the intentions of the tribal councils and the cultural gatekeepers.

THE EVOLUTION OF CULTURE

One of the most important books on this subject is the Wealth and Poverty of Nations by the economist David Landes. He argues that although climate, natural resources, and geography all play roles in explaining why some countries are able to make the leap to industrialization and others are not, the key factor is actually a country's cultural endowments, particularly the degree to which it has internalized the values of hard word work, thrift, honesty, patience, and tenacity, as well s the degree to which it is open to change, new technology, and equality for women. One can agree or disagree with the balance Landes strikes between these cultural mores and other factors shaping economic performance. But I [Thomas L. Friedman] find refreshing his insistence on elevating the culture question and his refusal to buy into arguments that the continued stagnation of some countries is simply about Western colonialism, geography, or historical legacy.

This paragraph too could be paraphrased and be adapted to reservation cultural situations:

> One of the most important books on this subject is the Wealth and Poverty of Nations by the economist David Landes. He argues that although climate, natural resources, and geography all play roles in explaining why some reservations are able to make the leap to industrialization and individual entrepreneurship and others are not, the key factor is actually that reservation's cultural endowments, particularly the degree to which it has internalized the values of hard word work, thrift, honesty, patience, and tenacity, as well s the degree to which it is open to change, new technology, and equality for women. One can agree or disagree with the balance Landes strikes between these cultural mores and other factors shaping economic performance. But I [Thomas L. Friedman] find refreshing his insistence on elevating the culture question and his refusal to buy into arguments that the continued stagnation of some reservations is simply about Western colonialism, geography, or historical legacy.

RETHINKING CULTURE

The following chapter by Rosemary Ackley Christensen provides an in-depth view of tribal culture and behaviors. Her suggestions for strategies and recourse for tribal colleges and universities provides the foundation for our work, much of it done and much to be done.

CHAPTER 8

WORLD VIEW AND CULTURAL BEHAVIORS

Strategies and Resources Determination in the Tribal Academy

Rosemary Ackley Christensen

In modern society, American Indians of traditional thought are functioning outside of their cultural worlds for a large percentage of their life. Furthermore, they are products of two educational means and two cultures. Initially, this is difficult as the traditional person strives to learn in the non-Indian educational system. But, once this is achieved, then this individual can draw upon the traditional knowledge and mainstream knowledge to put forth a modern Indian intellectualism.... The importance of Indian intellectualism is contributing answers to difficult questions today. (Fixico, 2003, p. 16)

INTRODUCTION/BACKGROUND

Back in the day when the indigenous people of Turtle Island (North America) controlled the education of their young, teachings reflected, replicated, reinforced and honored their holistic worldview. One could say that poli-

Tradition and Culture in the Millennium: Tribal Colleges and Universities, pages 93–106
Copyright © 2009 by Information Age Publishing
All rights of reproduction in any form reserved.

cies and practice were one. The Indigenous intellectualism that provided our stories, our teachings, and our way of life was strong and well.

It is time to discuss further and seriously encourage educational practice, teaching methods and techniques based on an American Indian world view. Eva Mackey (2002) notes ("Williams [1980] suggests) that 'in any society, in any period, there is a central system of practices, meanings and values, which we can properly call dominant and effective'. Such a dominant culture infuses multiple domains of everyday life. Its dominance is based, in part, on its ability to become common sense in everyday life. It is continually confirmed and relived in multiple dimensions of ordinary experience (p. xvii)." Mackey's provocative, interesting and perhaps controversial book is exploring the "cultural politics of Canadian identity (p. 3)" To consider identity issues in a Tribal institution might mean examining how one could explore injecting in-depth cultural beliefs and norms into the daily life of the institution. Mackey discusses how to proceed and notes that "Marcus (1989) argues for 'event-centred' and 'multi-locale' ethnographies that explore how any cultural identity or activity is constructed by multiple agents in varying contexts or places' and he suggests that ethnography must be 'strategically conceived' to represent such multiplicity 'in the network of complex connections within a system of places'" (p. 6).

It is a fatuous notion to anyone that knows and thinks about the complex American Indian culture and world view that ideas regarding cultural policy initiatives can be imposed on anyone as a blanket directive, but perhaps these suggestions could be discussed and investigated in Indian Country. A cultural initiative to consider increasing the context of teaching, for example, to reflect in a richer manner the behaviors, values and world view of American Indian people. Of course, not all American Indian people espouse the very same world view, although it might be that consideration of core values among Tribes are a useful way to look at cultural norms that might be represented in the Tribal academy. The world view and cultural norms represented in the Western Academy are mostly linear and reflect its proud European ancestry (see, e.g., Lucas 1994). Beck, Walters, and Francisco (1992) quote *Tewa* intellectual Alfonso Ortiz, "The notion 'world view' denotes a distinctive vision of reality which not only interprets and orders the places and events in the experience of a people, but lends form, direction, and continuity to life as well. World View provides people with a distinctive set of values, an identity, a feeling of rootedness, of belonging to a time and a place, and a felt sense of continuity with a tradition which transcends the experience of a single lifetime, a tradition which may be said to transcend even time (Ortiz, 1973, p. 91).... A world view—provides a people with a structure of reality; it defines, classifies, and orders the "really real" in the universe, in their world, and in their society... a world view embodies man's most general conceptions of order (Ortiz, 1972, p. 136). Consider Wiese (1996) who interviewed Elders and studied Elder knowledge, noted that knowledge "transmission goes beyond the written word for Indian people. . . . Oral transmission has been the major method of teaching and learning throughout Indian history. The elders have been the teachers of the knowledge. The knowledge-base of the American Indian is one that has grown out of the experiences of millions of Indian people over a period of thousands of years before European contact on this continent (p. 6)."

Several possibilities arise that could be reinforced and nurtured through cultural policy review and design in the Tribal academy, keeping in mind that as Thohahoken (2005) says, "Culture has two parts. What people from one society do for each other *goes without saying.* When one society is compared to another, culture becomes what *needs to be said*" (p. 177).

One suggestion concerns the institutional administrative/grant process, and the second examines briefly what might be considered in the form and function of teaching (including teaching techniques/strategies) relative to how context might be considered, with the ideas about techniques briefly addressed through a storytelling methodology discussion. Other techniques and strategies based on the circular form and function, particularly that of utilizing oral knowledge of elders through students interviewing elders, and an integrated learning technique that reinforce respect among participants, engages in exchanging information through an intergrouping process and utilizes spiral learning between instructor and student groups is discussed in, for example, Christensen and Oxendine (2005) and Christensen (2004). The third possibility involves institutional training functions to promulgate, design and agree to cultural competencies useful for teachers, staff and those who interact with the Tribal community on a regular basis (see, Christensen, 1991). These competencies reflect the cultural values the Tribal community celebrates within itself. The cultural competencies could be any number desired that reflect the cultural attributes of the Tribal academy as well as, if desired, that of the Western Academy. As Joseph P. Gone (2004) said when discussing how to indigenize psychology in the Academy, "I concede that the essence of professional psychology is fundamentally dependent on the Western rationalist and empiricist epistemologies that are largely incommensurate with Native ways of knowing. Instead my vision for a pragmatically beneficial professional psychology assumes that it will remain Western in essence, albeit tailored to appreciate and engage the local epistemologies and ethnopsychologies of Native communities in substantive, supportive, respectful, and constructive ways" (p. 140). In an overview brief (Christensen, 1986/2003) designed for use in a fusion project discussed below, for example, six competencies are listed "independence or personal sovereignty, connectedness, or interdependence of all living things, elder knowledge/age respect, indirect communication: key to interaction and relationship, Tribal language: understanding the thought patterns of Tribal people and spirituality: the holistic tribal world." In the competencies section being established for a fusion project, a seventh competency exploring the effect of colonization or the theory of Duran and Duran's (1995, pp. 27–29) internalized oppression appears necessary if Indians and non-Indians are to understand and work with each other. The *Decolonization Handbook* (Waziyatawin & Yellow Bird, 2005) is designed to help Indians in the decolonization effort, and may serve as important material for a seventh competency in the effort discussed, especially as it is includes activities and exercises in addition to valuable information.

INSTITUTIONAL EVALUATION EFFORTS

Evaluation is required in grant process and any institution needs to understand how to more effectively use evaluation to look at and solve problems. "Planning, preparing, publishing, and sharing evaluation and testing materials should be encouraged... (p. 184)" notes Behnam and Mann (2003) in their section on 'development of evaluation tools. The nature of the practice of the Tribal institution regarding evaluation efforts needs examination relative to cultural policy. It might be a simple yet effective way for an institution to increase cultural practice in work that must be completed anyway for the institution. We know we need to devise a solution, try it, monitor activities, look at results, and then use them to fix or restate the problem. Evaluation form and process then must be at least adequate in representing accurately what is being evaluated to correct problems. The National Science Foundation (2002) sponsored a workshop on the issues of "culturally responsive educational evaluation as they pertain to Native Americans" (p. 1). Ramaley, from NSF spoke to discussion issues by reminding the gathering "to reinterpret accountability to mean not only measuring outcomes but creating the capacity to continue to develop and improve a program once it is launched" (p. 8) is needed as well as to look at the ideas and principles behind current approaches, and discuss what kind of approach might be created to meet current needs in a more successful way. She identified four issues, "the adaptability question, scalability, sustainability and "the culture of the evidence—all of which depends on a strong, culturally valid context that supports the values, purposes and expectations of the people who are working together..." (p. 10). Later on, following the gathering and publication of the papers presented at the meeting, the American Indian Higher Education Consortium (AIHEC) agreed to lead an effort to develop an Indigenous Framework for Evaluation(IFE) funded by the NSF(REC-0438720). Recently, a LaFrance and Nicholas (2006) report detailed the project thus far in designing a cultural frame for evaluation that will "synthesize indigenous ways of knowing and western evaluation practice" (p. 4). As this effort moves toward fruition and makes available its culturally responsive model, administrators, teachers and others can rest assured there will be assistance and trained evaluators when they ponder possibilities for evaluation efforts that reflect Tribal cultural norms and practice in a way that provides helpful information for further learning and modification(s). For further detail regarding indigenous evaluation framework see also LaFrance's (2004) chapter on culturally competent evaluation.

TEACHING METHODS/TECHNIQUES

Anishinaabeg oral scholar Lee Staples when asked to describe or define teaching said,

- Gikinoo'aamaage—teach something to someone;
- Gekinoo'amaaged—teacher.

These two words are derived from:

- Giki (to move or transfer) as in the following:
- Gikissiton—I add to something by moving or transferring;
- Gikin na magoo—transferred over to me;
- Anooamaage—to point out or direct.

Teaching as defined then is more audience participation as in *gikinawaa-bi*-doing in a way that you have observed others do or *gikinootaw*—repeat what you have heard. Passing on the teachings is critical for us as a people. Our Elders insist we listen intently to assure that our teachings always survive. Teaching also means *Anishinaabeg* Thought or World View. The teachings are not to be taken lightly as the Creator gave them to us as a gift. Thus, we must keep still and listen, even to assuming a serious, overt demeanor of listening (Staples et al., 2005).

In the field of teaching methods, techniques and strategies that might be discussed within teacher ranks relative to what is possible over a period of time is a consideration. In some cases, methods and techniques might need tinkering, honing and perhaps tuneups, while in other cases, it might take some time to discuss, review and agree to appropriate cultural competencies in order to reflect these in strategies and techniques.

Academics interested in reflecting various aspects of that indigenous world view and indigenous passing of knowledge continue to learn, practice and hone various techniques of teaching that incorporate the holistic circular world view of ancestors. I call this kind of teaching, circle teaching, based on a circle instead of the more linear, well known and practiced Academic style. "The circular method is a circular philosophy focusing on a single point and using familiar examples to illustrate or explain the point of discussion. The circular approach assures that everyone understands and all is considered, thereby increasing the chance for harmony and balance in the community and with everything else" (Fixico, 2003, pp. 15–16). These teachers, if raised by parents and community utilizing and reflecting the holistic world view, will indeed replicate and imitate various aspects of this philosophy in their teachings; although it seems logical that given certain realities, the linear, categorical western world view or way of thinking is also present. This makes sense in that American Indians as with others in the United States have been in schools dominated by the western way of teaching since first the U.S. government in their policy demanded and forced American Indian children into that educational, schooling mode (see, e.g., Adams, 1995).

In the current world of the twenty-first century possibly no one worldview is *totally* dominant, but merging effects of various worldviews might be visible and observable in teaching methods. A way to image this is to think of the overlap that might be in evidence in a merging Venn diagram with one circle representing Indian world, and the other, the Non-Indian world; the overlap probably fits the daily thinking (and thus acting/and practice) of American Indians living and working within the academy.

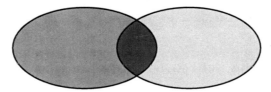

CIRCULAR TECHNIQUES

It makes sense that these formative times affect how, when, what and why these (and similarly experienced other) Indian academics might teach utilizing techniques Oral Elders taught and practiced in their earlier home environments. Circle teaching techniques (see, e.g., Christensen, 2004) are based on values and the intellectual construct of the indigenous worldview with the core value of personal sovereignty (and its practice of non-interference utilized through the structural elements of respect, reciprocity and relationship) being paramount. Elder Oral teaching passed through generational bundles of knowledge is an important intellectual construct and the value imbued practice(s) of respect, reciprocity and relationship expressed through distinct, particular behaviors are utilized in the methodology. Circle methodology includes oral traditional learning concepts. Teaching these values as cultural competencies is briefly addressed earlier. For further discussion on the conceptual points regarding circle classroom techniques/strategies and examples of other techniques see Christensen Techniques/strategies brief (Christensen, 2005).

The Academy (and reflected in grade school, middle and high school) throughout its long tenure has primarily used methods based on a linear worldview. These methods consisted primarily of lectures, with the teacher at the head of the room, with students in rows, asking questions, responding to the whole group, with individuals expected to deal with large numbers of students, limited time to seek learning from the teacher except through written word, and written exams. This is a commendable way to learn, but there are other ways, reflecting other worldviews.

The circle teaching method utilizes the "3r's" of oral learning: *reciprocity, relationship* and *respect*. The three Tribal R's of respect, reciprocity and relationship are the grid in the frame of the plan design. This allows usage of bonding method with students, a strategy that uses respect between teacher and student as a base premise. This cultural context needs to be part of instructional program coherence (IPC) within schools. IPC is defined as "a set of interrelated programs for students and staff that are guided by a common framework for curriculum, instruction, assessment and learning climate and that are pursued over a sustained period (Newmann et al., 2001, p. 297)." They suggest IPC may make a difference in school improvement.

STORYTELLING METHODOLOGY

Storytelling, an ancient Turtle Island teaching method incorporating oral tradition as constructive and dominant, reinforces the core value of personal sovereignty, allows for and encourages balance between young and old and teaches life's many lessons in a variety of ways. The method is only limited really by the variety and skills/talents of the human being. Our Elders told us stories when we were young. We learned to listen carefully and as we grow older still listening closely, we realize the stories grow with us. We get things out of the stories, as we need them. When young, maybe we just laughed at some of the antics told about in say coyote or trickster stories, but later as we grew older we realized these stories were imparting many useful, important things to us. I think of stories as if they were those vitamins we hear about that keep giving over time. We listen and ingest stories at a point, and they keep giving out good stuff long after we first heard them. It's almost as if stories are age-transportable. We portage them as we age, and these stories go on to help us understand our universe and our place in it as we continue to mature and further understand the teachings.

Consider the various aspects of storytelling methodology that might be reflected in the techniques and teaching methods of American Indians. For example, spiral communication is fostered in storytelling, with the teacher/storyteller in the middle, spiraling back and forth to the learners. I call a technique based on the storyteller method spiral lecturing. In this technique, the teacher is in the middle of the circle, while the students sit in the circle. Each student is invited to make a comment about ideas previously presented (either by the teacher or by student presentations) Teacher might comment to reinforce student idea, learning, or add onto the information provided to foster further learning, or correct an aspect that might be a little off, or just say, that's a terrific way to say it! In this way, the students are somewhat in charge of what is being presented by the teacher, thereby giving them some control over the discussion, a reciprocal event for both. In a circle, teachers can reinforce learning through a variety of ways.

Storytelling methodology reinforces listening skills, and makes a fine case for repetition as stories repeat similar teachings, sometimes in a humorous way, which makes the stories fun, and importantly, the teachings, easily recognizable. American Indian instructors normally and naturally may themselves use stories as a way of teaching, that is, stories of themselves, their families and their community members as a way of illustrating, and getting points across which might reflect their comfort in, and normal communicating manner on a daily basis. Some American Indian storytellers tend to change the story a little from the way they first heard it, they may add on something that seems right for the time, or eliminate another thing. Remembering the notion of personal sovereignty, it makes sense, that storytellers may see things differently in each generation and although the story may change a little, usually the core story remains the same, or provides similar teachings. Non-Indian scholars have difficulty with this way of doing things, because something isn't exactly the same as told before, and apparently, it then becomes more difficult to accept. The freedom to choose meanings from stories reflects again the personal sovereignty and living context of the individual; that is the age, the belief system and so forth. As stated earlier, meanings of stories may vary dependent on the age of the listener. Story telling methods create an appropriate context, establish a connection, merge time into one, reinforce values in an indirect method that reinforces the independence of the listener. Storytellers take the age of a listener into account in the length of a story, focuses on particular values, seeks and creates balance and harmony between teacher and learner, between young and old. The teacher takes time, interacts and is reciprocal with listeners. Listeners/learners take turns presenting materials orally, as story tellers do. The teacher makes decisions/offers choices and uses/teaches consensus, and listens and learns from students in a way the student can feel and see, while giving students equal time to speak and use oral skills.

RESOURCE IDEAS

We all need to know what resources are available when thinking about teaching techniques/methods that involve cultural context. I have found that Elder teachers are not only a great source of inspiration and a library of cultural verbal knowledge; they also are willing to assist with various techniques one may want to try. For example one could ask elders to evaluate teaching from time to time. This could be done by videotaping several classes, providing syllabi, and any explanations Elders may additionally need. I asked Elders to evaluate my teaching, and ended up with a procedure I call 'interactive grading' and it was thanks to Elder teacher evaluations that gave me the technique.

Other ways of utilizing these oral sources are to keep in touch with elder gatherings that occur from time to time which welcomes attendance from anyone that wishes to do so. The Elder gatherings that I have attended usually include Elders that speak their language(s) fluently,[1] and are eloquent in their teaching delivery. I note that the subtle nature of Elder teaching is a way of allowing holistic analysis, instead of analyzing things immediately, it provides an environment for each listener, person to decide on his/her own just what teaching might mean. Storytelling reflects this ingenious and restrained method as well. It is possible to ask various elders to come together for the express purpose of introducing colleagues (desiring learning lessons) to Elder teacher interaction.

Useful books, in addition to Elder oral knowledge are those that try and tell the story of our brilliant elders and how they set up our way to live. The Fusion project (see, Christensen et al., 2005) an interdisciplinary University five phase/2 level project teaches 4 pillars of American Indian knowledge (History, (indigenous traditional, contact and contemporary), Sovereignty, Indigenous Intellectualism and Laws & policy) to colleague faculty (presently we are working with Education faculty, History, Literature and Social Work faculty) who will then infuse this learning into their own curriculum so that their students will receive American Indian knowledge as a regular part of study of say, education, history, literature and social work. Thus, we are using the actual academy pipeline to meet the real intent of a WI policy that mandates teaching about American Indians at least three times before students graduate from high school.[2] Presently in phase three of a five-phase multi-year plan we are using Oral teachings from Elders in Elder summer seminars on a nearby reservation, and books/ materials that assist our non-Indian colleagues in understanding both content and cultural context. Some of these materials are discussed below.

Black Elk defines and describes the holistic world, and his courage, tenacity, shrewdness and brilliance in choosing Neinhart (2000) to insert Lakota living Thought into the changing world of North America. This could be viewed as not only verified, effective leadership, it demonstrates what can happen when someone believes in, listens to and works with (received) vision. Cajete (2000) gives credence to a maybe not so far out notion that the 'scientific' way of thinking, and the Indian way of thinking are not that far apart, just different in how it is said, and what it may furthermore mean in addition to what western scientists say it means and that we see more things as alive than they do. Deloria's (1999) *Spirit and Reason* is helpful in looking at cultural context in the contemporary world. Fixico (2003) makes the holistic world easy to understand, and he gives good examples. Peat's (2002) *Blackfoot Physics* is helpful in understanding the idea of the American Indian mind. He spent time, as anyone does that wants to understand the Indian mind, with Elders listening and participation learning in the traditional way.

Ross (1992) is a favorite book for use in discussing and understanding American Indian through and behaviors. Ross is a white man, a crown provincial judge in Canada. He worked on gaining his knowledge because he knew the criminal justice system way of dealing with Indians was incorrect; he just didn't know how to articulate it. This book and the next one, *Returning to the Teachings* (Ross, 1997) is his journey down that road of knowledge. He does what Peat did—found, listened, dialogued and participated with Elder teachers. The Education faculty colleagues in our fusion project liked the *Teaching* book very much. Swamp's (n.d.) *Great Law* was used to discuss with and demonstrate to teacher colleagues an intellectual exercise that is closely aligned to one of the western world's icons of intellectualism: the Constitution of the United States with some scholars (see, e.g., Grinde, 1977; Johansen, 1982) giving Indians credit for their influence on that paradigm or as Vine Deloria says in (Johansen, 1998) his Foreword, "...the Iroquois are finally credited with a powerful voice in creating the American government" (p. 4). Other scholars (e.g., Tooker, 1988) speak loudly in print against such an upstart idea. The parallel presentation provided in Swamp can foster a very active and involved discussion. Warrior (1995) tells us that Indians are intellectuals and Waters (2004) speaks to the issue as well with chapters by various authors. I specially like V.F. Cordova (one of the authors) and her definition and use of the term *reification* in explaining and understanding world view, as editor Waters says, "Cordova reminds us that ideas are nothing if taken out of context—it is context that allows us to recognize and understand ideas" (p. xix). Wiese (1996) uses Elder knowledge as the basis of her dissertation. Good ideas for cultural adaptation can also be gleaned from Mihesuah and Wilson (2004).

PEDAGOGY/CONCLUSION

A brief word about pedagogy is necessary. Pedagogy is defined in the dictionary as "the science of teaching" (Little Oxford Dictionary, 1998, p. 465). "Pedagogy is a technical and perhaps even fancy term for teaching and includes the concepts of how we decide what, when, and in which fashion we will be teaching our students while taking into account their levels of cognitive development" (Klug & Whitfield, 2003, p. 151). In the case of oral traditional teaching, the pedagogical base consists of a broad-based experience with dominant Indian community wherein the daily behaviors reflect the group's dominant values/practices and where Elders routinely pass life-needed information through oral discourse utilizing storytelling and participatory methodology. Or as defined in Grande's treatise, "red" pedagogy is distinguished by "its basis in hope. Not the future-centered hope of the Western imagination, but rather, a hope that lives in contingency with the past—one that trusts the beliefs and understandings of our ancestors as well as the power of traditional knowledge. A Red pedagogy is, thus, as much about belief and acquiescence as it is about questioning and empowerment, about respecting the space of tradition as it intersects with the linear time frames of the (post) modern world" (Grande, 2004, p. 28). Any pedagogical base includes categories of knowledge, which in this case are passed orally through a variety of means and using set-behavior patterns.[3]

A broad culturally-based pedagogy along with a cultural evaluation frame and a way to help others understand cultural context, such as, for example, choosing, designing and providing cultural competencies provides teachers and the Tribal Academy with sufficient pedagogical thrust to teach not only book/word knowledge or content, but provide within the Academy a pervasive, rich and enveloping *context*ual base. It is only with content and context that a person can make an informed decision and still remain personally sovereign. So it is with techniques and strategies teachers might pursue, design and use in the Tribal academy. Teachers using, teaching and refining circle techniques based and honed on Circle teaching methodology will have a wide-ranging, extensive and excellent base of knowledge gleaned from experience and participation with their home Indian community. The Tribal academy will have augmented education gleaned from the oral traditional way.

NOTES

1. For example, an elder at one gathering spoke to the teachings of the 13 moons, another spoke of Turtle Island star knowledge, and other provided teachings from the 7th Fire wampum belt.
2. WI Act 31(Chapter 115, 118 and 121) to address apparent racial conflict between American Indians & non-Indians citizens.
3. An example of a set behavior pattern might be using life skills gleaned through the work of the previous generation for making the world better for the next generation. Helping or working for the next generation(s) is an accepted moral imperative with many if not most American Indian Tribes, and people in their last stage (of four traditional stages) of this existence spend most if not all their time working for the betterment of the next generation.

REFERENCES

Adams, D. W. (1995). *Education for extinction: American Indians and the boarding school experience, 1875–1928.* Lawrence: University of Kansas Press.

Beck, P. V., Walters, A. L., & Francisco, N. (1992). *The sacred ways of knowledge, sources of life* (redesigned edition). Tsaile, AZ: Navajo Community College Press.

Benham, M. K., & Mann, H. (2003). Culture & language matters: Defining, implementing, and evaluating. In M. K. Benham & W. J. Stein (Ed.). *The renaissance of American Indian higher education: Capturing the dream* (pp. 167–191). Mahwah, NJ: Lawrence Erlbaum Associates.

Cajete, G. (2000). *Native science: Natural laws of interdependence.* Santa Fe, NM: Clear Light.

Cajete, G. (1994). *Look to the mountain: An ecology of indigenous education.* Skyland, NC: Kivaki Press.

Christensen, R. (2005, November). *Conceptual points for techniques/strategies employed In circle teaching methodology brief.* Presented at World Indigenous Education Conference, Hamilton, New Zealand.

Christensen, R. A. (2004). Teaching within the circle: Methods for an American Indian teaching and learning style, a tribal paradigm. In V. Lea & J. Helfand (Eds.), *Identifying race and transforming whiteness in the classroom* (pp. 171–191). New York: Peter Lang.

Christensen, R. A. (1991, June). *Five cultural competencies.* Paper presented at the American Educational Research Association SIG Research on Women and Education, San Jose, CA.

Christensen, R. A. (1986/2003). *Cultural competencies: An overview brief.* Unpublished manuscript.

Christensen, R. A., & Oxendine, L. E. (2005, November). *Teaching methods/techniques based on North American Indian Elder traditional knowledge and cultural values.* Paper presented at World Indigenous Peoples Education Conference, Hamilton, New Zealand.

Christensen, R., Poupart, L., & Kaufman, T. (2005). *Infusing American Indian knowledge into the curriculum: A model for teacher education.* Unpublished manuscript, University of Wisconsin, Green Bay.

Deloria, V. Jr. (1999). *Spirit and reason.* Golden, CO: Fulcrum Publishing.

Duran, E., & Duran, B. (1995). *Native American postcolonial psychology.* Albany: State University of New York Press.

Fixico, D. L. (2003). *The American Indian mind in a linear world: American Indian studies and traditional knowledge.* New York: Routledge.

Gone, J. P. (2004). Keeping culture in mind. In D. A. Mihesuah & A. C. Wilson (Eds.), *Indigenizing the academy: Transforming scholarship and empowering communities* (pp124–142). Lincoln & London: University of Nebraska Press.

Grande, S. 2004. Red pedagogy: Native American social & political thought. Toronto: Rowman & Littlefield Publishers, Inc.

Grinde, D. (1977). *The Iroquois and the founding of the American nation.* San Francisco: Indian Historian Press.

Johansen, B. E. (1982). *Forgotten founders: Benjamin Franklin, the Iroquois, and the rationale for the American revolution.* Ipswich, MA: Gambit.

Johansen, B. E. (1998). *Debating democracy: Native American Legacy of Freedom.* Santa Fe, NM: Clearlight Publishers.

Klug, B. J., & Whitfield. P. T. (2003). *Widening the circle.* New York: RoutledgeFalmer.

LaFrance, J. (2004). Culturally competent evaluation in Indian country. *New Directions for Evaluation, 102,* 39–50.

LaFrance, J., & Nichols, R. (2006, January). *Summary report: Stories from the focus groups on an indigenous framing for evaluation* (draft copy). Available from AIHEC 121 Oronoco Street, Alexandria, VA 22314.

Little Oxford Dictionary. (1998). Rev. Ed. New York: Clarendon Press.

Lucas, C. J. (1994). *American higher education: A history.* New York: St. Martin's Press.

Mackey, E. (2002). *The house of difference: Cultural politics and national identity in Canada.* Toronto: University of Toronto Press.

Marcus, G. (1989). Imagining the whole: Ethnography's contemporary efforts to situate itself. *Critique of Anthropology, 9*(3), 7–30.

Mihesuah, D. A., & Wilson, A. C. (Eds.). (2004). *Indigenizing the academy: Transforming scholarship and empowering communities.* Lincoln: University of Nebraska Press.

National Science Foundation. (2002). *The cultural context of educational evaluation: A Native American perspective.* Directorate for Education and Human Resources Division of Research, Evaluation and Communication. Contract No. REC-9912171.

Neihardt, J. G. (2000). *Black Elk speaks.* Lincoln: University of Nebraska Press.

Newmann, F. M., Smith, B., Allensworth, E., & Bryk, A. S. (2001, Winter). Instructional program coherence: What it is and why it should guide school improvement policy. *Educational Evaluation and Policy Analysis, 23*(4), 297–321.

Ortiz, A. (1973). Look to the mountaintop. In E. Ward (Ed.), *Essays in reflections.* Boston: Houghton-Mifflin.

Ortiz, A. (1972). New *perspectives on the Pueblos.* Albuquerque: University of New Mexico Press.

Peat, F. D. (2002). *Blackfoot physics: A journey into the Native American universe.* Grand Rapids, MI: Phanes Press.

Ross, R. (1997). *Returning to the teachings: Exploring Aboriginal justice.* Toronto: Penguin Books.

Ross, R. (1992). *Dancing with a ghost: Exploring Indian reality.* Ontario: Reed Books.

Staples, L., Ojibwe, St. Croix Band of Ojibwe Indians, Wisconsin Lake Superior Band. (2005, August 31). Oral scholar and advisor to the Chief, Mille Lacs Band of Ojibwe Indians, Minnesota, Mississippi Band, personal communication.

Swamp, J. (n.d.). *The great law of peace and the Constitution of the United States of America.* New York: Tree of Peace Society, Box 188-C, Cook Road, Mohawk Nation via Akwesasne, NY 13655.

Thohahoken. (2005). Organizing indigenous governance to invent the future. In A. W. Waziyatawin & M. Yellow Bird (Eds.), *For indigenous eyes only: A decolonization handbook* (pp. 157–177). Sante Fe, NM: School of American Research Press.

Tooker, E. (1988). *The United States Constitution and the Iroquois League. Ethnohistory 35,* 305–336.

Warrior, R. A. (1995). *Tribal secrets: Recovering American Indian intellectual traditions.* Minneapolis: University of Minnesota Press.

Waters, A. (Ed.). (2004). *American Indian thought.* Cambridge, MA: Blackwell Publishing.

Waziyatawin, A. W., & Yellow Bird, M. (Eds.) (2005). *For indigenous eyes only: A decolonization handbook.* Sante Fe, NM: School of American Research Press.

Wiese, D. P. (1996). *American Indian adults and the construction, structures, and meaning of knowledge.* Unpublished manuscript, Northern Illinois University.

Williams, R. (1980). *Problems in materialism and culture: Selected essays.* London: Verso.

PART III

LEADERSHIP

In Iroquois society, leaders are encouraged to remember seven generations in the past and consider several generations in the future when making decisions that affect The People.

—Oren Lyons, Seneca Nation

CHAPTER 9

INDIGENOUS GOVERNANCE

Linda Sue Warner and Kathryn Harris Tijerina

INTRODUCTION

Does indigenous governance in the United States mean that the people who govern are indigenous, or does it suppose a deeper, intellectually divergent system of governance, a system which found foreign the prioritization of Manifest Destiny and federalism? If the latter, what are some of the characteristics of this different system of governance? Are the tribal colleges the best representations of indigenous governance in the United States? This article will explore these questions in the context of policy development for tribal colleges.

Tribal people are inherently people of the group. Communal living gives rise to a value system that reinforces group behavior. This is not to be confused with a lack of strong individuals. In fact, strong individuals are encouraged because they have more to offer the group. But, the focus is on contributing back to the group. In terms of governance, these communal values are expressed in a consensus process. The individuals in the group would all participate collectively in the decision making process. The majority did not rule; rather all the people continue to engage until there is a general agreement.

This traditional consensus process is very different from the governance found in public education systems. It is interesting for native people to

Tradition and Culture in the Millennium: Tribal Colleges and Universities, pages 109–132
Copyright © 2009 by Information Age Publishing
109

observe the growing general dissatisfaction with public education. Increasingly, other people of color find that public education does not meet their needs. Now even mainstream Americans are finding that public education is not working for them. One result has been a growing search for other options. Many people in today's society are trying to re-envision public higher education; one of the successful aspects of the University of Phoenix is their use of collaborative learning which in some ways approaches communal processes.

Tribal colleges are another answer to the problems of public education, particularly in rural areas throughout Indian Country.[1] In their best examples, they embody communal public education. This has lead to consensus processes being used in the governance of some Tribal Colleges. An example in the Comanche Nation College is detailed later in this chapter.

The traditional consensus process is also very different from the governance found in United States legal and political processes and the resulting Federal Indian Law. Two crucial aspects of Federal Indian Law are self-determination and trust responsibility. Yet, there is an inherent tension between the legal concepts of self-determination and trust responsibility. This tension lends itself particularly well to the metaphor of a parent and child. Essentially it is the parent's responsibility to raise the child to be self sufficient, providing experiences and support along the way. The parent is entrusted with the child's physical, mental, and spiritual welfare. However, legally the parental responsibility ends at a specific date and the individual is considered to be self-sufficient. The individual may continue to seek advice from the parent, yet the parent and the child separate. In 1978 with the passage of the Indian Self-determination Act, Congress appeared to legislate that American Indian tribes had reached the date of legal maturity, if we continue our metaphor.[2] The law, however, does not eliminate the trust responsibility nor does it reinforce political sovereignty.

Self-determination or self-governance requires a political entity be entrusted with the authority to govern. Self-determination assumes prior informed consent from the group to be ethical and sustainable. The group must have enough information about a decision to make an informed, ethical, and sustainable decision. If we review the U.S. legal history of Indian self-determination, we would wrongly assume that American Indian tribes did not govern themselves except within the formal context of a federally imposed legal system in 1934.[3] This would be a false assumption; tribes have always governed themselves, with and without the knowledge and sanction of the federal governance system.

SELF-DETERMINATION IN INDIAN COUNTRY

The era of American Indian self-determination began in the 1960s. The decade of the '60s saw the founding of National Indian Youth Council (1961), the American Indian Movement (1968) and the passages of the 1968 Indian Civil Rights Act. Also founded in the '60s, Oklahomans for Indian Opportunity (1960) was the precursor to Americans for Indian Opportunity which was founded in 1970. The federal program "War on Poverty" resulted in new opportunities for young Indian leaders that had been previously shut out of the hall of power. It was the decade of the beginning of the Vietnam War which trained at least 43,000 American Indians. With this beginning, Indian self-determination was reinforced in the '70s, '80s, and '90s.

From self-determination in the '70s to self-actualization in current tribal agendas, the following law and policy initiatives continue to impact education: the American Indian Policy Review Commission (1975 1976) and the Indian Self-Determination and Education Assistance Act (1975) preceded the Indian Child Welfare Act (1978), the Tribally Controlled Community College Act (1978), the Indian Religious Freedom Act (1978),[4] the Indian Mineral Development Act (1982), the Tribal Tax Status Act (1982), the Native American Languages Act (1990), the Indian Arts and Crafts Act (1990), the Native American Grave Protection and Repatriation Act (1990), the Indian Tribal Justice Recognition Act (1991), the Tribal Self Governance Act (1994)—all designed to reinforce self-governance. Federal policy reports reflecting the changes mandated by legislation include The Kennedy Report (1969), Indian Nations at Risk (1991), and various executive orders, the most recent one signed by President Bush April 30, 2004.[5]

As policy and law reflected changes in Indian affairs in these decades, mainstream philosophy did not always reflect these changes. The United States is a nation that believes in property rights. Yet when American Indians obtain a property right, one often hears words like "giving," "welfare" and "Why should we give them things they didn't earn?" So it appears that the United States is also a country of profound double standards, or, at the least, one in which most do not understand the fundamentals of trust responsibility.

Many Indian Nations, including our tribe, the Comanche, signed treaties with the United States. In the hierarchy of law, treaties supersede a federal statute. Treaties with Indian Nations are sanctioned specifically in the United States Constitution. Simply put, the treaties embody property rights over time. In exchange for land an Indian Nation might receive among other benefits: health, water, hunting and fishing rights, housing, and education benefits. The citizens of the Indian Nations will continue to receive these benefits as long as the United States continues to benefit from the land.

If one did a cost benefit analysis of the value of the land and its minerals, Indian Nations have not fared well. For example, the health benefits are primarily conveyed through the Indian Health Services. In a recent federal study, researchers found that fewer dollars were spent for Indian health recipients than were spent for prisoners, yet the land benefits conferred to the US are still intact (U.S. Commission on Civil Rights, 2003). The trust responsibility is the fiduciary obligation of the federal government to hold these property rights for the benefit of Indian Nations and their citizens. For many years that trust responsibility was thought to reside in the Bureau of Indian Affairs or at most in the Interior Department. However, the trust responsibility is the responsibility of all of the federal agencies of the United States. Any of the federal instrumentalities, such as the Department of Education, share in the obligation of trust responsibility to Indian Nations.

Indigenous Governance

In the United States, the Harvard Project on American Indian Economic Development conducted research into the relationship between Indian/indigenous governance, sovereignty/self-determination, and sustainable economic development (Dodson & Smith 2003, p. 3). Indigenous governance is frequently conceptualized with economic development. Understanding local control of economies, particularly those without natural resources, requires a dialogue that focuses on human capital via education. Tribal colleges are the venue for such discussions and represent a key link in tribal economic development particularly as the world grows "flatter" through the use of technology (Friedman, 2005).

Tribal colleges exist as the embodiment of self-determination by tribal communities for the benefit of tribal communities. The creation of a tribal college requires vision, a plan for achieving this vision, desire and skill, and eventually materials. In many ways, creating the policies that produce the lifelong learners, the actualization of personal self-determination is a balance between this self-actualization and academic achievement. Whether or not governing boards create policies that produce this balance depends on the board's ability to establish policy and management systems that support student learning, often in venues that appear foreign to mainstream academe. This chapter explores the ways in which academic policy produces academic performance, and some of the factors tribal colleges consider essential to the development of lifelong learning.

Tribal College Policies for the 21st Century

Demographics for students in tribal colleges consistently report that tribal college students would be non-traditional students in mainstream institutions of higher education (IHE). Tribal college students are typically American Indian. Sixty-four percent of all tribal college undergraduates are female, and many single parents. Many attend part time and are first generation college students.[6] The unique characteristics of the students and the explicit mission of tribal colleges require particular attention to tribal college policies.

Educational policies are defined by Guba (1984) as:

1. Policy is an assertion of intents or goals.
2. Policy is the accumulated standing decisions of a governing body by which it regulates, controls, promotes, services, and otherwise influence matters within its sphere of authority.
3. Policy is a guide to discretionary action.
4. Policy is a strategy undertaken to solve or ameliorate a problem.
5. Policy is sanctioned behavior.
6. Policy is a norm of conduct characterized by consistency and regularity in some substantive action area.

This chapter focuses primarily on institutional level policies. At their creation, tribal colleges often rely on the established policies of a state, accredited institution. Tribal college policies may or may not remain coordinated with the original state institution and many policies evolve from the original set used in the founding of the institution. Policies that impact student performance may be found among the policies throughout an institution, including its personnel policies, its grievance policies, its facility usage, and even its travel policies.

The vision for student success is linked closely to all policies in a tribal college, regardless of the stage of evolution of these policies from the supporting state institution. Tribal college philosophy, and as a result, policies, interlock to create a holistic vision of lifelong learning. The uniqueness of these policies can be defined as this "interlock" between policy and practice to embody a successful tribal college, i.e., one whose students are lifelong learners and contributors to a community.

The strength of interlock between policy and practice can be defined as the magnitude of balance found around individual policies. Policies are often the result of problem identification. Someone identifies a problem and the next step is to create a policy which addresses the problem so that practice can enable a solution. Often the problems identified on a day to day basis are not linked in any obvious manner, so the interlocking required of a successful organization is complex. In mainstream academic orientation, administrators use the mandates, inducements, capacity building, and systemic change as policy tools to transform goals into actions.

Educational policy boards in IHEs[7] use policies to build institutions with a specific vision and values; such building creates conditions which allow practice to reinforce the policies. For student achievement, the policies that mandate specific test scores for admission to an institution allow administrators to practice a strategy which is designed to weed out less successful or under-prepared students, thereby making it easier for academic success in the institution. This type of exclusionary policy is often justified as support for "excellence." This type of policy is found more often when there is a state governing board for professional licensure at the end of the academic preparation. Mandating minimum tests scores are an example of policy to incentivize student achievement.

Hiring policies which use "Indian preference" is an example of a capacity building policy at a tribal college. Native ways of knowing, as a curricular emphasis, is an example of policy designed for capacity building. Native ways of knowing informs all aspects of pedagogy and builds on the traditions and cultures of the local community.

A combination of mandate, incentive, capacity building, and systemic change can be found in tribal colleges. In the 1990s, the National Science Foundation (NSF) provided incentives for tribal colleges to align policies and practice so that a seamless K–14 system of activities would increase student achievement, specifically in science, mathematics, engineering, and technology (SMET). With a specific set of "drivers" NSF combined policy mandates with incentives by awarding multiple grants of $2 million each year to tribal colleges through the Rural Systemic Initiative.[8] The singular most effective result of this combination of policy alignment was the use and ultimately the recognition of *native ways of knowing* as a viable philosophy, a teaching and learning tool, and a research method. The Tribal College Rural Systemic Initiative supported more than 100 focal K–12 schools in six states among 20 Indian nations in efforts to implement systemic change in mathematics and science standards-based curricula.

Culture and Tradition: Lifelong Learning

Governance can be defined as the processes and structures through which a group makes decision, distributes and exercises authority and power, determines strategic goals, organizes behavior, develops rules, and assigns responsibility (Dodson & Smith, 2003, p. 4). Indigenous governance contextualizes these processes and structures in a native culture and tradition that has been politically powerless in a nonnative society. The norms and values of Indian societies remain a vital part of the heritage of current tribes. Fundamentally, governance is about power, relationships, and processes of representation and accountability—about who has influence, who decides, and how decision-makers are held accountable (Plumptre & Graham, 1999).

Governance is not the same as government. Governance broadens the interaction to include more stakeholders (Sterritt, 2002). Indigenous governance infers lifelong learning. While "self-government" means having jurisdiction and a mandated control over the members of a group, its land, and resources, "governance" is about having the structures processes and institutional capacity in place to be able to exercise that jurisdiction through sound decision-making, representation, and accountability (Dodson & Smith 2003, p. 2). Cultural norms create the conditions for legitimate and capable rule through collective action. This leads to the social, cultural, and economic maintenance of native peoples through historical changes, such as from a nomadic, hunting society to a complex, multifaceted corporation.

Traditional Indian governance is situated within the context of kinship and its responsibilities. Families, and by inference extended families, form the foundation of all relationships within tribal communities. No one member of the family (council) has more power than another individual. Traditional American Indian governments, the councils involve people in the decision making (Washaba & Washaba, 1997). The primary task of the government is to protect and serve the community. Spirituality forms the center of indigenous knowing.

TRIBAL COLLEGES: FROM POLICY TO PRACTICE

To begin an explanation of an indigenous model for student performance that can evolve from institutional policies, it is important to begin with definitions for the following variables. A student is defined as the learner, regardless of the age of the student. The individual who learns in a classroom setting can be, and is defined for our discussion, any individual in the class, including the teacher. For institutional purposes, the student in a tribal college has the same identifiers as a student in any institution of higher education (IHE), including individual identification numbers, responsibilities for class assignments, and assignment and test performance indicators. Student success in tribal colleges is defined for institutional recordkeeping purposes in the same manner it would be for other IHE. Grades are distributed based on completed assignments and examinations.

Two examples of the use of indigenous policies to drive practice are described next. The first is The Achein in Santa Fe, New Mexico at the Institute of American Indian Arts (IAIA) and the second is the Comanche Nation

College in Lawton, Oklahoma.[9] Kirkness and Barnhardt (1991) argue that policies in traditional IHEs place the burden of success on the student, rather than the institution. Indigenous governance policies balance the burden.

These two examples use native ways of knowing in the policy structure of tribal colleges. Each of the thirty-five tribal communities linked with an IHE have variations that allow for the use of native ways of knowing in their philosophy, policies, and procedures. As a result of the authority of the local tribal councils and local governing boards, policies based on native ways of knowing often are tied to native languages and local traditions.

INSTITUTE OF AMERICAN INDIAN ARTS

The Institute of American Indian and Alaska Native Culture and Arts (IAIA) is a national art college, congressionally chartered. It is the only institute of higher education in the United States devoted solely to the study and practice of indigenous artistic and cultural traditions. IAIA was congressionally chartered and separated from the Department of Interior in 1988, although it had been operating in previous capacities in the 1960s.

In designing the policies and practices to accentuate student performance at the Institute of American Indian Arts (IAIA) in Santa Fe, New Mexico, the governing board and administration convened a national advisory group of approximately 100 individuals. Using native ways of knowing as the template for designing a lifelong learning center for multi-tribal students, the convocation members developed the following core considerations. The foundation for Achein, the Lifelong Learning Center (LLC) in Santa Fe was based on eight core areas. These are discussed, along with the recommendations from the convocation, in the following section. The Curricular Emphases, Examples, and the four crosscutting themes (Native Ways of Knowing, Leadership, Research, and Technology) provide powerful links to indigenous governance practices.

Education and Youth Development

Appliqué work, designed with mirror images, is a symbol of balance, a life of beauty that is also utilitarian.

Curricular Emphases Examples:

1. Educational tests and measurements as methods of accountability to tribal community.
2. Education law for Native communities.
3. Family-based education model in Native American student services.
4. Creating a scared place for children: a culturally based school improvement model.

Native Ways of Knowing. Many tribal communities work to sustain the youth in their care for seven generations. This responsibility is best carried out through educational programs that span generations and that seek to prepare Native youth to make decisions for their families, their tribes, and the next seven generations. Native ways of knowing as a pedagogy attends to the learner's individual style and emphasizes active participation in skill development.

Leadership. The development of leadership skills for youth is essential for tribes. With this understanding comes a responsibility to teach Native youth the traditions and practices of Indian tribes. Contextual leadership skills can be taught and the Achein Center can provide opportunities for various forums to explore leadership practices with students of all ages.

Research. Research projects in education and youth development will allow the Center to disseminate knowledge about indigenous learning to a broader public.

Technology. The Achein Center proposes youth development through practical skills in order that lifelong learning is actualized through productive adults and community leaders. Technology can empower youth by providing employment and life skills. Technology can be used to link cross-generational activities. Technology provides the opportunity for students to teach adults.

Art and Humanities

   The LLC will encompass freedom of spiritual places with healing environments; it is creating the way of beauty.
   Curricular Emphases Examples:

1. Native voices in history: First person perspectives.
2. Performing arts and Indian Country development.
3. World indigenous art.
4. Tribal museums place in history and community development.

Native Ways of Knowing. As pedagogical emphases, oral histories and storytelling connect current native teaching with more traditional methods. The preservation of these oral histories and cultural artifacts allows us to sustain cultures and to explore the connectedness in a contemporary forum.

Leadership. Individual exhibitions of the contemporary arts will develop individual styles of leadership that foster the growth of the community through active participation.

Research. Qualitative and quantitative research projects can be explored through the history of art and culture. These explorations can be cross-cultural or longitudinal and can add to a richer understanding of naïve pedagogy.

Technology.   Many current faculty members attest to the transformation in their teaching style that has occurred because of the availability of technology-enhanced instruction. Enrollment patterns for online enrollments throughout the country continue to increase as the templates for delivery become more sophisticated. The relationship of types of course/programs to the utility of online or hybrid online delivery can be enhanced with partnerships between disciplines and between other colleges and universities.

Culture, Language, Land
   Beauty is within.
   Curricular Emphases Examples:

1. Immersion teaching methods for native/indigenous language retention.
2. Action research methods.
3. Native sustainable architecture and land development.
4. Archival development/collections care and management.

Native Ways of Knowing.   Self-image and perception play persuasive roles in the Lifelong Learning Center's ability to educate, enlighten, and participate in tribal communities. An understanding of the critical need to foster the sustainability of tribal languages will benefit the IAIA's planning processes in the future. IAIA has a longstanding relationship with Indian educators within New Mexico and can be a model of the partnerships between an institution of higher learning and local communities.

Leadership.   The language of leadership found in indigenous languages may provide a situational context to leadership for communities. Understanding the language derivations and emphases allows for a more complete understanding of the basis for traditional tribal governments, as well as for all social interactions. Leadership may also be examined as relational depending on the cultural traditions of matriarchy or patriarchy found among tribes.

Research.   The Achein Center will foster the opportunity to research multilingualism and multiculturalism. By developing a knowledge base of second language acquisition, the Center will be able to conduct action research projects and to advance the quality of second language teaching and learning. This research will allow for an extension and application across disciplines and education systems.

Technology.   Technology provides a virtual learning environment for developing collaborative, constructive learning based on undertaking real tasks with other learners across the Internet. For language acquisition, it is possible to enhance learning strategies by solving real life problems, i.e., learning in a situated context. Learning through conversation and, through technology, asynchronous interaction, provides the learner with multiple opportunities for context driven learning.

Health and Wellness

Beauty is connection: connection with all living things, with the creator and with all parts of our lives.
Curricular Emphases Examples:

1. Diabetes prevention: cultural approaches to nutrition.
2. Traditional foods and culinary arts.
3. Traditional health and wellness initiatives.
4. Ethnobotany: medicinal plants.

Native Ways of Knowing. Indigenous health is not just the physical well-being of an individual. It includes the social, emotional, and cultural well-being of an entire community if the individual is to achieve a healthy, balanced lifestyle. Service providers need to be cognizant of the imperatives within tribal cultures if they are to assure that health care needs of communities are met.

Leadership. Indigenous knowledge systems accentuate an individual's relationship to the group as a whole and depend on interface between and among community members. The Achein Center can provide leadership in the improvement of service providers through licensure programs and professional development.

Research. The Achein Center's ability to provide thorough, high quality research in health and wellness with established partnerships will contribute to the knowledge base for health services policy, social services policy, and holistic health policy. Research will require knowledge translation from traditional cultures.

Technology. Technology has an impact on health and wellness in the areas of research practice. While the overall effect is not yet fully assessable due to lack of trained personnel, the presence of technology in so many different aspects of the health professions makes it important to more clearly recognize and appreciate its current and potential role.

Culturally Based Economic Development

Culturally based economic development is the path to beauty and spiritual health.
Curricular Emphases Examples:

1. Art Business Management.
2. Tribal cultural tourism.

3. Marketing Native American art.
4. Culturally based economies and economic development.

Native Ways of Knowing.   Economic development as a competitive method to acquire resources may seem at odds with native ways of knowing. In fact, understanding the balance of all systems is as essential in economics as it is in any of the social sciences. The balance of available resources and need is a basic economic question. Native ways of knowing can inform economic strategies and can be used as the basis for economic development.

Leadership.   Culturally based economic development is dependent upon resourceful, energetic leaders. As a direct result of the vision of tribal leaders, tribal communities have new opportunities today in areas of sustainable agriculture, resource management, and gaming in some of the poorest land base areas in the country. It is essential that tribal leaders temper the development of Indian country economics with the traditions and practices which have sustained them in order to build the future on the strength of the past.

Research.   Market research and resource identification are critical to an economically sound community. Expertise in these areas can be found with connections that the Achein Center has formed with private enterprise and with university expertise throughout the world.

Technology.   The Achein Center approach will capture the fusion of technology and economic development. Rapid technological development has fundamentally altered economic development principles. The use of technology is rapidly changing the way value is created and is also transforming the nature of dynamic competitiveness. A fundamental redefinition of the tools and strategies needed in Indian Country will improve tribal or individual efforts to define a position in the global marketplace.

Creative Leadership and Tribal Governance
A tribal code of ethics would be a source of beauty and spiritual health.
Curricular Emphases Examples:

1. Ethics and the law.
2. Cross-cultural models of executive leadership.
3. Repatriation challenges for tribal cultural and political leaders.
4. Native constitutions.

Native Ways of Knowing.   The Achein Center will provide opportunities to educate students with tribal governance perspectives that include the negotiation of relationships among individuals, groups, and governments. Indigenous governance systems are recognized as the framework for the republic form of government established in the United States, yet many of the subtleties remain unacknowledged or unexplored.

Leadership.   Leadership skills are critical in a contemporary era of self-determination by American Indian tribes. The variety of tribal structure throughout this country provides a wealth of resources for the identification and description of tribal leaders. The Achein Center can provide a forum for not only the study of leadership, but the actualization of leadership application in the development of policies for Native tribes.

Research.   The study of leadership in a society begins with a study of the society as a separate cultural entity. The Achein Center will have the opportunity to support leadership studies across 500+ indigenous communities in this country. The holistic study of leadership provides a unique opportunity to support indigenous knowledge systems and inform contemporary research methods.

Technology.   Tribal governments may find technology innovation to be risky and cost prohibitive. The ability to evaluate technological innovations before investments are made becomes even more requisite in times of declining resources. The Achein Center will develop decision-making skills that allow tribal government authorities the opportunities needed to strengthen management skills throughout their systems.

Law and Justice
  The building block of beauty is justice and freedom.
  Curricular Emphases Examples:

  1. Understanding tribal court systems.
  2. Management of Indian lands and natural resources.
  3. Ethics and the law on Reservations.
  4. Cultural property rights and sovereignty.

Native Ways of Knowing.   Students will have the opportunity to acquire a realistic understanding of the substantive aspects of law and legal professions, including those specific to tribal courts. Judicial decision-making and the principles of conflict management reflect various tribal perspectives. The indigenous justice paradigm is based on a holistic philosophy. Indigenous systems may be guided by the unwritten customary laws, traditions, and practices that are learned primarily by example and through the oral te achings of tribal elders. For indigenous systems, everyone connected to the problem is connected to the solution. From initial disclosure of a problem, to discussion and resolution of that problem, and, to making amends and restoring relationships, the focus is always on balance. The methods used are based on concepts of restorative and reparative justice as well as the principles of healing and living in harmony with all beings and with nature.

Leadership. Through a variety of forums, students will have the opportunity to build leadership skills essential to the practice of law. Such opportunities will include conducting legal research, oral and written presentations, and honing the skill of reasoning strategies. Leadership skills may be taught through internships in a variety of venues.

Research. The Achein Center would be positioned to analyze legal issues that currently confront tribal, state, and federal governments. The range of analysis would include responses to current legislative initiatives, i.e., red papers, to individual research projects by students.

Technology. Legal issues in technology include indigenous intellectual property issues. These issues continue to be debated throughout Indian Country. The Achein Center can provide a common forum for the development of policy and practice as it relates to the maintenance of language and culture. Technology is a means to accomplish a critical objective in preserving intellectual property.

Family, Community, and World Development

The paths to the source of beauty found at Achein allow learners a place to be themselves, a place to find out about themselves regardless of their origins.

Curricular Emphases Examples:

1. Traditional early childhood education methods.
2. Elder development and community modeling.
3. Culturally based natural resources management.
4. Cultural mapping in tribal communities.

Native Ways of Knowing. Significant community development activities originate from a commitment of time and resources at a local level. The internal assets of a neighborhood in a contemporary context are analogous to tribal emphases on social structures of family and extended family. Indigenous social structures value the community as a primary unit and the strength of this philosophy continues to sustain tribal communities throughout the county.

Leadership. Creative local leaders across Indian Country have sustained tribal communities through hard work and personal energy. They discovered that wherever there are effective community development efforts, those efforts are based upon an understanding of the community's assets, capacities, and abilities. One key to community regeneration and sustainability, then, is to locate all of the available local assets, to begin connecting them with one another in ways that multiply their power and effectiveness, and to begin building alliances with those local institutions that are not yet available for local development purposes. The Achein will facilitate structures and strategies for these connections.

Research. Research on family, community, and world development can lead to the development of activities based on the capacities, skills, and assets of local communities to interact in larger communities. Research on communities will be linked to research in areas of economic development, particularly efforts aimed at the grassroots of a community.

Technology. Family, community, and world developments merge philosophically in a lifelong learning center and sustainability of the policies and practices is critical. The relevance and importance of technology transfer to the process of sustainable community development continues to grow.

Technology

Beauty is empowerment for our people.
Curricular Emphases Examples:

1. Audio visual and computer use for cultural empowerment.
2. Tribal technology policy issues, planning, and management.
3. Distance education for knowledge acquisition and sharing.
4. Technology and indigenous communities: case studies.

Native Ways of Knowing. The ability to balance processes and to sustain a tribal community can be enhanced using technology as a tool to promote wellness. The traditions of Indian people can merge with contemporary community lifestyles to create a holistic perspective for the implementation and creative benefit of individuals and tribes using technology in Indian Country. Technology can provide a link for urban Indians who may be isolated from their culture and traditions.

Leadership. Technology provides the method for distance learning. Tribal leadership is necessary for technology incorporation in the core elements of preservation and communication. Leadership in the areas of infusion and incorporation of technology may be cross-generational as often younger students are the most aware of the methods used in current computer programs and software. While technology is not limited to computer use, tribal leadership across partners with the Achein will allow tribes to explore "trade routes" in a contemporary fashion. Composition and approaches for these connections will be facilitated by the Center.

Research. The preservation of traditional forms of art, story, and song remains a concern in Indian Country. Tribes can use technology to create a sense of common strength in the preservation and continuation of those practices which tribes may wish to highlight. The Achein Center can provide a common framework for preservation of tribal knowledge using technology and it can provide a resource facility as a clearing house for research.

Technology. Technology is a crosscutting theme and can be found in the recommendations of all groups. It stands alone as well. The nature and power of technology in a global economy remind us that our students' lives will embrace technology in a manner we realistically cannot conceive. Many rural communities have access issues with technology and it is important to create an atmosphere of advocacy for Native community members.

The Institute of American Indian Arts' new initiative in ACHEIN and the Comanche Nation College in Lawton represent recent developments in the tribal college movement. Each are uniquely linked to indigenous governance systems.

COMANCHE NATION COLLEGE

The second example is from Oklahoma's first tribal college. It was established by charter from the Comanche Tribe of Oklahoma on August 3, 2002. At Comanche Nation College (CNC), the policies of the institution which are specific to CNC and are separate from Cameron University are those policies which reflect traditional Comanche values: responsibility, reciprocity, redistribution, and relationships. The Comanche Nation College Council, the oversight authority for this college designed by the tribal council, consciously designed policies which reflected the traditional values of the tribe. Proposed policies which cannot be aligned with these four traditional values are not considered appropriate or viable in the day-to-day operation of the College.

Examples of policies and practices which impact student achievement reflect four traditional norms. These were articulated by LaDonna Harris and Jacqueline Wasilewaski and shape the paradigm used by the current Council to implement administrative structures. The explanations are provided here with examples linked to the Comanche Nation College.

Relationship—*Kinship Obligation:* Our relationships to others dictate our roles in society.
- All things are connected and we are related to all things—humans, all living things as well as rocks and Mother Earth. Native Americans have always known what scientists are just now learning, for instance humans share the same DNA with broccoli and that humans are made up of the very stuff of stars.

- Policies and practices which reflect kinship obligations can be found through the personnel policies for the College.

Responsibility—*Community Obligation:*   Our relationships to others determine our responsibilities to others.

- For instances if I call you my niece, then I have a kinship responsibility to you.
- Policies and practices which reflect community obligations to others include those found throughout the student handbook.

Reciprocity—*Cyclical Obligation:*   Our relationships and responsibilities are reciprocal.

- All things are circular in nature and all things are connected. If you are my niece, than you have an obligation to me as well. For instance, in the Comanche language the word for maternal grandmother and maternal granddaughter are the same word.
- Policies and practices which represent cyclical obligations include those outlining instructor/student dynamics.

Redistribution—*Sharing Obligation:*   We have a responsibility to share resources and information for the good of the whole.

- Policies and practices which reflect sharing obligations include budget allocations.

Most tribes were not hierarchal but flat societies that were communal. They owned and shared things in common. There were no poor people. There were no orphans. In today's society, we include non material wealth in this perspective but also information and resources should be shared for the good of the whole (Harris & Wasilewaski, 1992).

In practice, indigenous governance is confounded at times by the language of bureaucratic organizations and the language of a culture. For example, in a typical administrative Council meeting, a Council member might say, "It would be helpful to see an organizational chart that named the employees with the position." Council members agree and the conversation moves to the next topic. This is confounding if the school administrator hears this as rhetorical. It is phrased rhetorically, but culturally there is no doubt in the Council members' minds that a specific request has been made. At the next council meeting, it is expected by Council members that the organizational chart with names is provided. Administratively, it is important that the institutional bureaucracy respond to this request. The language of consensus is atypical for a governing body in mainstream organizations. This requires Council members, and college administrators, to consciously rethink and rebuild the language of institutional governance.

The combination of leadership and management in the development of policy is exacting and intricate if tribal colleges are to ensure that their institutions create the knowledge, skill, motivation, and context that result in student success. In institutions where policy and practice are linked through interlocking philosophies, such as native ways of knowing, policies will reinforce and accommodate the school context. The strength of the implementation of native ways of knowing within tribal colleges is that it supports local context with a directness and sensitivity that are inimitable in other community contexts.

The Comanche Nation College Council moved in consensus to configure all College policies within the framework of the four traditional cultural values of responsibility, reciprocity, redistribution, and relationship. To accomplish this, each of the College council members agreed to review chapters in the policy handbook and make an initial determination as to which core cultural value was represented. If we found a policy which could not be considered one of the four core cultural values, we discarded it. After the initial determination, each policy was reviewed in council work sessions and consensus was reached on the representation of the policy by a specific core cultural value. An example of how this is actualized can be found in Figure 9.1.

A separate example of how the core cultural values can be found in administrative practice is the alignment of the performance evaluation process with the core cultural values. An example of how this is actualized can be found in Figure 9.2. Subsequently budget line items, faculty performance, and student assessment will be aligned to the four traditional values.

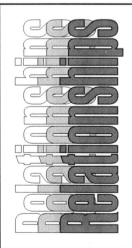

American Indian Preference in Hiring

1. The location of the Comanche Nation College as well as the nature of funding for the college, makes it attractive to utilize a locally derived employment applicant pool. The college will grant preference in hiring to qualified American Indian people.

The administrative staff shall develop a rating system for preference in hiring. The rating system shall include the following criteria in order of preference:

1. Candidate enrolled as a member of the Comanche Nation.
2. Candidate enrolled as a member of the in another tribe.
3. Candidate that is non-Indian.

Additional factors (i.e. education, experience, veterans) shall be added up the above criteria.

Figure 9.1 Example of format for policy handbook.

Procedure

American Indian Preference in Employment

A. Definitions

1. "American Indian" means a person who is a member of an American Indian tribe either recognized by the B.I.A. or state recognized. If the CNC has reason to doubt that a person seeking employment preference is an American Indian, the CNC shall grant the preference but shall require the individual within (3) days to provide evidence documentation from the tribe concerned that the person is proposing to be a tribal member of that tribe.

2. "American Indian Tribe" means an American Indian tribe, clan, band, Nation, or other organized tribal group or community, including any Alaska Native village or regional or village corporation as defined in or established as eligible for the special programs and services provided by the United State to Indian because of their status as Indians.

3. "American Indian Organization" means the governing body of any Indian tribe or entity established or recognized by such governing body in accordance with the Indian Financing Act of 1974 (88 Stat. 77: 25 U.S.C., 1451); and

4. "American Indian-owned economic enterprise" means any Indian-owned commercial, industrial, or business activity established or organized for the purpose of profit provided that such Indian ownership shall constitute not less than 51 percent of the enterprise.

B. Ethnic Fraud Policy

1. If an applicant indicates on an application that he/she is a American Indian, the search committee may consider this gesture in good faith and intent, if and when CNC Administration request the prospective employee to present their American Indian preference documents-thereafter the administration finds out the American Indian process has been falsified, then the employment process will be terminated immediately.

C. Recruitment

1. The responsibility for the recruitment of administrative, faculty and staff positions rest in the President of the Comanche Nation College. He/she will also have the responsibility for the implementation of the American Indian Preference Program.

2. CNC will inform its recruitment sources in writing and include a statement in all advertisement that American Indian applicants will be given preference in employment and training incident to such employment.

3. Written notices are to be placed in the college and appropriate tribal offices that sets forth approximate numbers of positions to be filled; types of employees needed; approximate duties of employment; experience and education levels; and, if appropriate, training opportunities that are available.

4. If necessary, CNC may request assistance from the Comanche Nation Complex in filling positions.

5. CNC will maintain written records of all American Indian seeking employment; the number and types of positions filled by Indian and non-Indian; and, the names and addresses of each American Indian employed.

6. CNC will give preference to American Indians who can perform the work required (subject to existing laws and regulations) regardless of age, sex, religion, or sexual orientation for training and employment opportunities.

7. CNC will also provide opportunities to American Indian organizations and Indian-owned economic enterprises in the awarding of counseling and contract agreements.

Figure 9.1 (continued) Example of format for policy handbook.

Comanche Nation College

Employee's name:	Classification:	
Institution/Division:	Evaluation period (From: To:)	Evaluation date:
Performance factors	**Performance indicators** Comments and/or examples (attach extra sheets if needed)	**Rating**
1. Responsibility • assures competence and thoroughness in organization • provides leadership in day-to-day operations • maintains communication with Council • protects health and safety of individuals in organization		☐ Outstanding* ☐ Exceeds expectations ☐ Meets expectations ☐ Needs improvement ☐ Unsatisfactory*
2. Redistribution • manages time on task • monitors and adjust productivity levels • meets schedules/deadlines • oversight of budget process		☐ Outstanding* ☐ Exceeds expectations ☐ Meets expectations ☐ Needs improvement ☐ Unsatisfactory*
3. Reciprocity • delegates • problem solves • trains and mentors employees • negotiates personnel matters		☐ Outstanding* ☐ Exceeds expectations ☐ Meets expectations ☐ Needs improvement ☐ Unsatisfactory*
4. Relationships • fosters academic culture and competence • maintains working relationship with all College communities • promotes positive public relations • maintains professional relationships with AIHEC/NCA/etc.		☐ Outstanding* ☐ Exceeds expectations ☐ Meets expectations ☐ Needs improvement ☐ Unsatisfactory*

Definitions of Performance Rating Categories

OUTSTANDING*—The employee has exceeded all of the performance expectations for this factor and has made many significant contributions to the efficiency and economy of this organization through such performance.

EXCEEDS EXPECTATIONS—The employee regularly works beyond a majority of the performance expectations of this factor and has made significant contributions to the efficiency and economy of this organization through such performance.

MEETS EXPECTATIONS—The employee has met the performance expectations for this factor and has contributed to the efficiency and economy of this organization.
NEEDS IMPROVEMENT—The employee has failed to meet one or more of the significant performance expectations for this factor.
UNSATISFACTORY*—The employee has failed to meet the performance expectations for this factor.
* Give specific examples of this employee's performance.

7. Specific Achievements (use additional sheets if necessary)		
8. Performance goals for the next evaluation period		
9. Training and development suggestions		
10. Attendance (Supervisor's comments)		
Rater's name (print or type)	Rater's title	Rater's signature*	Date rated
Employee's comments		
This performance evaluation was discussed with me on the date noted above. I understand that my signature attests only that a personal interview was held with me; it does not necessarily indicate that I agree with the evaluation.		
Employee's signature:		Date signed
Reviewer's comments		
Reviewer's name (print or type)	Reviewer's title	Reviewer's signature*	Date reviewed

Figure 9.2 Employee performance evaluation.

INDIGENOUS GOVERNANCE IN TRIBAL COLLEGES

Evidence of the early discussion of indigenous governance grounded in American Indian values and leadership and its departure from Western models can be found in the literature. Badwound and Tierney (1988) framed the "tribal college dilemma" concluding that the Western, rational model failed as a predictor of decision-making and governance in tribal colleges. This dilemma is being addressed through policy development and practice on a local level and on a national/international level.

Federal funding has consistently been tied to accreditation authority and tribal colleges have focused upon the regional accreditation agencies used by IHEs. These regional accreditation authorities rarely value culture and language programs necessary to the core of tribal college philosophy and indigenous governance. In the last five years, discussions and action, specifically the development of The World Indigenous Nations Higher Education Consortium (WINHEC) has revisited the idea of accreditation standards which rely on the culture of the people.[10]

As indigenous educators and as Council members for the Comanche National College, we have added to the engagement and reconstruction of indigenous governance systems to create an ongoing cultural dialogue. Tribal colleges begin the 21st century with the same tenacity that defined the struggles of the last 500 years. The diversity of cultures representing politically distinct self-governing communities still exists. Through the foresight of tribal college founders to the proactive next generation's collection of their graduates, the tribal college movement defines self-determination as self-actualization through indigenous governance. Graduates whom Cheryl Crazy Bull described as students . . ." we intended to raise (as) a bunch of radicals with the skills to recognize and address social justice (Ambler, 2005). It reaffirms what we intuitively knew all along— indigenous governance systems survive and thrive.

NOTES

1. Indian Country is defined sociologically to include urban regions, border towns, and checkerboard regions. It is not limited to the legal definition found in Arizona v. Blaze Construction Company (1998) codified in 18 U.S.C. § 1151 as including (1) federal reservations, whether created by statute or Executive Order, see *Donnelly v. United States*, 228 U.S. 243 (1913), including fee land.
2. Descendants of the indigenous peoples of the Americas have had various designations in historical documents and narratives. Indian, Native American and Native Peoples have been accepted as a collective designation throughout history. When citing other authors, we will use their original designation.

As a result, the terms American Indian, Native American, Native, Indian, Native peoples, and indigenous peoples may be found throughout. In original references, we typically use American Indian/Alaska Native/Native Hawaiian. These designations are preferred by the American Indian professors' group. We also try to use specific tribal references, if known and used by the tribe/individual.

3. Wheeler-Howard Act, June 18, 1934. Indian Reorganization Act. 25 USC § 461 through 479.

4. Kathryn Harris Tijerina was counsel to the US Senate Indian Committee and drafted this Act.

5. This Executive Order revoked Executive Order 13096 and called for an interagency Working Group to provide a Study and Report to the Secretary of Education for the purpose of improving American Indian and Alaska Native students' ability to meet the challenges of student academic standards of No Child Left Behind Act of 2001.

6. AIHEC. October 1988. Who goes to tribal colleges? Available at www.aihec. org/documents/PDFS/whogoestotcus.pdf

7. IHEs: Institutions of Higher Education.

8. The Division of Systemic Reform (ESR) of the National Science Foundation (NSF) considers successful systemic reform to result in full implementation of the six critical developments that drive systemic reform. These critical developments called "drivers" serve as the element of accountability across the 69 Systemic Initiatives (SI) funded by the National Science Foundation (NSF). *The first four are "process drivers" that focus on sustainable success in changing the system's approach to the teaching and learning of mathematics and science, K–1. The last two are "outcome drivers" that underscore the student-centeredness of the entire systemic reform effort.* The Rural Systemic Initiatives at NSF included tribal colleges and was established under the leadership of Luther S. Williams, EHR Director.

9. Kathryn Harris Tijerina served as President of IAIA from 1989 to 1993. She is a founding member of the Comanche Nation College governing board; currently both authors join Comanche colleagues on the governing board for Oklahoma's first tribal college.

10. The World Indigenous Higher Education Consortium can be found at www.win-hec.org. Also, see Ray Barnhardt's discussion of accreditation in this volume for more information.

REFERENCES

Ambler, M. (2005, Spring). Tribal colleges redefining success. Indigenizing education. *Tribal College Journal of American Indian Higher Education, 16*(3), 8–9.

Badwound, E., & Tierney, W. (1988, October). Leadership and American Indian Values: The tribal college dilemma. *Journal of American Indian Education, 28*(1), 9–15.

Dodson, M., & Smith, D. (2003, March). *Indigenous community governance: The key ingredients and principles for sustainable economic development.* Presented at Seizing our economic future indigenous forums: building a better territory. Northern Territory Government Workshop, Alice Springs, March 6–7.

Friedman, T. L. (2005). *The world is flat: A brief history of the twenty-first century.* New York: Farrar, Straus, and Giroux.

Guba, E. G. (1984, October). The effect of definitions of policy on the nature and outcomes of policy analysis. *Educational Leadership,* 63–70.

Harris, L., & Wasilewaski, J. (1992, August). This is what we have to share: Core cultural values. *AIO Tribal Governance Series.*

1990 Indian Arts and Crafts Act, 25 USC § 305 et seq

1978 Indian Child Welfare Act, 25 USC § 1901 et seq

1968 Indian Civil Rights Act, 25 USC § 1301 et seq

1975 Indian-determination and Education Assistance Act, 25 USC §§ 450–450n, 455–458e, PL 93-638

1982 Indian Mineral Development Act, 25 USC § 2101 et seq

1978 American Indian Religious Freedom Act, 92 Stat.469; P. A. 45 U.S.C. Chapter 21. Subchapter I.

1991 Indian Tribal Justice Reorganization Act of 1991, 1991 S. 963; 102 S. 963

Kirkness, V. J., & Barnhardt, R. (1991). First Nations and higher education: The four R's—respect, relevance, reciprocity, and responsibility. *Journal of American Indian Education, 30*(3), 1–15.

1990 Native American Graves Protection and Repatriation Act, 25 USC §§ 3001–3013

1990 Native American Languages Act, PL 107-477.

Plumptre, T., & Graham, J. (1999). *Governance in the new millennium: Challenges for Canada.* Project for the Policy Research Secretariat. Government of Canada. Institute of Governance.

Sterritt, N. (2002, April). *Defining indigenous governance.* Paper presented at the Indigenous Governance Conference. Canberra, AU April 2–5, 2002.

1994 Tribal Self Governance Act of 1994; PL 103-413.

U.S. Commission on Civil Rights. (2003, July). *A quiet crisis: Federal funding and unmeet needs in Indian country.* Washington, DC. Accessed: December 7, 2006. www.usccr.gov/pubs/na0703/na0204.pdf

Washaba, V., & Wabasha, E. (1997). *Tribal sovereignty and American Indian leadership.* American Indian Policy Center. http://airpi.org/projects/fall97wabasha. html

CHAPTER 10

OKLAHOMA TRIBAL COLLEGE EXPANSION

Later than Sooner
Comanche Nation College

John W. Tippeconnic III

INTRODUCTION

Comanche Nation College (CNC), founded in 2002, was the first tribal college to become operational in the state of Oklahoma. Given the American Indian presence in Oklahoma and the rich history of Indian nations in the state, it was just a matter of time before a tribe chartered and operated a college. The Comanche Nation, based on their sovereignty status and self-determination power of tribal control in education, exercised their right to establish a college to meet the educational needs of tribal members, other Indians and non-Indians living in Comanche country.

The first tribal college, Diné College, was established as Navajo Community College in 1968. Today, there are 35 tribal colleges, located in 10 states and Canada serving more than 30,000 undergraduate and graduate students (AIHEC, http://www.aihec.org/). There is great diversity among

Tradition and Culture in the Millennium: Tribal Colleges and Universities, pages 133–146
Copyright © 2009 by Information Age Publishing
133

the tribal colleges; they are different in many ways depending on their tribe and local conditions. Yet, there are common elements that unite them and give them strength as tribally controlled institutions. Among the common elements are:

- Indian control of Indian education.
- The emphasis on tribal cultures and languages.
- A strong relationship between education and economic development.
- Developing and providing Indian leadership.
- Meeting community educational needs.

The higher education experience for many American Indians and Alaska Natives in mainstream institutions has been difficult and too often leads to recruitment and retention issues, dropouts, the lack of "Indianness" in the curriculum and few AI/AN faculty members and administrators. Granted, there are more AI/ANs attending colleges and universities today compared to years past, and there are some very good Indian studies programs and Native faculty that help ensure student success and graduation. However, we are not where we want to be in higher education, especially in building and developing tribal cultures and languages as strengths in the learning process.

The tribal college movement has not been easy. Many of the tribal colleges continue to struggle in many areas, including inadequate facilities, lack of funding to support basic operations, program support, limited funds to support faculty and staff, and the need for consistence leadership. The persistence, sustainability, and success of tribal colleges and universities have been truly remarkable given the challenges they have and continue to face.

OKLAHOMA

A tribal college was slow to come to Oklahoma; CNC was founded 35 years after the Navajo Nation established a college in 1968. One can only speculate as to reasons why it took so long, and it is not because there was no interested. There has been awareness of tribal colleges and their educational benefits by tribes and Indian educators in Oklahoma. Perhaps a key reason is that Oklahoma is different when compared to reservation states since major colleges and universities are in closer proximity to many tribes and tribal communities. The isolation factor has been a key reason in the development of most tribal colleges. Also, colleges have improved their AI/AN programs and increased their Indian student enrollment over the years, e.g., The University of Oklahoma, Oklahoma State University, Northeastern State University, etc. If mainstream institutions are more responsive to students and tribes, why establish a college? Other reasons may be that when compared to other tribal needs, especially economic development, establishing a tribal college is often lower in priority. Perhaps the lack of resources, like funding and facilities, are other possible factors. Other tribes in Oklahoma are also interested and have established tribal colleges. They, along with the Comanche Nation College, formed an Oklahoma Tribal College Coalition to provide support and serve as a resource for each other.

COMANCHE NATION COLLEGE

CNC Philosophy

The foundation of learning, teaching, conducting research and all other activities of the College are based on the culture and language of the Comanche Nation. The College recognizes the strength inherent in Comanche culture and language therefore; the basis for teaching and learning is Comanche-Centered (see Appendix B for a description of Comanche Centered Education).

Mission Statement

- The mission of the Comanche Nation College is to provide educational opportunities in higher education that are combined with the traditions and customs of the Comanche Nation and other Native American beliefs. Comanche Nation College provides lower division programs and educational opportunities in higher education that meet the needs of Comanche Nation tribal members, all other tribal members, and the general public. The following institutional functions have been approved by the Comanche Nation College Council which acts as the governing body of the institution.
- To provide a lower division program of higher education with a Native American culture basis for the traditional and non-traditional students in South western Oklahoma.
- To provide a general education that enables students to become informed responsible citizens.
- To provide programs of education in the liberal arts and sciences leading to the Associates in Science degree through campus-based and distance learning.
- To provide career and technical programs to enable students to seek employment in various job fields, with completion of such

      programs culminating in the awarding of the Associate in Applied
Science degree or an appropriate certificate.

- To provide transfer programs which include liberal arts, sciences,
and pre-professional subjects, thus enabling students to pursue
completion of baccalaureate or professional degrees at four-year
colleges and universities.
- To provide courses, services, and programs in remedial education
for individuals who require such assistance in order to function effectively at the college level.
- To provide guidance services and a program of student activities
for the promotion of personal development and tribal cultural
awareness.

CNC Beginnings

      The development of a tribal college from scratch is not easy and is to
be undertaken after serious consideration of its need and benefits to tribal
members. It requires a significant investment of time, energy, and financial and human resources. There are significant challenges along the way,
including funding, facilities, building connections with other institutions,
leadership, faculty and faculty development, accreditation, data collection
and research, etc. (Benham & Stein, 2003; Shanley, 2003; Boyer, 1997;
Stein, 1992, 2001).

      The focus of the rest of this paper is on ten developmental areas or chal-
lenges that CNC faced and continues to work through today. The 10 areas
are in no particular order or priority nor do they represent all the challenges before the college. However, each is important and gives an indication of
the development of CNC.

TEN FUNDAMENTAL DEVELOPMENT AREAS

Local Leadership

      The concept of a Comanche college originated within the tribe with the
Education Programs Director, Ron Bugress, taking the lead in 2001 to advance the vision forward. As Wayne Stein (1992) pointed out, "Tribally controlled community colleges would not have come into existence without
the support of two important groups: tribal councils and tribal communities" (p.143). This was true for CNC, as the Comanche Business Committee
(CBC), the tribal Chairman, and the Comanche communities were supportive of the idea of establishing a college. In November 2001 Ron Burgess

noted that Southwestern Oklahoma University, Langston University, and Cameron University were approached and all were willing to help in the development of a Comanche college. Burgess also emphasized the point that we, as Comanches, must take the lead in establishing the College when he stated:

> This college must be created by NUMUNU. In the beginning we must be the ones to assume responsibility. We have other professional friends who want to help and perhaps in the future they will. It is so important for Comanche educators to lead the way so our people will feel pride and ownership of this important institution.[1]

On May 4, 2002, the CBC approved a resolution that stated that the CBC was "acting for and on behalf of the Comanche Indian Tribe, hereby fully commits, supports, and approves the development and establishment of a Comanche tribal college." Chairman Johnny Wauqua signed the resolution. It was recognized that the college must operate and "function independently of the Comanche Business Committee in order for the Comanche Nation College to acquire academic accreditation and maintain its autonomy." In addition, $185,000 in tribal funds was approved in the resolution for "planning and implementation" of the College.

On August 3, 2002, the CBC and the Tribal Chairman adopted a charter establishing the Comanche Nation College. The charter stated:

- The Comanche Nation is established by the Comanche Nation pursuant to the Nation's sovereign right of self-government and its authority to foster the general welfare and education of the Comanche citizens.
- [The philosophy and] foundation for learning, teaching, research and all other activities of the College shall be based on the culture and language of the Comanche Nation. The College recognizes the strength inherent in Comanche culture and language and therefore, the basis for teaching and learning is Comanche-centered.
- The purpose of the College is to provide educational opportunities for Comanche tribal members, members of other tribal nations, and others to learn the necessary knowledge and skills to be successful in a multicultural society.

College Governance

The charter also established a Comanche Nation College Council to "manage the affairs of the College, including setting policy and shall have all powers of the College not expressly otherwise delegated." The Council is the overall governing and policy authority for the College and comprises eight members, including the tribal chairman, two members of the CBC, and five at large members. All members are required to be citizens of the Comanche Nation. Initial members on the Council were appointed by the tribal Director of Education. Current council members are from Oklahoma, New Mexico, Arizona, Pennsylvania, Tennessee, and Kansas (see Appendix A). The charter also stated that the "Council meetings shall be conducted according to a consensus process." This has worked well for the Council, even when there are differences of opinion among Council members. Dialogue, respect for each other, commitment to the philosophy and purpose of the College, focus on the students, and an understanding of "consensus" are some key reasons why consensus decision-making works for the Council.

The Council is an active and working group, assisting and providing direction to the College in a number of areas, e.g., in the development of policies and procedures, budget development and implementation, building external and internal relationships, defining Comanche-Centered Education, identifying funding sources, etc. The Council meets in face-to-face meetings four times a year and often holds conference calls and uses technology tools to facilitate communication and to conduct business.

One of the first challenges of the Council was to select a founding President. Ron Burgess, the former tribal Director of Education for the tribe served as our interim President, followed by Charles Tippeconnic who also was an interim President. The Council understood, as Wayne Stein (2001) pointed out, that the selection of the President must be done with great care and that a wise choice must be made because of the nature of the job. A majority of the CNC Council members have higher education experience and are familiar with tribal colleges and mainstream colleges. A national search was conducted. Although our salary and benefit's package were less than ideal and our expectations high, the search yielded a small but strong pool of applicants. Dr. Kim Winkelman, Vice President for Instruction and Academic Affairs at Oglala Lokota College was selected as the first official President of the College. Dr. Winkelman not only brought tribal college experience to CNC but also an academic background in education, technology, and the military as a retired Army officer, and he is of Oglala Lakota heritage. Dr. Winkelman reported to work at the College in November 2004. The inauguration of President Winkelman took place on April 30, 2006 at the 1st Annual Spring Comanche Nation College Powwow.

Building Relationships

Building relationships internal to the tribe and tribal community and external to other Indian and non-Indian communities and to higher education institutions in the state is essential and ongoing. Developing internal relationships comes first in order to get tribal government and tribal community support for the college. As the first tribal college in Oklahoma, building relationships in the state became an educational process to inform others about tribal colleges and universities and, in particular, about CNC.

The College was initially set up as a satellite of Cameron University, using Cameron's professors, curricula and accreditation. CNC also entered into an agreement (MOU) and contract with Great Plains Technology Center in Lawton, Oklahoma to use instructors, curricula and accreditation from that Institution. After three years of start up status, the Comanche Nation has now taken the required legal and financial steps necessary to create a Tribal College with the groundwork in place to begin the path toward full accreditation as a stand alone higher education institution. We will continue to work with our existing education and training partners, and uphold their and our standards through the growth and transition of the College.

Fiscal Resources

Adequate funding for education programs has been a long-standing concern in Indian education, including tribal colleges and universities. Jim Shanley (2003) estimated that, at a minimum, it takes around $560,000 to develop a tribal college using 2–3 part time faculty serving 100 to 125 students. CNC was fortunate because the Comanche Nation clearly demonstrated its commitment by allocating gaming revenue to support the operation of the College. The initial appropriation was $185,000. The appropriations from the tribe increased each year to the current level of $1,200,000. Additional funds from grants bring the total CNC 2006–07 revenue budget to more than $3,071,000. We are very appreciative to the tribe for their support; however, we also realize the tenuous nature of gaming revenue and the need for us to develop other sources of funding in the future.

Language and Culture Focus

The foundation of learning, research and all other activities of the College are based on the culture and language of the Comanche Nation. The College recognizes that the Comanche culture and language are strengths that enhance teaching and learning and should be integrated throughout all College activities. We call this approach Comanche Centered Education.

In defining and making Comanche Centered Education operational the CNC Council took a number of actions to ensure the philosophy was implemented throughout the College. One action was the adoption of "retraditionalization" and "empowerment" as two domains that are used to provide guidance and direction to College activities. The second action was to identify and use Comanche values that could be used to integrate Comanche Centered Education. The four values of "relationship," "responsibility," "reciprocity," and "redistribution" were identified (see Appendix B) and are being used as we continue to develop as a College. For example, the values are currently being used to provide the framework as we develop and refine our policies and procedures and as we develop job performance criteria for our President and other employees.

Political Considerations

One of our challenges, as it is in many tribal communities, is to be aware of and develop strategies to deal with the political nature of the community, tribe, state, and national environments. We understand that tribal politics are influenced by many factors that could have a positive or negative effect on the College. In general, our approach has been to focus on education and the programs we provide; to be aware of, respect, and attempt to minimize local politics; to develop working relationships with tribal officials and offices; and to articulate our vision and demonstrate our successes to the community. Since the tribal chairman and CBC members are members of the College Council, tribal politics are built into our governance structure.

At the state and national levels we continue to work with and inform our Congressional delegation and members of the state legislature about CNC. We realize the importance of developing positive and supportive relationships in the political arena as we continue to develop as a college.

Students

Our primary purpose is to provide educational services to tribal members, other American Indians, and non-Indians. We opened the college doors in the Fall of 2002 to 23 students. Each year the number of students has increased significantly. There were 62 students enrolled during the 2004 Spring semester. A year later, Spring 2005, there were 278 students. Our students tend to be older than tradition college students with an average age of 29, 68% were female, 63% were full time students, and approximately 60% were American Indian. During the Fall 2005 semester, the student enrollment increased to 285.

We anticipate that student enrollment will increase in the future as we continue to develop our academic program.

Because we are a tribal college and plan to meet the criteria established by the American Indian Higher Education Consortium (AIHEC) and the provisions of the Tribally Controlled College or University Assistance Act, our student body must be majority or at least 51% American Indian. As will be noted below, this was a concern expressed by AIHEC during their site visits in 2004. We are aware of this requirement and monitor it closely since we have found that non-Indians find our college inviting and attractive because of our small classes, cultural focus, and the curriculum offered. We have developed classes and programs that reach out to Comanche communities; this helps to keep our Indian enrollment above 51%, but more important, it provides educational opportunities for our tribal members close to their homes and communities.

Facilities

Finding a place to call home gave us not only a physical location, but a presence in the community that people could "see" and recognize as Comanche Nation College. We were fortunate to identify a former elementary school building for sale in Lawton, Oklahoma and to have a donor, Mr. John Harrington, a Comanche tribal member and Vice President of Integrity Gaming provide $800,000 to purchase the facility. The facility includes 16 classrooms, an auditorium, kitchen, and office space. The building met our immediate needs and provided enough space for future growth, although there are recent indicators that we may be outgrowing the building. Even though we have had to make repairs to an older building, we sincerely appreciate the support given by Mr. Harrington.

Accreditation/Planning

Accreditation was something that was considered early in the development of College. The College Council and the administration of the College realized the importance of accreditation in developing our independence and recognition of a quality program for our students. It was also understood that achieving accreditation from the North Central Association of Colleges & Schools would take time, a lot of work and the allocation of resources. A necessary step in working toward independence was the establishment of a business office and obtaining authority from the CBC to handle our own business accounts. This was accomplished by tribal resolution in 2002.

Becoming a member of the AIHEC also became a major goal. After some interaction with AIHEC and reviewing their membership criteria, we decided to seek membership at an early stage in our development because by doing so it would give us a sense of where we were and what we needed to do in the future. In September 2003 we informed AIHEC of our intent to apply for membership. AIHEC conducted site visits in March 2004 and September 2004. AIHEC recognized that CNC was in its early stages of development and that there was "very strong commitment and support" from the tribe, tribal chairman, and the CNC governing board. As a result, AIHEC granted CNC applicant membership status.

Accreditation and AIHEC membership became major goals in the planning process for the College. The development of a comprehensive strategic plan was also a priority.

Key planning actions for us included the hiring of a President, accreditation, AIHEC membership, program and curriculum focus, budget planning and responsible implementation, use of technology, determining key partners and others we need to develop relationships with, etc. Strategic plan goals include:

- Define, Develop, Integrate and Institutionalize a Culturally Based System of Learning, fully Accredited, with Capacity to Foster CNC Student Excellence and to share our Expertise with Partners.
- Accreditation by Appropriate Nationally Recognized Authorities and Organizations.
- Integration of Existing And New Resources for the Foundation of an Effective and Efficient Learning Organization that serves the CNC Student Population, the Comanche Nation and the surrounding Community.
- To Provide a vehicle for the Comanche Nation to Preserve, Maintain and Disseminate Comanche Tribal Heritage and Learning, now and into the 21st century.

Curriculum, Courses, Programs and Staffing

Because we are not yet accredited, Cameron University, located in Lawton, Oklahoma supported our accreditation efforts and agreed to be our partner host college. Cameron agreed to reimburse CNC for instructor costs for courses taught by our faculty. Courses are offered at the Associate Degree level and include basic English, reading and math courses. Art, speech, history, government, psychology, and economics were also offered, as was Comanche language I and II. Part-time or adjunct faculty taught the courses, until the Fall of 2006 when four full time faculty were hired to teach courses in math, science, English, and Comanche culture and language.

External resources are used by colleges and universities to support institutional teaching, service and research activities. CNC is no different as funds and collaborative efforts provide educational opportunities for students while meeting community needs. One example is the development of a practical nursing program through a partnership between CNC, Great Plains Technology Center, and the Indian Health Service.

Special programs include the Council on Law Enforcement Education and Training (CLEET), which provides casino security training for five tribes in southwestern Oklahoma, Medical Billing and Coding Training, and a Department of Labor grant that provides computers and training to the Comanche, Navajo, Sioux, Three Affiliated and Washoe tribes.

An Office of Student Services has also been established that provides "support and resources for students as they acclimate into their new college environment to ensure their success academically, socially and professional" while instilling Comanche values.

Leadership and Staff

As noted, President Winkelman was hired early in the development of the College to provide the necessary permanent leadership and to work with the College Council. Instructors were employed to teach courses and staff hired to provide support and leadership in the various CNC offices. Other key staff includes a Business Manager, IT Director, Academic Advisor and a Financial Aids Officer in the Office of Student Affairs, Development Officer, Administrative Assistant, Receptionist, and Custodians.

The Dean of Academic Instruction was considered another important leadership position in overseeing the development of the academic program. Dr. Cornel Pewewardy, a Comanche tribal member, became the Dean during the Fall of 2005. Dr. Pewewardy was an original member of the CNC Council and was previously a faculty member in the School of Education at the University of Kansas. He has also been instrumental in developing and implementing the concept of Comanche Centered Education at the College.

CONCLUSION

Comanche Nation College is a young developing institution. There has been significant progress made since its founding in 2002. This has raised the expectations from the tribe, the community, the College Council, and others that there will be even more successful in the future. We are optimistic that CNC will become recognized as a place where tribal members, other

American Indians and non-Indians can receive a Comanche Centered Education in any academic discipline. The ten fundamental development areas mentioned above, and others, will continue to be challenges in the future as we work toward accreditation, full AIHEC membership, achieving recognition, earning respect from others, and to serve as a successful example of tribal control of education. We take great pride in CNC as our college and welcome the challenges before us. Access the Comanche Nation College website at http://www.cnc.cc.ok.us/ to track our progress, receive updates and other relevant information about the College.

NOTE

1. Letter from Ron Burgess to John Tippeconnic dated November 11, 2001.

REFERENCES

American Indian Higher Education Consortium website at http://www.aihec.org/

Benham, M. K., & Stein, W. J. (Eds.). (2003). *The renaissance of American Indian higher education: Capturing the dream.* Mahwah, NJ: Lawrence Erlbaum Associates.

Boyer, P. (1997). *Native American colleges: Progress and prospects.* Princeton, NJ: Carnegie Foundation for the Advancement of Teaching.

Comanche Nation College website at: http://www.cnc.cc.ok.us/

Shanley, J. (2003). Limitations and alternatives to developing a tribally controlled college. In M. K. Benham & W. J. Stein (Eds.), *The renaissance of American Indian higher education: Capturing the dream.* Mahwah, NJ: Lawrence Erlbaum Associates.

Stein, W. J. (2001). It starts with a dream...road map to initiate a tribal college. *Tribal College Journal of American Indian Higher Education, 12*(3), 10–14.

Stein, W. J. (1999). Tribally controlled colleges. In K. G. Swisher & J. W. Tippeconnic, III (Eds.), *Next steps: Research and practice to advance American Indian education.* Charleston, WV: ERIC Clearinghouse on Rural and Small Schools.

Stein, W. J. (1992). *Tribally controlled colleges: Making good medicine.* New York: Peter Lang Publishing.

APPENDIX A

Comanche Nation College College Council Members

Current Members	Past Members
Dr. John Tippeconnic III, Council Leader Pennsylvania State University	**Ms. LaDonna Harris** Americans for Indian Opportunity
Mary Jo Tippeconnic Fox, Council Second Leader University of Arizona	**Dr. Cornel Pewewardy** University of Kansas
Dr. Lotsee Patterson, Council Secretary/Treasurer University of Oklahoma	
Mr. Garrison Tahmahkera, Council Historian Mesa Community College	
Dr. Katheryn Harris-Tijerina University of Phoenix	
Dr. Barbara T. Hobson University of Oklahoma	
Dr. Linda Sue Warner Tennessee Board of Regents	
Mr. Wallace Coffey Chairman, Comanche Nation Tribe	
Darrell Bread Vice-Chairman, Comanche Nation Tribe	
Eddie Mahseet Comanche Nation Tribe	
LaNora Parker Comanche Nation Tribe	

APPENDIX B

Two Domains that Provide Guidance and Direction to Comanche Centered Education are (Comanche Nation College website at http://www.cnc.cc.ok.us/):

Retraditionalization

Includes the emersion of all Comanche language courses, use of Indigenous peace-making strategies, learn from Elders, integrate past Comanche traditions into a modern Comanche worldview.

Empowerment

Includes to indigenize all core courses, affirm cultural equality, foster a healthy self-esteem in all students, foster intellectual growth, analyze historical and contemporary development in the United States from the perspective of the Comanche people, rewrite and teach history from a Comanche perspective, decolonize ourselves, promote and respect the Comanche Nation's legal status as a sovereign nation, and teach to the spirit of every student by seeking harmony, balance, and equity in all religious and religious groups.

Four Comanche Values that help define Comanche Centered Education

Relationship
Kinship Obligation: Our relationships to others dictate our roles in society.

Responsibility
Community Obligation: Our relationships to others determine our responsibilities to others.

Reciprocity
Cyclical Obligation: Our relationships and responsibilities are reciprocal.

Redistribution
Sharing Obligation: We have a responsibility to share resources and information for the good of the whole.

CHAPTER 11

STUDENT RETENTION INITIATIVES AT TRIBAL COLLEGES AND UNIVERSITIES AND STRATEGIES FOR IMPROVEMENT

Robin Williams and Cornel Pewewardy

INTRODUCTION

Despite civil rights legislation, the national goal of providing ethnic minorities with equal access to quality institutions of higher education and opportunities for academic success has yet to be realized. Actualizing this educational vision requires understanding the forces that preclude and those that promote equal opportunity and academic success. Higher education dropout rates, lower levels of academic preparation in high school, lower socioeconomic status, and greater alienation or isolation in the white college environment have been cited as problems facing ethnic minority college students (Pewewardy & Frey, 2002; Loo & Rolison, 1986). This problem has no where been so great as in American Indian college students (Pewewardy & Frey, 2004; Lin, LaCounte, & Eder, 1988).

Tradition and Culture in the Millennium: Tribal Colleges and Universities, pages 147–159
Copyright © 2009 by Information Age Publishing
All rights of reproduction in any form reserved.

The complex issue of student retention is a principal component of the access-retention-graduation mosaic and few other issues in higher education generate as much interest, argument, and inquiry from inside and outside the academy. For American Indian students, tribal colleges and universities (TCUs) may offer a more supportive educational setting for students encountering some difficulty in realizing their full academic potential and needs (Pavel, Inglebret, & Banks, 2001). TCUs generally offer a broad range of effective remedial programs for students. Many TCUs have established developmental centers, reading laboratories, and expanded tutorial and counseling services to accommodate the special needs of educationally disadvantaged students. In addition, a strong commitment by many TCUs to serve American Indian students has resulted in high rates of graduation.

This chapter provides an overview of retention initiatives in which many TCUs face as they carry out their unique mission. The information will allow the reader to consider TCUs as a valid choice in meeting the educational needs of American Indian students in higher education. Further, this chapter offers recommendations aimed at strengthening TCUs.

HISTORICAL CONTEXT

TCUs were created over the last 30 years to serve the higher education needs of American Indian students, particularly serving geographically isolated populations in the United States. Over the years, TCUs have become essential to educational opportunity as they have become unique institutions that combine personal attention with culturally responsive teaching (Pewewardy & Hammer, 2003).

Campus environment is a central feature in the academic experience of all students. According to the American Council on Education (2000), since the late 1980s, Students of Color have made varied but steady progress in college attendance. From 1988 to 1977, the overall enrollment of Students of Color in higher education increased 57.2%; this included an increase of 16.1% during the last five years. From 1996 to 1997, the enrollment of Students of Color increased 3.7%. Specifically, American Indian experienced a 54% increase in college enrollment during the past decade, including an increase of 3.6% from 1996 to 1997, which brought the total enrollment of American Indians in higher education to 142,000. Alarmingly, this is barely 1% of all college students (American Council on Education, 2000). American Indians are one of the smallest ethnic minorities of the United States population (U.S. Department of Commerce, 2002), and American Indian students are among the most underrepresented groups in academe (Tierney, 1992; U.S. Department of Education, 1998). For Indigenous Peoples who have suffered the ravages of colonization, the history of higher education becomes the foundation to rebuild their educational institutions (Stein, 2003).

LITERATURE REVIEW

One cannot look at higher education for American Indian students without examining the history of federal policy toward American Indians from the late eighteenth century onward. "The deliberate and premeditated genocide of the early years of invasion and theft, however, has moved on from religious fervor and ethnic and racial hatred to economic genocide and ethnocide" (Cook-Lynn, 2001, p. 193). That American Indians were subjected to cultural genocide is self-evident, although it has been rarely articulated as policy (Tinker, 1993). "Since its invasion of America, white society has sought to justify, through law and legal discourse, its privilege of aggression against Indian people by stressing tribalism's incompatibility with the superior values and norms of white civilization" (Williams, 2000, p. 103). Moreover, prior to the invasion of the American Indian settlements in the Americas (Zinn, 1999) and the imposition of Euro-American educational systems, many tribal nations had their own very diverse educational systems that were culturally and linguistically designed to provide education informally through parents, extended families, elder members of the tribe, and religious and social groups (Dejong, 1993).

Historically, the challenges to educating American Indian students were/are vast and based on 500 years of mistreatment of American Indian people (Adams, 1995; Huff, 1997; Spring, 2001; Stannard, 1992; Thorton, 1987; Tinker, 1993; Zinn, 1999). American Indians have had negative relationships with federal government agencies, and many American Indian people are likely to be realistically cautious with white institutions due to the destruction of culture, language, and human lives inflicted on all American Indian populations throughout U.S. history. The early educational history of American Indians is about the use of the schoolhouse, specifically the boarding school, as an instrument for acculturating Indian youth to "American" ways of thinking and living (Adams, 1995). Termination policies and those aimed at limiting tribal self-determination were also based on attempts to "Americanize" Indians (Deloria, 1995).

The history of higher education for American Indian students in the twentieth century shows a slow progression from total assimilation to tribally controlled (Stein, 1999; Tippeconnic, 2000). Today, tribal colleges seek to celebrate their tribal cultures by offering a culturally-based or tribally-specific curriculum in higher education. Tribal colleges do not, however, fill for all American Indian students the social, educational, and economic chasms created by this oppressive history (Viznor, 1994). Given this externally imposed history of educating American Indian students, the long-range outcome has resulted in limited educational opportunities today.

We believe the identification of the historical barriers to academic success is a first step in addressing the current problems of retention with American Indian students in higher education.

FACTORS RELATED TO RETENTION

There are a number of factors related to retention as found in the research literature. Here is a summation of major findings within TCUs.

Academic Preparedness. Academic integration and preparation are primary features of many models of retention. Research shows that between 30 and 40% of all entering freshman are unprepared for college-level reading and writing and approximately 44% of all college students who complete a 2- or 4-year degree had enrolled in at least one remedial/developmental course in math, writing, or reading.

Campus Climate. While researchers agree that "institutional fit" and campus integration are important to retaining college students to degree completion, campus climate mediates undergraduates' academic and social experiences in college. Minority and low-income students inadequately prepared for non-academic challenges can experience culture shock. Lack of diversity, with regard to income and race/ethnicity, in the student population, faculty, staff, and curriculum often restrict the nature and quality of minority students' interactions within and out of the classroom, threatening their academic performance and social experiences.

Commitment to Educational Goals and the Institution. Tinto (1993) hypothesized that commitment to occupational and educational goals and commitment to the institution in which one enrolls significantly influence college performance and persistence. The stronger the goal and institutional commitment the more likely the student will graduate. Research shows that congruence between student goals and an institutional mission is mediated by academic and social components, and that increased integration into academic and social campus communities cause greater institutional commitment and student persistence.

Social and Academic Integration. The process of becoming socially integrated into the fabric of TCUs has also been found to be both a cumulative and compounding process, and the level of social integration within a given the first year of study is part of a cumulative experience that continues to build throughout one's college experience. The establishment of peer relations and the development of role models and mentors have been defined in the literature as important factors in student integration, both academically and socially.

Financial Aid. Attending college and persisting to degree completion is most often rewarded with higher annual and lifetime earnings. But for many low-income and minority students, enrollment and persistence decisions are driven by the availability of financial aid.

Low-income and minority students who receive grants generally are more likely to persist than those who receive loans. However, given the rising costs of attending college, it is unlikely that low-income students will be able to receive bachelor's degrees without any loan aid. At the same time, the research also suggests that the shifts in aid from grants to loans and from need-based to merit-based programs adversely affects both enrollment and persistence for minority students, especially American Indian students. Reversing these shifts may be needed to increase college access and success for low-income and minority students.

The bottom line—which we hope to highlight in this chapter—is that the cost of prevention attrition (when it can be prevented) easily outweighs the costs of status quo (or doing nothing). This is an important statement that is lost on many administrators. And secondly, an institution must be willing to spend money (or redirect) to save or earn money. If we can get past these two statements, we're half the way to success.

Transfer is often cited as an issue in retention of American Indian college students. In order to improve transfer rates for American Indian students, several suggestions include: strengthening articulation agreements with four-year institutions, implementing stronger counseling and remediation services, and improving special activities for American Indian students that increase peer support.

CURRENT PRACTICE

Current practices that address retention within TCU's has been a prominent and recurring issue for American Indian students, faculty and staff within these higher education institutions. Many TCU's have begun to look at what is deemed best practices between current retention efforts. In general, best practices that have been found within TCU's are that over half have obtained the TRIO federal grant specifically in the Student Support Services area, which allows for advisement, tutoring, career assessment and remedial courses that are often needed as many TCU's have open enrollment and serve adult learners. As well, other best practices that are an intricate part of the make up of TCU's is that there are American Indian staff serving these students and American Indian faculty instructing and teaching these courses who are from the respective tribe or local community who have personal ties with a sincerity that is brought into the classroom (AIHEC, 1999).

Recently in the last ten years, a consortium of tribal colleges and universities have worked together with a state affiliated institution to create what is commonly known among TCU's as the Family Education Model. This model is known for its emphasis on replicating the support networks of the American Indian family and incorporating the family of the students within the functions of the institution. As well, the focus of the family education model is to build on the strength of the cultural resiliency of the students. Cultural resiliency can best be defined as the strength that exists from an individual who can identify with their tribal culture and values, from this identification, have the confidence to move forward successfully with goals they set before themselves and overcoming obstacles that may arise (De-Celles & HeavyRunner, 1994).

Other current practices that have been identified within TCU's are programs housed at the Crown Point Institute of Technology (CIT) located on the Dine reservation and at Northwest Indian College on the Lummi reservation. CIT has an Alternative Livestock and Veterinary Science program that explores reproductive and genetic technology of elk and llamas. The uniqueness of this program that has been attributed in retaining students is within the curriculum of this program in which it incorporates Dine elders to assist in telling the history of the tribe and the teaching of traditional practices used in healthcare for animals (Ambler, 1988). Northwest Indian College, whose environmental science program integrates the local tribe's culture within the teachings of this unique program, is designed to increase the presence of American Indian students in this field. The historical background of TCU's is founded on this rationale of integrating the tribal culture within the curriculum of the institution to assure cultural relevancy and that students can attribute their cultural values into the discipline being studied. For these vary reasons, many TCU's have experienced high retention rates because of the cultural relevancy and tapping into the cultural resiliency of the individual student (IHEP, 2006).

Another current practice of TCUs is the recruitment efforts to increase enrollment into certain programs where there is a high need for these professionals in their community. For instance, efforts by Northwest Indian College and Washington State University collaborated to form the effort of OKSALE to increase the number of K–12 teachers within their Native communities has been ongoing. The other unique factor of this program is the incorporation of tribal government officials in the guidance of the program objectives and assuring the method for increasing the presence of American Indian teachers succeeds. Another program that encourages the presence of American Indians in education is the Oyate Consortium which includes: Oglala Lakota College, Si Tanka College, Sitting Bull College, Sinte Gleska College, and Sisseton Wahpeton Community College; who provides a graduate education opportunity for teachers to become education administrators within the state of South Dakota (Tate & Schwartz, 1993).

Other methods used to increase retention of American Indian students are to offer flexible education opportunities by TCU's via distance learning to American Indian students. Many TCU's are currently offering on-line courses such as Salish Kootenai College, who offers two upper division baccalaureate degrees to other TCU's who are only able to offer associates of arts degrees. Also, the North Dakota Intertribal College Partnership, a consortium of six tribal colleges in North and South Dakota, have developed a methodology for these TCU's to share online courses so that education is more accessible to their American Indian populations (Ewen, 1997). Another tribal college offering more opportunities via distance learning is Bay Mills Community College who has recently began to offer free online classes to anyone who fulfills their admissions requirements with free tuition and the materials required for these courses. This unique online approach is offering a window of opportunity to American Indian students who may be considering higher education and this will allow them that exposure (www.bmcc.edu, 2006).

INTERPRETATION

The current practices that have been adopted by the TCU's have been designed to fit their respective student populations. The historical background of tribal colleges was to provide more access and opportunity to these tribal communities while including the culture and language of their tribe. What is unique about the historical background for many staff in tribal colleges is a unique family support factor that has to be included along with being cognizant of the cultural values these students bring with them. One common trait of many TCUs is that they build on the strengths of their students and providing them the basic knowledge of the higher education process, while encouraging and building on their cultural resiliency. Subsequently, they are ready to transfer to a four-year university because they have experienced success at TCUs (DeCelles & HeavyRunners, 1994).

The uniqueness of TCUs should be seen as a strength to catapult the number of tribal members seeking higher education. Simultaneously, many TCUs continue to seek out emerging patterns of best practices. For American Indian students, it is often hard to separate one part of our lives from the other because it is all connected and when one part is suffering the rest will be affected (Larimore & McClellan, 2005). There is a new theory that will be emerging in the near future, the Pretty Paint Theory on Educational Persistence is one that is considerate of this, the three areas of focus are (1) visions of success, (2) circles of relations and (3) personal faith and optimism. It also includes factors of retention and protective factors that would enable students to be successful. As we begin to see more of this theory, its relevancy will be seen as it was designed by the study of one tribal college, it may find immeasurable value among the other tribal colleges in the United States (PrettyPaint, 2006).

RETENTION ASSESSMENT METHODS IN TCUS

The current practices that exist within tribal colleges to address retention as well as emerging concerns and findings have become known to the public recently, through the publication of books and most commonly the Tribal College Journal (TCJ), which has began to educate and bring awareness to those who serve students in these institutions. These publications have caused the TCU communities to seek assessment methods of how to gauge success in retaining their respective student population and their effectiveness in fulfilling their institutional mission. From this curiosity and the creation of support networks between departments of the TCU communities, there are conferences that have become tradition to cross collaborate and share what is needed across TCU's, what is an institutional fit, and what policy implementation is needed; conferences such as the "Student Services Conference" hosted by Salish Kootenai College and the most recent "Convening for Student Success Conference" hosted by the Institute of American Indian Arts.

From these conferences and the presence of the governing board of tribal colleges, the American Indian Higher Education Consortium (AIHEC), the creation of the American Indian Measures for Success (AIMS) report was born. AIMS was created through a partnership from the Lumina Foundation which will enable TCU's to assess their current institutions enrollment, retention status, and to look internally at what changes need to occur and what is currently effective. This will also allow for capacity building through this data collection process via the systemic research collected from each tribal college, this will also enhance communication and awareness of each TCU's status, as there is a mechanism for shared information (Lumina Foundation, 2006).

The issue that prevails for TCU's among other higher education institutions in assessing retention is a methodology needed that can be used to define what retention is and how to measure success in retaining students. The uniqueness of tribal colleges also calls for an in-depth look at what each institution would use to measure retention. For instance, many TCUs serve adult learners who may have children or are taking care of their families, so these students may be part-time and/or may "stop out" to accurately gauge success for TCU's will differ from other public mainstream institutions.

RECOMMENDATIONS

As of today, the growing success and need for TCU's is omnipresent among American Indian communities. As tribal college administration and staff continue to build on our successes and look at areas that we have been ineffective, it is necessary in order to ensure the growth of tribal colleges will have the lasting impact on our communities to bring economic growth and build healthy families. What is needed among TCU's is the continual fight for recognition of our success nationally for an increase in funding and the acknowledgment that in the last century this creation is best suited for American Indian people to grow and prosper. As we continue to gain recognition nationally, we also need to have continued support from tribal officials and members, where there may be a division of opinion on the existence of these higher education institutions. A tribal college provides the self-confidence to students to create a needed change in the crime and unemployment rates and empowers students to make a positive change within them. As the support nationally and locally is built, it would assist in the building of support networks within the community and within the family that many tribal colleges are in need of. As each tribal college graduates one student at a time, they will find they are continuing to build the positive role models within our tribal communities that will trickle down into the seventh generation.

There are several important factors in the design of an effective TCU retention effort that include:

- Assurance that all elements of TCUs recognize that effective equity group retention efforts invariably have a "ripple" effect, resulting in enhanced retention of all students;
- The importance of continuous collection and analysis of retention data;
- Implementation of proven retention programs; and
- The need for enhanced student tracking and collection of information regarding the specific factors which contribute to attrition and retention.

More and more TCUs are adopting the following goals and strategies.

Goal: *Create a more welcoming nurturing campus climate in which all students can flourish.*

Strategy
- Continue sponsorship of diversity workshops for student leaders for each academic year.
- Continue the focus on leadership at annual student leadership retreats.

- Continue to invite scholars who can enlighten TCUs on issues relating to diversity, pluralism, and cultural pride.
- Expand campus involvement during ethnic holidays and events.
- Sponsor diversity workshops/lectures for all official student organizations.
- Provide ongoing support workshops for all students that address issues of racism, isolation, anger and fear which may be concern to American Indian students.
- Continue support for mentor groups established to respond to issues specific to Native students.

Goal: *Expand the formalized mentoring program for American Indian students to involve more faculty, staff and alumni in an effort to support career goals, enhance personal confidence and enlarge the vision of American Indian students.*

Strategy
- Through TCU funding and a grant from the State System of Higher Education, select, train and educate faculty and staff as mentors to support and nurture American Indian students throughout their academic stay at TCUs.

Goal: *Assist the TCU-wide retention program.*

Strategy
Offices of Student Affairs and Cultural Diversity will assist retention efforts developed by TCUs to enhance the effectiveness of the following programs and services:

- Strongly encourage students to meet with advisors and others in developing a personalized academic plan.
- Strongly encourage students to take advantage of tutoring and other support services designed to help students achieve academic success.
- Continue to reinforce among students the necessity to accept and act upon those responsibilities required for academic success.
- Continue to counsel students and help them develop strategies for becoming more self-reliant.
- Continue to be an advocate for students to ensure that the living and learning environment is a positive one in which they can reach their full potential.
- Continue mentoring programs and expand it to include parents.
- Continue to provide:
  a. leadership training,
  b. career exploration,

c. personal counseling,
d. personal development workshops,
e. mentoring, and
f. tutoring assistance.

SUMMARY AND CONCLUSION

Research reviewed in this chapter strongly suggests that there is much need for, and room for, improvement in the quality of academic advisement and the rate of student retention for American Indian students in TCUs. The research also suggests that improvement in the former is associated with improvement in the latter. However, to promote extensive and enduring gains in American Indian student retention, academic advisement programs need to undergo systemic change at four foundational levels: (a) recruitment and selection of advisors, (b) preparation and development of advisors, (c) recognition and reward for advisors, and (d) advisor assessment and program evaluation. These four elements are also the cornerstones and building blocks that under gird construction of any high-quality advising program. Only when sufficient institutional attention and resources are devoted to securing each of these foundational features of program development will the quest for quality academic advisement be successful and it's potential for promoting American Indian student retention be fulfilled.

Along with the development of advisement programs, so is the need for continual development of support networks within and external to the TCU. It is essential that all entities understand their role and important contribution to retention. It is the commitment by all individuals who support our students that ensure their success and retention.

REFERENCES

Adams, D. W. (1995). *Education for extinction: American Indians and the boarding school experience, 1875–1928.* Lawrence: University Press of Kansas.

Ambler, M. (1998). Land-based colleges offer science students a sense of place. *Tribal College Journal of American Indian Higher Education, 10*(1).

American Council on Education. (2000). College enrollment. In D. J. Wilds (Ed.), *Minorities in higher education 1999–2000: Seventeenth annual report* (pp. 17–22). Washington, DC: Author.

American Indian Higher Education Consortium and the Institute for Higher Education Policy. (1999). *Tribal colleges: An introduction.* Washington, DC: Author.

Bay Mills Community College. (2006). www.bmcc.edu

Cook-Lynn, E. (2001). *Anti-Indianism in modern America: A voice from Tatekeya's earth.* Urbana: University of Illinois Press.

DeCelles, R., & HeavyRunner, I. (1994). Family education model: Meeting the student retention challenge. *Journal of American Indian Education, 1*(2).

Dejong, D. H. (1993). *Promises of the past: A history of Indian education in the United States*. Golden, CO: North American Press.

Deloria, V. (1995). *Red earth, white lies: Native Americans and the myth of scientific fact*. New York: Scribner.

Ewen, A. (1997). Generation X in Indian country. *Native American Times, 14*(4) 24–29.

Huff, D. J. (1997). *To live heroically: Institutional racism and Indian education*. Albany: State University of New York Press.

Institute for Higher Education Policy. (2006). *Championing success: A report on the progress of Tribal college and university alumni*. Washington, DC: Author.

Larimore, J. A., & McClellan, G. S. (2005). Native American student retention in U.S. postsecondary education. In S. J. T. Fox, S. C. Lowe & G. S. McClellan (Eds.), *Serving Native American students* [Special Issue]. *New Directions for Student Services, 109,* 17–32.

Lin, R. L., LaCounte, D., & Eder, J. (1988). A study of Native American students in a predominantly white college. *Journal of American Indian Education, 27*(3), 8–15.

Loo, C. M., & Rolison, G. (1986). Alienation of ethnic minority students at a predominantly White university. *Journal of Higher Education, 57*(1), 58–77.

Lumina Foundation for Tribal Colleges and Universities. (2004). *AIMS: American Indian measures for success*. Alexandria, VA: Author.

Pavel, D. M., Inglebret, E., & Banks, S. R. (2001). Tribal colleges and universities in an era of dynamic development. *Peabody Journal of Education, 76*(1), 50–72.

Pewewardy, C. D., & Frey, B. (2004). American Indian students' perceptions of multicultural support services, racial climate, and ethnic fraud at a predominantly white university. *Journal of American Indian Education, 43*(1), 32–60.

Pewewardy, C. D., & Frey, B. (2002). Surveying the landscape: Perceptions of multicultural support services and racial climate at a predominately white university. *Journal of Negro Education, 71*(1/2), 77–95.

Pewewardy, C. D., & Hammer, P. C. (2003). Culturally responsive teaching for American Indian students. *ERIC Digest*, Clearinghouse on Rural Education and Small Schools (EDO-RC-03-10), Charleston, WV.

PrettyPaint, I. (2006). Convening for student success: The 1st year tribal college student. Santa Fe, NM.

Spring, J. (2001). *Deculturalization and the struggle for equality: A brief history of the education of dominated cultures in the United States*. New York: McGraw Hill.

Stein, W. J. (2003). Developing action for implementing an Indigenous college: Philosophical foundations and pragmatic steps. In M. K. Benham & W. J. Stein (Eds.), *The renaissance of American Indian higher education: Capturing the dream* (pp. 25–59). Mahway, NJ: Lawrence Erlbaum Associates.

Stein, W. J. (1999). Tribal colleges: 1968–1998. In K. Swisher & J. Tippeconnic (Eds.), *Next steps: Research and practice to advance Indian education* (pp. 258–269). Charleston, WV: Clearinghouse on Rural Education and Small Schools.

Stannard, D. E. (1992). *American holocaust: The conquest of the new world*. New York: Oxford University Press.

Tate, D. S., & Schwartz, C. L. (1993). Increasing the retention of American Indian students in professional programs in higher education. *Journal of American Indian Education, 33*(1), 21–31.

Thornton, R. (1987). *American Indian holocaust and survival: A population history since 1492.* Norman: University of Oklahoma Press.

Tierney, W. G. (1992). *Official encouragement, institutional discouragement: Minorities in academe—the Native American experience.* Norwood, NJ: Ablex Publishing Corporation.

Tinker, G. E. (1993). *Missionary conquest: The gospel and Native American cultural genocide.* Minneapolis, MN: Fortress Press.

Tinto, V. (1998). Colleges as communities: Taking research in student persistence seriously. *The Review of Higher Education, 21*(2), 167–177.

Tippeconnic, J. W. (2000). Towards educational self-determination: The challenge for Indian control of Indian schools. *Native Americas, XVII*(4), 42–49.

U.S. Department of Commerce. (2002). *The American Indian and Alaska native population: 2000.* Census 2000 Brief. Washington, DC: U.S. Census Bureau.

U.S. Deparment of Education. (1998). *American Indian and Alaska natives in postsecondary education.* National Center for Educational Statistics 98–291. Washington, DC: U.S. Government Printing Office.

Viznor, G. (1994). *Manifest manners: Postindian warriors of survivance.* Hanover, NH: Wesleyan University Press.

Williams, R. A. (2000). Documents of barbarism: The contemporary legacy of European racism and colonization in the narrative traditions of federal Indian law. In R. Delgado & J. Stefancic (Eds.), *Critical race theory: The cutting edge* (pp. 94–105). Philadelphia, PA: Temple University Press.

Zinn, H. (1999). *A people's history of the United States, 1492-present.* New York: HarperCollins Publishers.

CHAPTER 12

LEADERSHIP IN AMERICAN INDIAN HIGHER EDUCATION

Gerald E. Gipp

EVOLVING ROLES

Leadership is inherent in all cultures; however, the development of contemporary leadership in Indian country is not occurring by design. As a rule, tribal communities are not systematically selecting future leaders and then nurturing them to serve the people. The evolving role of American Indian leadership in today's society has not been well documented, but there is agreement among various scholars that there are significant differences between American Indians and Euro-Americans. American Indian leadership has a foundation in traditional culture. Just as other tribal values and traditions have been handed down from one generation to the next, tribal cultures also have expectations of leadership skills and abilities.

Vine Deloria, Jr., Lakota philosopher and scholar, and others have articulated that traditional leadership was based on relationship and kinship responsibilities. Those who served the people best were chosen as leaders. Expanding upon this view, Indian leaders often emerged through a Darwinian form of natural selection where the most bold and courageous individuals,

Tradition and Culture in the Millennium: Tribal Colleges and Universities, pages 161–170
Copyright © 2009 by Information Age Publishing
161

and also those who had special healing powers (e.g., warriors and medicine men) often assumed leadership positions. In most cases, these individuals received unheralded support from fellow tribal members and performed various leadership functions on their behalf.

REVISIONING AMERICAN INDIAN LEADERSHIP

Tribal people over the past five hundred years have been forced to adapt to a continually changing environment. In the brief history of early contact with non-Indian people, the new immigrants of the continents of the Americas halted the natural evolution of indigenous cultures, including the evolution of governance systems and the development of new leaders. With the establishment of the federal government came edicts forbidding native people to practice their traditional ways.

The establishment of reservations ended a subsistence way of life leaving tribal people in a state of dependency on the federal government. This loss of freedom created an environment that devalued the traditional social structures of tribes and families. Historical evidence of federal intervention in attempts to eradicate American Indian cultures is plentiful. Ironically, isolated reservations lands became islands of hope where tribal people were able to continue to practice to some degree their own beliefs, traditions, and ceremonies. Nevertheless, this did not prevent a continuing loss of cultural structures and languages, and the breakdown of tribal and family infrastructures including the identification and nurturing of future leaders. By the end of the 19th century, native people were living in a dominant society that was often contradictory to the traditional ideals, values, and customs.

Indian leadership took a more significant turn with the passage of the Indian Reorganization Act of 1934. In many ways this law undermined the traditional leadership paradigm in tribal communities because it prescribed governing processes for tribal governments that mandated the development and ratification of tribal constitutions. This law set the stage for the public elections of tribal leaders, while at the same time limiting tribal sovereignty by allowing for the U.S. Government, through the Department of Interior, to approve the results of tribal elections.

The role of American Indian leadership in today's society has evolved dramatically and while it is not well studied, it is generally accepted that today's American Indian leaders have a special challenge to use traditional culture as a foundation for leadership. Indian leaders are expected to not only know their traditional communities, but there are an implicit expectation and responsibility to provide for all the people in the community. Those who served the people best are viewed as successful leaders.

Tim Begaye, like many non-Indian researchers, asserts that the term "leadership" is difficult to define because it is abstract, broad, and subjective. Translating leadership discussions from English into tribal languages further complicates the subject. An in-depth study of leadership is usually limited to analyzing the tangible characteristics of individuals or organizations. A thorough understanding requires the study of individual and collective values, norms, and beliefs. It also requires studying how an institution and community's objectives are prioritized and accomplished. Begaye further states, in reality, understanding leadership requires comprehensively analyzing social, economic, and political factors and relationship dynamics. He identifies a number of mainstream institutions that have become well known for preparing American Indian leaders over the past several decades, notably, Pennsylvania State University, Harvard, Minnesota, and Arizona State University (Begaye, 2002).

From the outset many of these graduate school programs were not fully prepared to deal with the special needs of training Indian leaders. Fortunately, those that have proven to be successful have adapted their leadership training to address the contemporary issues of Indian students. Leaders such as Joe Abeyta, David Beaulieu, Rosemary Christensen, Bill Demmert, Lloyd Elm, Grayson Noley, Bruce Ramirez, Karen Gayton Swisher, John Tippeconnic, Linda Sue Warner and a cadre of administrators, academicians, policymakers, and researchers have been instrumental in impacting national education policy and guiding the development of new and culturally relevant educational programs at different levels.[1] Regardless of these efforts there continues to be a dearth of leadership in Indian country as programs expand and current leaders complete their careers in public service.

Despite the complexity of defining Indian leadership, it has been argued that one expectation that still holds true within the Indian community is that contemporary Indian leaders in the face of operating in a Euro-American environment must recognize the value systems and interconnectedness and holistic approach lifestyles of their communities. Former President of Bay Mills Community College, Dr. Martha McLeod, in her article on native leadership finds that Indian leadership is different in the following ways:

a. Indian leaders need to know both their own community (values and history) as well as the Euro-American community because they must function in both societies;
b. Indian leaders need to be holistic because Indian communities are small, Indians value interconnectedness, and Indians work on a wide variety of issues;
c. Indian leaders belong to communal societies that must accommodate both tribal values and Euro-American systems in which Indians and non-Indians coexist.

Dr. McLeod further concludes that these experiences exemplify the complexity of tribal leadership roles. Their insights illustrate that tribal leadership is not simply an act or a series of acts; it is not merely directing a process; it is not playing a role. Tribal leadership is the embodiment of a lifestyle, an expression of learned patterns of thought and behaviors, values, and beliefs. Culture is the basis; it formulates the purpose, process, and ultimately, the product (McLeod, 2002).

The leaders of the American Indian tribal nations from the past are many. Each tribe has its story of heroic leaders in their struggles and display of skills necessary to survive the overwhelming force of a growing American nation. Confronted with the doctrine of Manifest Destiny, Native leaders fought to protect and preserve their homelands; eventually realizing the need to adapt to survive the cultural and social genocide imposed by a dominant culture.

The requirements to persevere under dire and changing circumstance created tremendous pressure on tribal leaders in the 1800s. Leaders like Sitting Bull, Crazy Horse, Chief Joseph, and Geronimo and others fought to prevent the complete annihilation of their people. Today, the struggle for survival continues, but the arenas of battle differ for contemporary Indian leaders in all walks of life. The skills necessary to survive in today's world require a wide range of expertise and knowledge ranging from the class room to the courtroom, in matters related to political, financial and organizational management. Along with the contemporary tribal leaders emerging over the past four decades are the presidents and administrators of the 35 American Indian tribal colleges and universities.

TRIBAL COLLEGE LEADERSHIP

Since the birth of the first tribal college on the Navajo reservation in 1968, a grassroots movement has spawned 35 tribal colleges and universities (TCUs) across 13 states. These institutions of higher education have made significant contributions to American Indian communities and tribal nations through presidential leadership (e.g., President Lionel Bordeaux, Sinte Gleska University; President David Gipp, United Tribes Technical College; President Joe McDonald, Salish Kootenai College; and President James Shanley, Fort Peck Community College;) among many others who have steadfastly insisted on a unified movement while welcoming the inclusion of new colleges despite continuing funding limitations. Other new and dynamic TCU leaders are exemplified by the current officers of the AIHEC, President Cheryl Crazy Bull, Northwest Indian College, Vice-President Ferlin Clark, Diné College, Secretary, Dr. Cynthia Lindquist-Mala, Candeska Cikina Community College, and Tom Short Bull, Oglala Community College.

The Importance of Collaborative Unified Leadership

The success of the grassroots tribal college movement was initially dependent on a handful of educational leaders that recognized the need and value of unity. As a minority among minorities, these Indian leaders waged a long and difficult battle to overcome stereotyping and the disbelievers who felt that American Indians were not capable of creating and managing institutions of higher education. At the same time the first TCU leaders realized the importance of seeking out collaborative partnerships. During the early 1970s and decades to follow, nearly every tribal college that was created was assisted by leaders in mainstream institutions of higher education who accepted the notion of American Indians having the opportunity to provide relevant education for their students on their own terms. Despite differing interests among the TCUs, the themes of unity and partnerships have been central to the successful growth of new tribal colleges and universities. Since the inception of the first tribal college on the Navajo reservation nearly four decades ago these guiding principles have contributed to the success of the tribal college movement.

Through their leadership, tribal colleges and universities have become centers of education on their respective reservation lands and are viewed as legitimate institution of higher education among their students; assisting tribal governments to train people for developing businesses and providing economic alternatives; while supporting the health, welfare and spiritual well-being of tribal members. The leadership of these grass roots institutions of higher education are fundamental to keeping the vision of culturally relevant education alive for Indian country for the all people. This idea is reinforced in the philosophy statement guiding the Lakota Leadership/ Management Development Program of Oglala Lakota College:

> The curriculum is guided by the principle that traditional Lakota beliefs recognize a leader as someone who works for, with, and among the people rather than above them, someone who lives for the people and takes action that is for the people rather than for personal or material gain. The OLC program encourages the full exploration of Lakota culture into contemporary society and contributes to the advancement of knowledge through reservation-based research, promotes the integration of rigorous theory and quality practice, and provides a critical foundation for life-long learning.

Organizations reflect the people who exist within them. It is important for organizations established to serve American Indian people to have leaders who embody Native ideals and reflect the Indian people within those organizations. John L. Phillips in his writing quotes Maenette Benham, an education professor studying leadership and diversity that leadership is "interactive and inclusive, and has at its focus the health and welfare of people, the good of the community, and the celebration of life" (Phillips, 2005).

Tribal colleges and universities resemble mainstream higher education institutions structurally, but there are significant differences. For example, the mission statements of these institutions emphasize the strengthening and retention of tribal culture, which in turn requires leaders who recognize and understand these cultures.

Dr. Verna Fowler, President of the College of Menominee Nation in her study of tribal college leadership further supports the expectation that Indian people look forward to tribal colleges and universities serving the entire community. This is reflected in the wide variety of services, including forums focused on diabetes, early childhood education, child care, economic development, and sovereignty. Cultural expectations, values, and mores are important considerations that influence work at the local level (Fowler, 2002).

In most communities, the tribal colleges play a vital role in the lives of tribal members by offering unique course offerings and important ancillary functions that are not found in mainstream institutions. For example, by providing culturally-relevant education and necessary support systems (such as student housing, child care, and wellness programs) students' basic needs are met, affording them the opportunity to focus on their career goals. Furthermore, because colleges embed native culture, language and tradition into their curricula, students may celebrate their heritage, while building their self-esteem and attaining their educational goals in a familiar learning community. As Dr. Jim Shanley, President of Fort Peck Community College has stated: "tribal colleges are in the business of not only educating students, but we are educating the entire family."

In a study of tribal college presidents Tom Allen and Dave Archambault found that TCU presidents were unanimous in the opinion that the tribal colleges themselves are playing a major role in developing tribal leaders and leadership modes for the future through their classes, tribal forums, modeling, and student government. They also found that tribal college presidents draw the leadership qualities they need from their past experiences, their education, their on-the-job training, and their tribal cultures. Accordingly all presidents interviewed believe that "Traditional tribal leadership teaches many lessons for today's leaders" (Allen & Archambault, 1998).

The Future Role of Leadership

The leadership role for American Indians is increasingly complex for a wide variety of reasons. Lack of resources tends to be the central issue for most tribal institutions of higher education, followed by the need for leadership with an understanding of the unique differences and special needs of Indian communities and their students. Well-prepared leaders with knowledge and experience with cross-cultural issues are fundamental to the future growth and sustainability of tribal colleges and universities. The need for Indian professionals to play this role is paramount to developing a learning environment that is meaningful and relevant for their community members.

Tribal Colleges and universities offer such an environment to begin a systematic approach to preparing future leaders in all endeavors of life. One mandate for TCUs is to determine the role and responsibility their institutions play in the preparation of educational leaders in their communities. This effort is underway with several colleges designing and offering degrees in teacher education at the K–12 level, which is supported by the U.S. Department of Education. In some cases these opportunities are being strengthened by collaborating and partnering with mainstream institutions to ensure that all available resources and learning opportunities are made available to Indian students. This baseline program is the first step to developing a new educational workforce that will have opportunities to emerge as future leaders.

Formal Leadership Development

In 2003, the American Indian Higher Education Consortium (AIHEC) and the tribal colleges and universities began to address the challenge of developing and enhancing the leadership capacity in Indian country with the assistance of the W. K. Kellogg Foundation. In collaboration with the Historically Black Colleges and Universities and the Hispanic Association of Colleges and Universities, AIHEC initiated a leadership program designed to train future TCU presidents or senior college administrators over a three-year period. The program came to a successful close during 2006 with the identification and training of 30 new Indian professional leaders, most of whom have assumed new challenging leadership positions as presidents, vice-presidents and academic leaders.

The Kellogg initiative provided an important opportunity to design a leadership program to successfully address the unique needs of the TCUs that can serve as a model for the large tribal community. However, the focus was limited to highest level of management in the tribal colleges. In addition, the issue of sustainability remains as a paramount concern as limited discretionary resources come to an end.

Tribal colleges have the capacity to expand leadership and capacity-building activities into all areas within the colleges, from students to top managers in fundamental areas such as the principles of American Indian leadership and administration, financial management, government relations, strategic planning, assessment, board and council training and governmental relations. In order to fully address the leadership demands in tribal colleges, opportunities must be developed for mid-level managers such as department chairs, deans, financial aid officers, and registrars, as well as for faculty, counselors, and other support staff. Student leadership is yet another critical area of leadership development that must be pursued.

AIHEC also recognizes that in order to transform the poverty-stricken environments to ones of self-sufficiency for many of our reservations and Indian communities, core areas of leadership need to be identified and designed to reach beyond higher education to provide leadership development to tribal administration and other entities serving American Indian people. Consequently, the development of new leadership and human resource development must extend to our tribal governments and federal agency personnel that serve our communities.

Indian Nations view the tribal Colleges as a viable mechanism to achieve their goal of reestablishing healthy viable communities and thus, healthy nations. Healthy in terms of developing a well-educated citizenry, revitalizing the business and economic environments on and near the Indian reservations, regaining physical, mental, and spiritual health of each and every tribal member. The tribal colleges and universities and AIHEC recognize that effective leadership is essential to achieve this vision for Indian country.

Designing culturally relevant leadership programs is a prerequisite for offering and sustaining successful opportunities for new leaders. While there are many potential venues for the development of American Indian leadership, i.e., tribal governments, mainstream institutions of higher education and the federal agencies themselves, all have the potential and some responsibility to participate in this important endeavor. However, the tribal colleges and universities are in a unique position to play a major role in leading the effort of developing future leaders.

CONCLUSION

Leadership is intrinsic in all cultures, including American Indian cultures, which have yielded significant numbers of effective contemporary tribal leaders. However, leadership development is not occurring by design. As a rule, tribal communities are not selecting future leaders and nurturing them systematically to serve the people. The development of tomorrow's leaders is essential for the continued growth, survival, and success of American Indian Nations. It is important that new programs be envisioned to offer the opportunity to create not only tomorrow's chiefs and visionaries, but highly qualified administrators and managers to serve their people. Programs that reflect training in the areas of not only Tribal higher education, but also in Tribal business and economic development, Tribal health care programs, and Tribal and Federal program administration are equally important.

The tribal colleges and universities are developing the necessary infrastructures to play a leading role in providing quality post secondary education in an environment sensitive to the cultural, economic, and technical needs of American Indians and Alaska Natives. Through advocacy and technical assistance, AIHEC assists its member institutions in strengthening their infrastructures, and helping the colleges meet their individual educational goals. Thus, the tribal college movement is uniquely positioned to address the tribal communities and their specific leadership needs. Such an endeavor can be accomplished by providing tailored services in a cost-effective manner on a comprehensive and collaborative basis with other colleges and agencies.

As the tribal colleges and universities enter a new era of accountability and increased expectations, there are new challenges to be met. The colleges are gaining the capacity to design American Indian leadership programs at several levels and across a variety of professions. Such an effort requires a long-term commitment that must extend over the next decades to effectively address the leadership needs of native communities. It is envisioned that future leaders will bring new visions of hope to Indian Country for new generations.[2]

NOTES

1. This list is considered representational; many other leaders were products of these programs as well.
2. Portions of this article were developed with Debra His Horses Thunder for use in AIHEC's leadership initiative article: Chiefs & Visionaries: AIHEC molds leadership initiative to match tribal values.

REFERENCES

Archambault, D., & Allen, T. (2002, Summer). Politics and the presidency: Tribal college presidents share their thoughts. *Tribal College Journal, 13*(4), 14–19.

Begaye, T. (2002, Summer). Resources for Native American leaders. *Tribal College Journal, 13*(4).

Deloria, V., Jr. (1997). *Tribal sovereignty and American Indian leadership.* URL: www.airpi.org/projects/fall97deloria.html. St. Paul, MN: American Indian Policy Center.

Eagleeye, D., & Stein, W. (1993). Learned leadership: Preparing the next generation of tribal college administrators. *Tribal College Journal, 5*(2), 33–36.

Fowler, V. (1992). *Leadership of American Indian presidents of accredited tribally chartered community colleges.* Unpublished doctoral dissertation, University of North Dakota.

McLeod, M. (2002). Keeping the circle strong: Learning about Native American leadership. *Tribal College Journal, 13*(4).

Phillips, J. (2005, Winter). Developing leadership for the 21st century. *Tribal College Journal, 17*(2).

PART IV

OUR FUTURE

We are what we imagine.
—N. Scott Momaday, Kiowa

CHAPTER 13

SUCCESSION OF THE TRIBAL COLLEGE PRESIDENCY

Phil Baird

INTRODUCTION

A significant issue emerging in the 21st century for American higher education is the preparation of future presidents of this country's tribal colleges
and universities (TCUs). With the longtime tenure and "advancing tribal
elder status" of TCU presidents, there is an emerging need for discussion
about the succession of TCU presidential leadership. What attributes need
to be considered for future TCU presidents? Is there a difference between
preparing tribal college presidents and the higher education leaders of
mainstream institutions? Does a tribal college president become totally disengaged from the institution after a successor is selected? Or is the incumbent president involved with mentoring the successor? What roles, if any,
does the incumbent president have in the transition process serve? What
about life after the TCU presidency?

Tradition and Culture in the Millennium: Tribal Colleges and Universities, pages 173–187
Copyright © 2009 by Information Age Publishing
173

BRIEF HISTORICAL BACKGROUND

The Dine Nation was responsible for establishing the first tribe college in America—Navajo Community College—in 1968. Thereafter, Indian tribes of the northern Great Plains began organizing tribely-chartered institutions of higher education in the early 1970s. Most of these colleges started as affiliate institutions of mainstream colleges and universities through articulation agreements, and then evolved as independent post-secondary institutions. The need for American Indian leaders at TCUs was established early on since the philosophies of most TCUs advocated for culturally-based education under tribe control. This could only be affirmed in a large way with Native American board members, presidents, and educators in charge of policymaking, administration, teaching, and support services.

By 2003, there were 35 tribal colleges and universities participating as institutional-members of the American Indian Higher Education Consortium (AIHEC). The TCUs provided a broad array of postsecondary academic opportunities from vocational certificate and two-year degree programs to master degree level programs. The TCUs served predominantly American Indian students from rural communities located on or near federal Indian reservations. Student populations ranged from less than 100 to more than 1,500 and were predominantly female, single parents with dependents, and economically disadvantaged. Collectively, tribal colleges and universities now serve more than 30,000 students.

Given the mission and tribal population base served by the TCUs, there has been and continues to be the need for American Indian educational leadership uniquely prepared with the knowledge and experience working at tribal colleges and universities. This suggests that leaders must not only be familiar with higher education systems, but they must understand those unique and diverse characteristics of TCUs that are different from mainstream postsecondary institutions.

The evolution of the TCU presidency has mirrored the history of tribal colleges and universities as developing postsecondary institutions. The knowledge and skills needed for this presidency have been, for the most part, cultivated as the colleges evolved. The executive leadership role has been a "work in progress." To be sure, some colleges were fortunate to employ individuals with prior experience in mainstream higher education systems. However, the challenge of developing a new multi-cultural postsecondary education model administered under tribal control remains a "work in progress." And so are the leadership roles of the TCU president.

Dr. Wayne J. Stein presented the early history of TCUs in his doctoral dissertation turned into the book, *Tribally-controlled Colleges: Making Good Medicine* (1992). His research documented the leadership activities during the formative years of several institutions. As TCUs were established, prospective presidents were either identified from within the tribal, or recruited from other Indian programs. Some tribal colleges started with non-Indian presidents and others with tribal members serving in the executive administrator role. A common element of this early history was that the tenure of the first TCU presidents was brief, lasting in most cases no longer than two years. The succession of the TCU presidency at this time was centered on finding tribal educators, and preferably tribal members, with the commitment, cultural sensitivity, academic credentials, and experience more conducive to developing higher education institutions serving American Indian people.

Half of the six TCUs profiled in Stein's book were eventually successful in employing tribal members who have served for an extended period of time, in some cases more than 20 years. Lionel Bordeaux, president of Sinte Gleska University (formerly Sinte Gleska College) since 1973, is the longest tenured president. Dr. Gerald Monette assumed the presidency at Turtle Mountain Community College in 1978. Tom Short Bull, president of Oglala Lakota College (initially known as Lakota Higher Education Center), came into his present role twice, accumulating time of more than three decades now. The tenure of these individuals, and now others in the contemporary tribal college arena, suggests that the succession of leadership will need to be addressed within the next 5–10 years.

With the proliferation of tribal colleges, the succession issue has emerged steadily and touched nearly all the tribal colleges. There have been several succession pathways; some were planned but all-too-many times, unplanned and unexpected. An ever-present factor creating change in the TCU presidency has been the intrusion of tribal politics. TCU presidents have resigned or been fired because of political pressures from within the institution (e.g., conflicts with the college board) and outside the college (e.g., tribal government interference). In most cases, there was no formal succession plan beyond unilateral appointments or standardized employee recruitment practices to fill the position.

Transitions in TCU presidencies have been attributed to other factors such as sabbaticals, voluntary resignations due to age or poor health, financial mismanagement, and unexpected deaths. To a small degree, because of the lack of Indian candidates, succession became an issue when colleges employed non-Indian professionals until a qualified Indian president could be recruited. Regardless of the reasons for presidential transitions, wellconceived succession plans have not emerged between tribal colleges and universities. The absence of such plans creates a myriad of problems for an institution—leadership conflicts, low staff morale, loss of funding opportunities, accreditation stipulations, public relations issues, gaps in institutional history, and diminished credibility and public confidence to name but a few.

A significant issue in Indian education leadership is that no model has been developed specifically for the succession of the presidency at tribal colleges and universities. This is critical since at least one-third of the TCUs are presently addressing position vacancies or will be facing leadership succession situations in the next ten years due to the tenure of their presidents (Ambler, 2002). For the latter situations, there are at least five institutions— Fort Peck Community College (MT), Salish Kootenai College (MT), Sinte Gleska University (SD), Turtle Mountain Community College (ND), and United Tribes Technical College (ND)—that have presidents with tenures of 20 or more years. Four other tribal colleges have presidents who are 60 years of age or older. Five colleges are presently engaged in presidential search modes. There are at least two new tribal colleges on the horizon of being established, and these will require qualified leadership.

Only one tribal college among all these institutions has acknowledged that an active succession plan is being considered. A discussion about such a plan is timely, and perhaps a framework can be shaped for the succession of future tribal college presidents.

INFORMATION GATHERING

Given the fact that tribal colleges and universities are relatively young institutions within the American higher education system, it should be no surprise there is little available research information specifically about the succession of tribal college presidencies. There has been good information compiled and written about K–12 Indian school leadership, and about Indian leadership in general. Yet in the context of the tribal college experience, there is a void.

One indicator about the tribal college leadership dilemma can be viewed from the information about the future of community college and minority higher education leadership. In a report published by the American Association of Community Colleges, a 2001 study indicated that 45 percent of community college presidents were planning retirement by 2007. The same report said those incumbent presidents involved in the study thought that one fourth of their senior administrators would be following retirement paths during the next five years.

These situations are of particular concern to the leadership representing the nation's 450+ minority-serving institutions (MSIs) of higher education. They recognized that the demand for college leaders among MSIs "far exceeds the supply; yet there has been little attention paid to task of identifying and educating the next generation of leaders" (AEHE Press Release, August 2003). Three national MSI organizations—the American Indian Higher Education Association (AIHEC), the Hispanic Association of Colleges and

Universities (HACU), and the National Association for Equal Opportunity (NAFEO) in Higher Education—came together to address this situation.

The Alliance for Equity in Higher Education, organized by the three national MSI organizations, established a four-year initiative in 2003 with support from the W.K. Kellogg Foundation aimed at cultivating the next generation of presidents and senior executives. The Kellogg MSI Leadership Fellows program began in August 2003 with the first class of 33 Fellows representing Hispanic-serving institutions, historically Black colleges and universities (HBCUs), and tribal colleges and universities. The project entailed a series of seminars, national higher education and organizational events, an international experience, and mentoring activities focused on providing information and "seasoned" expertise about key significant issues in the higher education world.

The development of a research paper about the succession of TCU presidencies was identified by the author as one outcome of the Kellogg MSI Fellows program for AIHEC participants. For this topic, the primary information-collecting methodologies selected were . . . (1) conducting literature searches about TCU presidential leadership, and (2) engaging in formal and informal discussions with tribal college presidents and other leaders through the Fellows program activities. The end product of these activities would be a discussion paper to be shared with the leadership of tribal colleges and universities about the succession of the TCU presidency.

As an initial approach to the topic, information was searched to answer the question—what leadership qualities should a tribal college president possess? Some information was obtained by reviewing what was published about Indian educational leadership in general. In their monograph, Robbins and Tippeconnic (1985) presented a set of characteristics of effective Indian educational leaders:

1. A leader must be able to recognize that differences between native and nonnative people exist.
2. A leader must possess skills in cross-cultural communications.
3. A leader must be able to translate theory into practice.
4. A leader must maintain a positive attitude toward and a deep commitment to the education of, by, and for American Indians.
5. A leader must have creativity and vision.
6. A leader must demonstrate patience and tolerance with regard to various opinions and positions.
7. A leader must possess self-confidence and pride in being a Native American.

As a former president of the Institute of American Indian Arts (IAIA), Dr. Perry Horse suggested the following Indian leadership attributes: An individual must be competent, committed, able to demonstrate courage, a good listener, multi-talented, and able to demonstrate a sense of humor. Demonstrating a love for the people served was listed as "often overlooked" but essential—"otherwise good leaders would give up" (Horse, 2002).

Other tribal college presidents have offered information about the qualities needed in the role of American Indian higher education leadership. In *The Tribal College Journal* edition titled "The Many Faces of Leadership," several TCU presidents offered their perspectives drawn from their education, experiences including on-the-job training, and from their indigenous cultural bases (Allen & Archambault, 2002). Some key thoughts and ideas are summarized as follows:

1. Traditional leaders were respectful, visible in the community, and accessible. (Dr. James Shanley, president, Fort Peck Community College).
2. A leader is willing to be one of the people and provide leadership in a humble way. (Tom Shortbull, president, Oglala Lakota College).
3. A leader has to be patient, model what you preach, and focus on the mission. (Dr. Gerald Monette, president, Turtle Mountain Community College).
4. A leader should practice participatory management and have the courage to delegate. (Dr. Joe McDonald, president, Salish Kootenai College).
5. A college president must be honest, consistently show integrity, and have a sense of humor. (Dr. Verna Fowler, president, College of Menominee Nation).
6. The president's loyalty is to the college and the students. (Dr. Martha McLeod, founding president, Bay Mills Community College).
7. Future TCU presidents need an overview of the tribal college movement itself, its history, purposes, struggles, and triumphs. (Lionel Bordeaux, president, Sinte Gleska University).

Information specific to a tribal college presidential position were offered during a 2003 Kellogg MSI Leadership session for the AIHEC Fellows at Greensboro, N.C. Several current and past TCU presidents talked about skills and experiences necessary in the following areas:

1. Budget development and monitoring.
2. Academic/Instructional leadership.
3. Fund-raising.
4. Strategic planning.
5. Active participation in accreditation activities.
6. Community leadership.
7. Negotiation skills and experiences.

The focus of information-gathering at this point has been centered on ideal Indian education leadership qualities. However, to address the challenge of preparing for the succession of a TCU president, there was a need for information specific to this situation.

The next approach was to interview a tribal college president who was actively considering retirement and the issues of succession.

Dr. Joseph McDonald, founding president of Salish Kootenai College, began in 2003 the transition process for a new college president for the second time. When he previously entertained the idea of retirement, he had identified his successor, the late Jerry Slater, who served for many years as the SKC academic vice president. Unexpectedly, Jerry passed on, leaving Dr. McDonald to postpone retirement plans and to continue carrying on with the urgent business of his college. At 70 years of age, the former teacher, basketball coach, and recipient of many national and state awards were again approaching the process for identifying and transitioning a new president of SKC.

Because he was dealing with a succession situation, President McDonald agreed to participate in an interview with the author in April 2004. A three-day on-site visit was made to conduct personal interview activities on the SKC campus at Pablo, Montana. The first activity was to jointly review and discuss information collected on tribal leadership attributes by the author. The second activity centered on Dr. McDonald responding to four questions in an interview manner. The third and final activities were to summarize the findings in a research paper and then prepare this discussion paper.

FINDINGS

As a result of the interview with SKC President Dr. Joe McDonald, a summary of his responses to selected questions is as follows:

1. **What options does SKC have regarding the succession of a new tribal college president?**

There are basically three options for the tribal college to consider in the selection and transitioning of a new president. These are:

A. With preselected qualifications and processes, the TCU board will pick the successor and the incumbent president will be retired from the position, becoming totally disengaged from the institution. This is the "move out of the way" approach recommended by the Association of Governing Boards, leaving the successor to carve out his/her own space at the college.

B. With preselection qualifications and processes, the TCU board will pick the successor as an administrative vice president to be mentored directly under and by the incumbent president for a certain length of time. When the successor is determined to have the knowledge and experience to assume duties, the successor will step into the role of president. The incumbent will become totally disengaged from the institution.

C. The processes for Option C are nearly the same as Option B, except that post-presidential duties would be considered for the retiring president. Under this scenario, the incumbent does not become totally disengaged if he or she is a residential tribal member willing to assume another supporting (i.e., non-presidential) role at the college.

In the review of these options, Dr. McDonald indicated that he preferred Option C, envisioning opportunities for the incumbent president to assist with a variety of important institutional functions such as fund-raising, governmental liaison activities, accreditation processes, etc. He also identified the need for and advantage of maintaining institutional history, which could be served by having the incumbent involved with the college in non-presidential roles. President McDonald also concurred with the author's perspective that Option C may be culturally-appropriate for some indigenous tribal groups that embrace the value of tribal elders in supporting community roles. Under Option C, the board should be involved with the important task of clearly delineating expectations, roles, responsibilities, and any administrative authorities of the retiring TCU president.

The common disadvantage for all three options is that without a clear, well-thought succession plan, the tribal college could end up with a new president who does not understand the challenges of the TCU presidency, who is reluctant to make changes, or who takes the institution "down the wrong path." Dr. McDonald acknowledged there is no guarantee that a successor will work out. But at least with a succession plan that includes mentoring, he feels a prospective presidential candidate can acquire some degree of on-the-job training and experience that could be measured prior to the transition phase.

2. What tribal leadership qualities, skills, and experiences are unique and necessary to the TCU college presidency?

After reviewing previously collected information about tribal educational leadership, Dr. McDonald felt it was important to consider those attributes important to the TCU presidency of the 21st century. Since tribal colleges and universities have evolved to become more and more complex, he felt that TCUs now require more knowledgeable and sophisticated leadership.

He offered his perspectives about those attributes essential for the TCU president of the future.

"An emerging tribal college president should effectively possess and demonstrate. . . ."

General familiarity with indigenous cultural philosophies and perspectives. The ideal candidate will have knowledge about the general history of tribes, tribal cultures, and tribal education philosophies. These serve as the foundation of tribally-controlled education, which defines TCUs as distinct from mainstream higher education institutions.

Understanding key characteristics, needs, and trends (e.g., cultural, political, social, economic) of the tribe community base served by the college. A successor should have an understanding about the tribal communities and the constituents served by the college. The political aspects would very much include the principles about tribal sovereignty and the unique political relationship between the federal government and Indian tribes. An effective president must also become familiar with the "political culture" of the tribe or tribal community served.

Familiarity with the institutional history of the tribal college movement. Future tribal college presidents should have basic understanding about how tribal colleges evolved, what successes and accomplishments have been achieved (institutionally and collectively), and what critical issues TCUs must face (e.g., funding, assessment, accreditation, grants management, etc.).

Sense of place of TCU students. It is worthwhile to assess how a potential successor views the roles and responsibilities of TCU students. These views will influence policies and decisions about how the college will serve its students, a majority of who are American Indians and Alaska Natives learning in a multicultural education setting.

Familiarity with tribal Land Grant status. Being recognized as 1994 Land Grant institutions, Tribal colleges and universities have the potential to broaden roles in tribal human and land resources development toward the goal of rebuilding Indian Nations (Baird, 1996). The successor needs to be familiar with needs and trends of Indian communities, and with opportunities and resources available among federal agencies, especially the U.S. Department of Agriculture.

Capabilities of networking. The TCU college president of the future must effectively network with a broad array of private and public section entities. Advocacy, marketing, collaboration, and fund-raising will drive networking activities. This means the TCU president must have strong communication skills (e.g., oral, written, technological).

Flexible leadership styles and skills. The college presidency requires an understanding of leadership styles, interpersonal skills, and style shifts to interact in a variety of organizational settings. One leadership behavior (e.g., to be humble, walk softly, be reflective) may fit well with a tribal elder group; another constituent group may expect a more outgoing, assertive, and vocal leader.

The aforementioned attributes were identified as specific to the TCU presidency. Both President McDonald and the author concurred that there were other attributes essential for any college or university presidency, including the following: Knowledge of higher education systems; prior participation in accreditation processes; familiarity with academic programs, student assessment, and curricula development; experience with higher education strategic planning; understanding of fiscal management practices; basic knowledge about technology applications; and familiarity with educational research.

There was one other dimension of the succession process discussed by President McDonald. This dimension was related to the "values orientation" of the presidential candidate. He indicated that tribal college boards might be concerned with background and reference checks revealing "question marks" about the character of a successor. Questions could arise about such things as an individual's financial history (e.g., bad checks), family history (e.g., domestic violence), and health history (e.g., substance abuse treatment). Boards could be concerned about how the community, in particular an Indian community, might perceive, albeit subjectively, the values of the prospective successor. Dr. McDonald believed any assessment of values-orientation would become more evident, and perhaps more weighted, when considering *residential tribal members* as candidates for the TCU presidency.

3. Is there any value in having a tribal member selected as a successor versus a non-tribal member versus a non-Indian?

The succession of a president for a reservation-based tribal college or university should in most cases invoke "Indian preference." This means that in a situation with equal credentials possessed among a pool of qualified candidates, a tribal college board should exercise Indian preference by first selecting a tribal member, a member of another tribe (non-tribal member), or a documented descendant (non-enrolled) of an Indian tribe for the position. The history of tribe college presidencies will reflect that those tribal colleges' presidents with the longest tenures are tribal members of the community served. This history will also show that non-tribe members and non-Indians have served as TCU presidents.

As a member of the Indian tribe he serves, Dr. McDonald felt there was potentially great value in his successor being a tribal member of the Salish and/or Kootenai Tribes. In the eyes of the community, tribal affiliation of the college president demonstrates direct connectiveness to the tribal cultural base by having "one of our own" in a high level position. tribal affiliation also provides a community and family base that are needed for cultural, social, and political purposes. Because of this base, the college president has a network of people that can be called upon. The tribal member as college president can also serve as a positive role model for students and community members.

Does tribal affiliation provide the tribal college president with any advantage in dealing with tribal government? This is perhaps better determined by the political astuteness of a TCU president. Some TCU presidents have successfully served on tribal councils; others have a preference to minimize any interaction with tribal governments. Dr. McDonald, a former tribal council member, and the author recounted several situations in tribal college history where tribal college presidencies were sustained, and terminated, in the arena of tribal government.

As for considering non-tribal members and non-Indians for a tribal college presidency, Dr. McDonald believed that tribe college boards must decide how tribal higher education institutions will affirm the principles of tribally-controlled education. This will be reflected in hiring decisions. He said he has heard from board members of other TCUs about a perceived lack of qualified Indian candidates to be considered for TCU presidencies. While this may be true in some cases, Dr. McDonald and the author concurred there were most likely other mitigating factors (e.g., community leadership conflicts, board instability, financial management problems, accreditation issues, etc.) that inhibited qualified Indian educators from pursuing presidential positions at certain tribal colleges.

4. **What roles do you believe you have as the incumbent TCU president in the succession process?**

Dr. McDonald and the author identified at least four basic phases of the succession process: pre-recruitment, search and selection, transition, and succession. Each of these phases could include the active participation of the incumbent president, dependent upon (a) the administrative environment of the college, (b) the relationship between the incumbent and the college board, (c) the experience of the president, (d) the desired extent of board involvement, and (e) the work delegated to a presidential search committee or to an external consultant if these are to be used.

Assuming the retiring president will be involved, there are key contributions that can be provided by the incumbent for each phase. Qualifications and tribal leadership attributes of the ideal TCU presidential candidate can be identified with the college board. Duties and responsibilities involved with the search process can be clearly outlined if a committee or consultant is utilized. In the selection process, the retiring president can provide an important assessment of each candidate's experience, or potential experience, in the tribal college world. Whether or not there is a mentoring period, the incumbent president can facilitate the flow of information and key documents for the successor during the transition phase. In the ideal situation, one might expect the retiring president to be involved with formal transition activities and ceremonies.

The tribal college board will ultimately need to determine the value of any post-presidential duties for the retiring president. There are advantages and disadvantages in creating life for a "TCU president emeritus" who retires from the position. Again, there appear to be more distinct advantages with an incumbent president who is a tribal member and does not expect to relocate from the tribal community. For the tribal college or university that has enjoyed institutional success because of an effective tribal college president, a formal effort should be made to explore and assess all options for ensuring continued success after a new tribal college president takes office. One approach is to determine a supporting role(s) of a retiring TCU president that can be directed in a positive and constructive manner.

CONCLUSION

Total disconnection of the retiring or incumbent college president from the institution is what's recommended by mainstream higher education experts. This course of action is what has been observed during the past 30+ years of tribal college history when a tribal college president has voluntarily or involuntarily stepped down. Is this the best approach for tribal colleges and universities that have the opportunity to prepare for the retirement of a long-tenured president and the succession of a new president?

The lack of a model for the succession of the TCU presidency represents a serious challenge for tribal colleges and universities in the future. Given the diversity of TCU institutions and the tribal communities being served, it may be fair to say that no one model will fit all. What may be the best approach is to say what is best for the institution, considering all factors. And therein lies the key—there is a need for a succession plan, and the development of such a plan should consider all those factors affecting not only the presidency, but all dimensions of the college influenced by the president. The lack of succession plans among today's TCUs points to the value of discussions and research about the potential framework of a plan.

As a result of the information-gathering activities leading to the development of this paper by the author, perspectives by tribal college presidents and other educational leaders became clearer about the succession of the TCU presidency:

- The evolution of tribal colleges and universities has occurred in a relatively short time span compared with American mainstream higher education institutions. As the TCUs are regarded as developing institutions, so are the evolving roles of a TCU president. These roles will be shaped by the developmental activities and progress of a given tribal college. Roles can also be expanded to include participation in national organizations (e.g., AIHEC) and in international developments such as those of the World Indigenous Nations Higher Education Consortium (WINHEC).

- There are valuable perspectives to be learned about the traditional and contemporary qualities of tribal leaders. Along with these qualities, there are skills and experiences tribal college presidents must have to be effective. These all must be considered as priority attributes for the tribal college presidency. Advocacy activities with such issues as tribal sovereignty, racism, land reclamation, and natural resources development are other important considerations. The relationship between gender and cultural philosophies of tribal leadership is another perspective to be considered.

- The attention and focus on tribal culture, language, history, and communities cannot be overly stated or emphasized as the foundation of tribal colleges and universities. If not for this foundation, tribal colleges would be just another community college.

- There are TCU leadership attributes, skills and experiences common to the presidency of mainstream higher education institutions. These will need to be weighted in the selection process in comparison to those attributes unique and necessary for a tribal institution of higher education.

- The role of tribal college boards in the succession process is of utmost importance. Given the "tribalism" and "community orientation" of TCUs, it is perhaps better for an informed board to proactively oversee the search and selection process as opposed to outsourcing these roles to a committee or external consultant not familiar with the "big picture." On the other hand, board members with little experience or with political agendas may prove to be counterproductive to the succession process. Board training must be strongly considered.

- While the role of tribal communities has not been explicitly discussed, tribal college presidents in various forums have repeatedly emphasized the importance and "place" of tribal communities in the work of tribal colleges. There is a fundamental need for decision-making to be inclusive of community stakeholders if the colleges are to be successful and progressive. When asked if they aspired to tribal college presidencies, the 2003–2004 AIHEC/Kellogg Fellows acknowledged the place of tribal communities, agreeing that "the people" of a tribal community will have a strong say,

directly and indirectly, about who will be accepted in tribal leadership roles.

- Future discussions about the succession of the TCU presidency
  could become more difficult for the incumbents as they realize they
  have more years behind them in their careers, and in their lives.
  This realization, and the ability to cope with this reality, has implications that will touch each incumbent differently—professionally,
  emotionally, psychologically, economically, spiritually. For those who
  wish to continue contributing to the tribal college movement, and
  to their respective tribes and tribal communities, there should be
  situations considered for "life after the tribal college presidency."

RECOMMENDATIONS

There is much more to be explored about developing viable and relevant
succession models. The literature review and interview activities served to
formulate some initial recommendations that will hopefully expand the inquiry process. These recommendations are:

1. Tribal colleges should identify the standards and methodologies to
   be used to measure the competencies of tribal college presidential
   candidates as these competencies relate to knowledge, understandings, and the degree of familiarity with tribal philosophies, cultures,
   histories, sovereignty, and tribally-controlled education.
2. Knowing that a candidate cannot possibly meet all qualifications and
   selection criteria, tribal colleges must identify and prioritize the most
   important factors in the selection of the new tribal college president.
   The screening process might have to involve establishing increased
   value or "weight" for those skills and experiences absolutely critical to the TCU president's role. The value of certain factors will be
   perceived differently from college to college because of the varying
   institutional development levels among the TCUs. There also could
   be consideration of other factors such as the "political culture" of
   the tribe or tribal community, and the issue of gender as this might
   pertain to cultural philosophies, roles, and trends of tribal leadership.
3. With priority order and value attached to selection criteria, a "TCU
   Presidential Selection Matrix" could be developed as an assessment
   tool, providing more structure for candidates as well as for college
   stakeholders involved in the selection process. Board training in the
   selection of an institutional president would be highly recommended.
4. The college board and incumbent should define what types of professional activities and outcomes would be established for the succes-

sor who is being mentored by an incumbent TCU president. Clear expectations and time lines should be established.

5. A college board should establish parameters and methodologies for determining "when the successor has arrived" to step up into the TCU president's role.
6. Tribal colleges should determine if there is a productive role for the retiring TCU president within and/or outside the college.
7. After the transition process, a tribal college should embrace the opportunity to capstone the succession process in a culturally-appropriate way by acknowledging the spirit world, by recognizing past and present tribal college leadership, and by publicly celebrating one of the most significant events of the institution—moving forward in a positive way with new tribal college leadership in the 21st century.

Mitakuye Oyasin (All My Relatives).

REFERENCES

Allen, T., & Archambault, D. (2002, Summer). Politics and the presidency. *The Tribal College Journal of American Indian Higher Education, XII*(4), 14–19.

Ambler, M. J. (2002, Summer). Today's educators creating the leaders of tomorrow. *The Tribal College Journal of American Indian Higher Education, XII*(4), 8–9.

Baird, P. (1996, September). What is a tribal land grant college? *Sinte Gleska University Concept Paper.* Rosebud, SD.

Benham, M. K. P., & Stein, W. (2003). *The renaissance of American Indian higher education: Capturing the dream.* Mahwah, NJ: Lawrence Erlbaum Associates.

Boyer, P. (1997). *Native American colleges—progress and prospects.* Princeton, NJ: Princeton University Press.

Deloria, V. (1997, Fall). Tribal sovereignty and American Indian leadership. *American Indian Policy Center Forum Report.*

Gambler, C. (2004, February/March). About this issue. *Community College Journal, 74*(4), 2.

Gregnon, G. (2002, Spring). Keeping the tribe colleges tribe. *The Tribal College Journal of American Indian Higher Education, XII*(3), 38–41.

Horse, P. (2002, Fall). Leadership challenges in Indian country. *The American Indian Graduate, 2*(1), 8–9, 28.

McLeod, M. (2002, Summer). Keeping the circle strong: Learning about native american leadership. *The Tribal College Journal of American Indian Higher Education, 13*(4), 10–12.

Robbins, R., & Tippeconnic, J. III. (1985). *American Indian education leadership.* Tempe, AZ: Center for Indian Education.

Stein, W. (1992). *Tribally-controlled colleges: Making good medicine.* New York. Peter Lang.

World Indigenous Nations Higher Education Consortium. (2004). *WINHEC Accreditation Handbook.* First Edition.

CHAPTER 14

THE ROLE OF THE *TRIBAL COLLEGE JOURNAL* IN THE TRIBAL COLLEGE MOVEMENT

Marjane Ambler and Paul Boyer

INTRODUCTION

For 17 years, The American Indian Higher Education Consortium (AIHEC) has published a quarterly magazine chronicling the stories, issues and challenges faced by the tribal colleges. Since the Tribal College Journal's inception in 1989, the scope of the journal has steadily progressed from serving the specific needs of the tribal college administrators to informing a larger audience about the tribal college movement and the challenges facing American Indian higher education today. Over the years, the AIHEC board and journal staff have considered hard questions about purpose and audience. Should the journal mimic other scholarly journals? Or should it promote a distinctly "Native" approach to scholarship? Should it be inward looking (writing primarily for an Indian audience), or should it be outward looking (writing for non-Indians and offering a window into the tribal world)? If it is read by non-Indians, should it strive toward an honest

Tradition and Culture in the Millennium: Tribal Colleges and Universities, pages 189–200
Copyright © 2009 by Information Age Publishing
All rights of reproduction in any form reserved.

portrayal of the community—blemishes and all—or stress a positive, public relations role? Finally, can the journal sustain itself financially and still fulfill its mission?

The history and mission of the journal also illuminate larger issues within the tribal college movement. Leaders have struggled since the beginning to define the movement's relationship with mainstream colleges and universities, with their own communities, and with the nation as a whole. Who are we? How do we want to be viewed by others? Where do we find the resources to stay alive, and how does that affect our self-determination efforts? What is our unique contribution to education? The journal confronts these issues in a very public way, four times a year, and by 2006, it had an audience of some 18,000 readers.

CREATION STORY

The idea for a tribal college magazine emerged when Paul Boyer was conducting site visits of tribal colleges during the spring of 1988 for the Carnegie Foundation for the Advancement of Teaching. The Princeton, New Jersey-based foundation had hired Boyer to visit the tribal colleges and write a report on the status and needs of the movement entitled Tribal Colleges: Shaping the future of Native America (1989).

By traveling from campus to campus, spending several days at each, he quickly learned a great deal about each institution. Despite their differences, all shared a similar philosophy of education. While resources were limited, all were attempting to offer an education grounded in the tribal culture and, for most, community development was a priority. Yet, as he traveled from campus to campus, Boyer began to realize that faculty and administrators within the movement knew little about the work of their sister institutions.

The epiphany came to Boyer when he was talking with an employee at Navajo Community College (NCC, now Diné College) in Tsaile, AZ, about that college's plan to sponsor a public television station. He had just visited Salish Kootenai College (SKC) in Pablo, MT, which had just started broadcasting PBS programming over the Flathead Reservation. Yet staff at NCC had no idea that another tribal college had a station up and running. Clearly, there was a gap that needed to be filled. Since he had a master's degree in communications, his natural impulse was to create a magazine.

Boyer took the idea for the journal to Dr. Joe McDonald, president of SKC, who agreed that it should be considered by the board of AIHEC. In 1989, AIHEC endorsed the idea, set up an advisory board of tribal college presidents, and voted to increase the membership dues to pay for it.[1] Seed money from the Carnegie Foundation covered the cost of printing the first edition—a modest black and white publication designed on an early Macintosh computer.

Looking back, it was an improbable project. The tribal colleges were struggling financially, and their consortium had even fewer resources—no full time employees and no office.[2] How could they afford a national magazine, even the small sum of $15,000 a year? By choosing to have an advisory board of presidents, they were choosing not to have experts in marketing, fundraising, or publishing on their board as other nonprofit magazines often do.

But these people were accustomed to making improbable ideas reality. They also recognized the need for the colleges to have a public face. At this time, there was no central repository with information about tribal colleges. AIHEC had no office and the American Indian College Fund was just being created. Because of their limited resources, the tribal college founders built their institutions based on passion, commitment, and ability to stretch a dollar. They expected the young editor to do the same.

DEFINING THE INITIAL MISSION AND AUDIENCE

The magazine was named Tribal College: Journal of American Indian Higher Education.[3] As the name suggested, the focus of the journal was on the work of the tribal colleges. Boyer always had assumed that a core function of the journal was to help colleges communicate with each other, and the colleges also recognized this was important. But from the very beginning, it was clear that the journal had to serve a variety of roles and reach a wider audience. Indeed, the dilemma faced by the journal in its early years was not that it lacked a purpose, but that it had so many different roles to play.

For example, some felt strongly that it should be a true scholarly journal. Sinte Gleska College (later to be Sinte Gleska University) President Lionel Bordeaux expressed hope after the first issue came out that the journal would include more articles "with footnotes." For him (and others), academic writing tangibly demonstrated the colleges' commitment to scholarship and their status as serious institutions of higher learning. Through the ensuing years, longtime Tribal College Journal Advisory Board member Dr. Gerald "Carty" Monette often insisted upon using the term "journal" rather than "magazine" when describing the publication.

At the beginning, others assumed the journal would play a public relations role. Georgiana Tiger, AIHEC's legislative representative for several years, handed out journals to members of Congress during her visits to Capitol Hill. Few policy makers knew about the colleges, and the journal helped her tell the story of the movement and build the case for increased federal funding. Before long, AIHEC asked the journal to add members of Congress from tribal college states to its complimentary subscription list.

In 1991, Boyer was approached by Barbara Bratone, the founding executive director of the American Indian College Fund, about printing enough journals for mailing to College Fund donors. The fund would cover the cost of printing and mailing the copies they ordered. Boyer was delighted because larger print runs would be more economical, greatly increase readership, and make the journal more attractive to advertisers. But Boyer wondered out loud if donors would be interested in the kind of articles that were then being printed. He proposed developing a separate publication for the fund's donors. She rejected that idea and emphasized that the journal was fine as it was. The donor subscriptions soon represented more than half of the readership.

Although there were no reader surveys at that time, Boyer inevitably started thinking about what donors and members of Congress would want to read. He began including more articles that he called "Tribal College 101." All of these roles had to be balanced in a single publication.

FREEDOM AND FLEXIBILITY

In the early years, the journal could not pay writers and relied on the kindness of current and past tribal college presidents and faculty to set aside time and write articles. Jack Barden, Dr. Wayne Stein, Dr. James Shanley, and Sky Houser were among the many tribal college leaders who addressed subjects such as spirituality, Native ways of knowing, assessment in a cultural environment, leadership, indigenous math and science, accountability, and economic development.

From the beginning, the editor focused each issue upon a specific theme. As might have been expected of a journal for tribal colleges, some of the themes of the early years centered on administration, curriculum, and culture—for example how to run a tribal college, international indigenous education, art, spirituality, indigenous math and science, Indian history traditions, and Indian research.

Tribal colleges are committed to play broader roles in community development than other community colleges. Therefore, the journal also covered issues beyond what would normally be considered "education," such as economic development; management across cultures; alcohol, drugs, and family violence; and leadership.

But Boyer's time as an editor was limited by all the administrative tasks —from billing, to design, to mailing. For the first two years he personally sorted the magazine by zip code on his living room floor. The magazine gradually grew, from the initial 24 pages and a mailing list of 1,000. As it grew, he was able to hire some part-time help and some professional writers, but he worked outside of any bureaucracy.

In these and other ways, the journal reflected what was happening in the movement during the late 1980s and early 1990s. There were a can-do spirit and a sense of importance that inspired loyalty to the movement even when money was tight and the future seemed unclear. Boyer started the journal at the age of 22. Some of the tribal college founders were not much older than that when they created their colleges. As a young person involved in a young movement, he felt they were doing something of great importance. They didn't have a lot of funding, but they had enough to create something. There was a strong feeling that they were building something entirely new while struggling against people and institutions that would rather see them fail. They felt that they were helping to create a better life for whole communities.

There was also a sense of freedom and flexibility within the movement. Creativity and individual initiative were encouraged. In part, this simply reflected the lack of an infrastructure within AIHEC. Without a centralized administration of AIHEC, Boyer (and others) worked with almost complete autonomy. They handed him a check, and he handed them a magazine. This had its down side; by running the journal as his own business, he was personally paying taxes on the journal's income. But the ability to experiment and innovate more than compensated.[4]

SCHOLARLY ROLE

After a few years, Boyer began to think more deeply about the journal's scholarly role. It was a unique hybrid, mostly journalism reviewed only by the editor with a few scholarly articles refereed by a Research Review Panel. Being a hybrid created problems. At first, refereed articles were included because they gave the colleges prestige and because American Indian faculty in mainstream universities needed to publish in refereed journals to gain tenure. At least one faculty member at a state university cobbled something together just before a tenure review specifically with the journal in mind.

However, with a few exceptions, the journal did not attract top quality research. When Boyer solicited submissions from well-established scholars who were doing cutting edge work, he was rebuffed. They didn't need the journal—there were other, far more influential and prestigious journals where they could publish. At the same time, some tribal college scholars did not submit their papers because only a portion of the journal was refereed and it was not perceived as an academic journal.

In the early 1990s, there was growing discussion of scholarship within academe. A few interesting books were coming out talking about different "ways of knowing." Do women scholars have different "ways of knowing," for example, and what are the implications for scholarship? The same question was being asked of minority groups, such as Indians, but asking the question was not the same as accepting the answers. When tribal colleges were invited to submit grant proposals focusing upon their tribes' ways of knowing, the grantors rejected the proposals, saying, for example, that oral histories did not qualify as real scholarship.

Thinking about all this, Boyer hoped that the journal could help define and publish new models of research. He envisioned the journal helping to articulate a "Native" philosophy of scholarship and becoming a forum for new approaches.

However, before this dream could be realized, Boyer decided to leave the journal in 1995. Creating a new journal and getting it on its feet had excited him, but he was ready for new challenges. After seeing the important role that tribal colleges played in addressing social change, he felt a fire burning inside to explore social change in other communities.

FINANCING THE GROWING JOURNAL

Before he left, Boyer succeeded in getting a grant from the Lannan Foundation that substantially changed the journal. It provided funding for administrative support. The new editor, Marjane Ambler, had freelanced for the journal since 1993. She lived in Mancos, Colorado. Since the magazine always had been published in the editor's home, the journal moved to southwest Colorado, near the Navajo Reservation and two Ute reservations, which made it easier for the journal to recruit Indian staff and adjunct staff. In 1998, with help from the Kellogg Foundation's grant to AIHEC, the journal moved into its permanent home, a Victorian-era house in Mancos.

Prior to her work at the journal, Ambler had "boot strapped" another nonprofit publication, serving as an editor of the *High Country News* but also helping to promote subscriptions to keep the newspaper alive. The Lannan grant made it possible for the journal for the first time to hire a full-time person to market subscriptions and sell advertising. After some initial turnover, the journal hired Felicity Broennan (then Kurth) in 1997. She was followed by Rachael Marchbanks as the marketing manager.

While most scholarly journals do not devote a lot of effort to marketing, the journal staff and the Tribal College Journal Advisory Board recognized the importance of attracting a larger constituency for the tribal colleges and universities. The mission statement adopted by the advisory board stated, "On behalf of the American Indian Higher Education Consortium's member tribal colleges and universities, we provide information for everyone interested in American Indian higher education. Our culture-based publication addresses subjects important to the future of American Indian and Alaska Native communities utilizing both journalistic and scholarly articles."

Few people knew that tribal colleges existed, and fewer still understood their significance. When the tribal college founders initially approached Congress in 1970s, one member told Sinte Gleska College President Lionel Bordeaux, "You Indians are good with your hands. Why don't you forget about colleges and get into the chicken business?"[5]

By the 1990s, the college administrators rarely encountered such blatant racism. However, they sometimes spent hours explaining other questions. Sending the journal to members of Congress and College Fund donors was not enough. Tribal college administrators constantly struggled with people at federal agencies, mainstream universities, accreditation agencies, and state legislatures who did not understand why tribal colleges existed. Why can't Indian and other local students attend mainstream universities? Isn't this a form of segregation? Doesn't the federal government take care of all the financial needs of Indian students? Why don't students graduate in two years and immediately get jobs? Why is there still high unemployment on reservations with tribal colleges? Wouldn't Indians be better off if reservations were abolished? Are these real colleges?

The tribal colleges depended upon their publication to tell their story. They could not expect readers to find the journal. Finding and keeping subscribers in this difficult market took resources. The journal placed advertisements in other publications, sent journals with presidents when they spoke at conferences, and conducted direct mail campaigns at least once a year.

To make it attractive to readers and advertisers, the journal added color pages and high quality photographs and hired talented American Indian-owned design firms (G+G Advertising in 1995 and Nakota Designs in 2002). Kurth and Marchbanks discovered that many advertisers wanted to reach the journal's audience. Federal agencies and mainstream universities sought to recruit students and faculty. Tribal colleges wanted to publicize their programs and new initiatives to potential supporters and student prospects. Others wanted to sell products or services to the tribal colleges. The increasing ad revenues supported most of the increasing costs.

The Tribal College Journal Advisory Board wrestled with advertising policies. How much advertising should there be? Should the journal accept advertisements from casinos? Tobacco companies? The Central Intelligence Agency? Ultimately, the advisory board members established an open policy, saying they did not want to be in the business of censoring which choices their students and other readers could make. The advisory board initially limited the amount of advertising in the journal (30% advertising/70% editorial). Later (spring 2004) this percentage of advertising was raised to 40% so that the journal could better support itself.

Reader research in recent years found—somewhat to the staff's surprise—that members of focus groups specifically mentioned advertising as a reason for reading the journal. Readers (even those with terminal degrees) at focus groups said they appreciated the journalistic style and accessibility. Readership statistics showed that 61% of the journals went to tribal colleges, 18% to individuals, 8% to other organizations, 6% to schools, 4% to government organizations, and 3% to libraries. In later years, the journal had subscribers in a dozen foreign countries, including many from Canada.

ROLE OF TRIBAL COLLEGE JOURNAL ADVISORY BOARD

Initially, the advisory board acted primarily as editorial advisors, helping the editor to select themes and article topics. In 1998, the College Fund board began to question the amount of money being spent sending the journal to its donors. The costs of printing and postage for each donor copy were growing, and the number of donors was also growing rapidly. Focus groups held by the fund indicated that some readers did not want a lot of money spent on gifts for them; they wanted the money spent on scholarships.

The discussion became a defining period for the journal partly because it forced the Tribal College Journal Advisory Board to become much more actively involved in the journal's business. The College Fund board asked the journal staff to prepare a five-year business plan, which was completed and adopted by the advisory board and by the full AIHEC board in 1998.

The business plan analyzed the potential for future revenue from selling advertising, subscriptions, and back issues and concluded that while growth was likely, the journal was unlikely to ever be fully self-supporting.[6] Its primary mission was serving the tribal colleges' needs, not making money. This conclusion provoked a serious discussion amongst all the tribal college presidents on the AIHEC board. It gave the board members another opportunity to discuss whether it was important to them to have a journal that required a heavy subsidy.

After a lengthy and sometimes heated discussion at the July 1998 AIHEC Board meeting, the members decided they wanted the journal to continue. They passed a resolution saying that the costs of the journal would be distributed among four entities (self-generated revenue, AIHEC, the College Fund, and tribal colleges).[7] Four years later, the College Fund felt compelled by increasing costs to discontinue sending the journal to its donors.[8]

The College Fund's decision made the journal more dependent upon AIHEC; the tribal colleges; and its own sales of advertising, subscriptions, web advertising, and back issues. AIHEC increased its subsidy, and more tribal colleges started taking a bigger role in helping to support the journal by taking out ads and purchasing more subscriptions.

Like the tribal colleges, the journal staff always had stretched each dollar: The editor and her husband arranged family camping trips around visits to the tribal colleges; the staff donated furniture and equipment; and they relied upon volunteers to help prepare renewal mailings. After the 2002–2003 financial crisis, the staff tightened the journal's belt even more and found a more economical printer. The staff's efforts and the tribal colleges' support paid off. While the journal only produced enough revenue to cover 44% of its costs in Fiscal Year 2002, this was up to 82% four years later in 2006 with the other 18% provided by AIHEC.

Looking back, the College Fund support had helped the journal grow during a critical period of time, perhaps making the difference between life and death for the fledgling publication. It had also contributed to the journal's editorial mission. The editors addressed articles to the general public rather than an insider audience. When the journal was no longer sent to College Fund donors, the impact on the content was minimal. By then, the audience already included many people from the general public.

Despite the number of readers from outside the tribal college community, the Tribal College Journal Advisory Board did not want the journal to avoid potentially embarrassing topics. This was their magazine, and they insisted that the journal cover certain topics critical to them. As a result, the journal covered subjects such as lessons learned from bad college investments and the politics of board/college relations in Indian communities.

EVOLVING EDITORIAL MISSION

By 2006, the journal had grown from its initial 24 pages to 64 pages, but the number of colleges had expanded, too, from 25 to 37. The programs at the colleges increased: In 2006, eight offered accredited four-year degrees, and two offered accredited masters' degrees. They were at the vanguard of new education technology. With the help of AIHEC and the College Fund, many had new campuses, some of which were designed as "green" campuses, using dramatically less energy and water.

There were never enough journal pages to cover all of them. The journal continued to serve many purposes and audiences. It periodically carried articles about the history of the tribal college movement, such as the winter 2002 issue (Vol. 14, N.2), which was devoted to the 30th anniversary of AIHEC. It also printed memorials for historic leaders of the movement. By the late '90s, the journal hired journalists to interview the presidents about these and other topics, rather than depending upon the busy presidents to write such articles themselves. Nevertheless, some tribal college presidents continued to write some of the most requested articles for the journal, such as Dr. James Shanley, Dr. Joe McDonald, Dr. Richard Littlebear, Cheryl Crazy Bull, and Dr. Karen Swisher.

Few articles in later years addressed "Tribal College 101." By that time, AIHEC Central had begun producing documents that explained the reasons for tribal colleges, such as *Tribal Colleges: An Introduction* (AIHEC, 1999). Boyer had published a second report for the Carnegie Foundation (*Native American Colleges: Progress and Prospects*, Jossey-Bass Inc. Publishers, 1997). And the College Fund also raised the public's awareness of the tribal college movement. However, the journal continued to serve as a clearinghouse sometimes for researchers and funders with questions about tribal colleges. For example, in 2005, the journal staff met with a journal subscriber from Switzerland whose organization had been sending financial contributions to certain tribal colleges and wanted to expand that role.

Initially the journal had published a separate journal with student creative writing. Beginning in summer 1999, this was incorporated into *Tribal College Journal* in an annual student edition, mailed for the first time to regular subscribers. Most readers responded positively, saying the students' writing gave them insights into the students' thoughts and feelings and into what tribal colleges provided for them, as well as appreciation for the students' artistic expression.

The Tribal College Journal Advisory Board wanted the journal to emphasize cultural topics. They felt the journal should show case best practices in developing cultural curriculum and culturally appropriate operating practices, from leave policies to architecture. They also wanted the journal to serve their faculty; a majority was non-Indian at some institutions. Each college's mission required the faculty to integrate culture into the curriculum, and the journal devoted many pages over the years to models for indigenizing education. Sitting Bull College instructor Lanniko Lee said the journal served as a "mentor of the desk" for faculty.

Tribal colleges became increasingly involved in international indigenous education over the years. The first journal focusing upon this topic was in fall 1991. Then in 1999 the W.K. Kellogg Foundation arranged a historic meeting in Hawaii between the Maori higher education leaders from New Zealand and tribal college leaders. This meeting led to several exchange visits and eventually in August 2002 to the formation of the World Indigenous Higher Education Consortium. SGU President Lionel Bordeaux served as one of the founding co-chairs of this international organization, and he was followed in 2005 by another tribal college president, Dr. James Shanley. As this relationship developed, the journal covered the global exchange of ideas, most notably, perhaps, WINHEC's indigenous accreditation process (Vol. 15, N.3), a model that could help achieve a long-standing dream of AIHEC founders.

FUTURE

Through the years, the journal has reflected the issues shaping the tribal college movement in that era and the resources available to the colleges at that time. Inevitably, it also reflected each editor's own interests, strengths, and weaknesses. In the future, the journal will continue to explore how best to fulfill its expanding role while staying afloat financially.

Despite their growing sophistication, the tribal colleges' and universities' financial struggles persist. Their prestige has improved due in part to the efforts of AIHEC, the American Indian College Fund, and the journal. However, they still frequently have to prove their credibility to some government officials and mainstream institutions.

At an AIHEC strategic planning meeting in 2004, tribal college presidents said they wanted AIHEC to begin publishing books. Although most of the tribal colleges produce their own curriculum materials, language tapes, and tribal histories, only a few (such as Diné College and Salish Kootenai College) offer them beyond their own reservations. With its network of editors, proofreaders, copyeditors, printers, and designers, *Tribal College Journal* could serve this function, providing another avenue for increasing the colleges' credibility while possibly also increasing revenue for the journal.

The journal covered research and the Native philosophy of scholarship as themes in several issues during both Boyer's and Ambler's tenure. Refereed research papers never played a central role in the journal. The journal had more success writing about research than publishing any leading-edge research models. Perhaps covering research issues achieves the colleges' goals without requiring the lengthy, scholarly articles. With limited pages to work with, being a hybrid between journalism and research may not be a practical or workable concept.

Future Tribal College Journal Advisory Boards and staff will continue to deal with the persistent question of audience. The journal provides boxes of magazines to the tribal colleges and universities at cost, but the number of copies ordered each year varies widely from institution to institution, depending upon their financial resources. At some colleges, the faculty and students depend upon the library to provide them with access. Others purchase hundreds of copies and make them widely available.

Student readership is limited both by this access problem and by the lack of student writing in three-fourths of the issues each year. Although *Tribal College Journal* is the de facto archive for the tribal college movement, access to back issues is limited. It is cataloged by several online companies, such as EBSCO HOST, Ethnic NewsWatch, and LexisNexis, but until its back issues are available online, researchers have difficulty searching and finding the articles they need. In the future, the journal might choose to publish online exclusively, but reader surveys indicate that current readers depend upon the printed copy.

Through the 17 years of its history, the journal has covered broad themes of concern to tribal communities, such as reforming K–12 education, contemporary heroes, sovereignty, AIDS and HIV, leadership, and agriculture. Most of the feature articles have focused on tribal colleges, but many have not. Some departments (such as the On Campus Department) are designed to cover primarily the tribal colleges and their affiliated organizations while others (such as the Resource Guide) serve all higher education audiences.

In recent years, other national magazines have emerged that cover minority education. WINHEC began publishing an international journal online. When these other magazines carry stories about tribal colleges, they deliver the tribal college story to additional readers, which is a good thing. At the same time, such magazines compete for the same advertisers and subscribers as the journal.

While challenges always exist, it is something of a miracle for AIHEC to have kept its journal alive for 17 years. In the media world, the list of publications that fold far outnumbers those that survive.[9] After 17 years, it is still possible that one tribal college will.

NOTES

1. AIHEC Board of Directors meeting minutes, Nov 14, 1989.
2. AIHEC's Denver office had closed in 1983 when the organization lost its grant funding. It wasn't until October 1994 that the consortium established a permanent office by purchasing an office building on the Potomac River near Washington, DC.
3. In 2000, the journal was redesigned with TCJ as the registered trademark.
4. Later when Paul Boyer suggested setting up as a separate nonprofit magazine, the AIHEC board decided that the magazine should be part of the AIHEC organization, a department of the consortium.
5. *Tribal College Journal, 14*(2).
6. In fact, according to a 2003 survey by the American Society of Association Executives, most association publications receive heavy subsidies from their associations and 73% are not mandated to generate profits.
7. AIHEC Board of Directors meeting minutes 7/98.
8. At the time, the College Fund subscribers represented two-third of the total journal subscribers. It stopped sending the journal to donors in December 2002 and stopped giving an annual gift in December 2003.
9. Amongst American Indian publications, two of the casualties were the *Navajo Journal of Education* (Fall 1983–Spring 1996) and *Native Americas* (1995–2004), a quarterly at Cornell University covering the Western Hemisphere, which stopped publishing after it was taken over by First Nations Development Institute.

CHAPTER 15

TECHNOLOGY AT THE TCUs

Carrie L. Billy and Al Kuslikis

INTRODUCTION

For centuries, the indigenous people of the Americas—American Indians—have demonstrated remarkable resilience, ability to adapt, and even a little acknowledged capacity to develop and use new technologies. Over a millennium ago, the Anasazi of the Southwest experimented with different combinations of clay, sand, and water, eventually initiating a new era in the storage and transportation of goods: ceramic bowls, pots, and dishes—indispensable tools of everyday life and a continuous source of innovation as more specialized forms of ceramic were developed for specific social, ceremonial, and trade uses. The ongoing refinement of ceramic technology may have helped move Anasazi culture to developments such as the complex grouping of communities that inhabited Chaco Canyon in New Mexico and hundreds of smaller communities that depended on the trade networks supported by the people of Chaco Canyon.

Today, just as centuries ago, new technologies are expanding the range of possibilities for participating in a rapidly expanding horizon of educational, economic, and community-building opportunities. The current range of technologies and their applications are broad, and just as before, the future of Indian Country will be intimately bound up with how new technologies will be adopted, and adapted to meet the needs of American

Tradition and Culture in the Millennium: Tribal Colleges and Universities, pages 201–208
Copyright © 2009 by Information Age Publishing
All rights of reproduction in any form reserved.

Indian people and their communities. Tribal Colleges and Universities are playing a pivotal role in the process of innovation and adaptation by using technology to reach more students, serve their communities, conduct research, and build an infrastructure of opportunity for American Indians. Importantly, Tribal Colleges are also exploring strategies for using technology to strengthen and preserve language and traditional culture.

Southwestern Indian Polytechnic Institute (SIPI) in Albuquerque, NM, exemplifies the pace at which Tribal Colleges are adopting new technologies. SIPI's Monte Montieth, Education Program Specialist (Technology), recently told the story of his school's growth: In 1993, the Institute had less than eight computers on its entire campus. Through several grants and funding sources, the institute tied all of its campus buildings together via fiber to enable Internet access, putting a computer lab in every academic building and all the residence halls. Today, SIPI has a robust technology infrastructure with more than 200 computers—a 1:4 ratio of computers to students, all of which are networked and connected to the Internet. Through distance learning, SIPI provides classes and training opportunities to reservations throughout the Southwest. SIPI recently opened a state-of-the-art science and technology building which houses an engineering program in which students are working on robotics projects in collaboration with partners such as NASA's Jet Propulsion Lab.

This success, like much of the success of the Tribal Colleges and Universities, is due to a simple, yet resilient, vision that Tribal College leaders have identified for the future. Almost a decade ago, a handful of Tribal College presidents and staff refused to accept the "digital divide" as in inescapable reality for Indian Country. Rather, they saw an opportunity. They shared their vision and growing awareness about emerging technologies with the broader Tribal College community, who together initiated a planning process intended to move Tribal Colleges and communities toward a "Circle of Prosperity," in which tribal traditions and new technologies could be woven together to build stronger and more sustainable communities.

Through a series of meetings in 1999 and 2000, Tribal College presidents identified two goals, which are the core of AIHEC's technology initiative:

1. To enable each Tribal College to improve its technology infrastructure in a manner that fulfills its mission and objectives related to the needs of its students and community.
2. To develop tribally and culturally centered applications of information technology.

To achieve these goals, these presidents reached out to 11 major local, national, and international stakeholder groups and invited more than 150 representatives to participate in a "Prosperity Game" event. The Prosperity

Game is a fast-paced, interactive simulation of real-world negotiation and relationship brokering processes developed by Sandia National Laboratory from strategic war games, and is designed to create and sustain productive change through strategy development and commitment by participants to specific action steps. During the three-day Prosperity Game in October 1999 and follow-up meetings, participants developed the "Tribal College Framework for Community Technology," a comprehensive planning document that includes strategic partnerships, resources, and tools to help create locally-based economic and social opportunities mediated by information technology and use of the Internet.

TRIBAL COLLEGE FRAMEWORK FOR COMMUNITY TECHNOLOGY

To achieve the identified goals for TCU technology, AIHEC developed eight strategy areas within the TCU Technology Framework.

Leadership & Coordination: To guide the technology initiative, AIHEC established a technology office, largely through support from the National Aeronautics and Space Administration (NASA). The office's functions include strategic technology planning, initiative development and partnership building.

Continuous strategic technology planning is absolutely essential to any effort on the part of higher education institutions to effectively respond to rapidly-evolving opportunities and challenges associated with emerging technologies. At the very minimum, colleges must ensure that their academic programs are keeping up with new developments in science and technology. Through support from NASA and NSF, AIHEC has been providing strategic planning expertise to help ensure that colleges develop strategic technology plans that are community-based and integrated with the institutions' overall strategic plans. These plans in turn are helping to guide AIHEC's technology initiative into the future.

Infrastructure: To help ensure that resources exist to develop and sustain a technology infrastructure at each Tribal College, AIHEC and their Circle of Prosperity partners worked to establish NSF-TCUP, which has led to more than $50 million in science education and technology-related funding for the Tribal Colleges between fiscal years 2001 and 2006. AIHEC also worked with the Department of Education to ensure a strong technology focus to the Tribal College Institutional Development program, and worked to ensure $3–4 million/year in technology and science equipment funding for Tribal Colleges through the Department of Defense.

Navajo Technical College in Crownpoint, New Mexico is implementing their "Wireless Internet to the Hogan" project, which will effectively saturate the entire New Mexico portion of the Navajo Nation with wireless broadband Internet access to every home, school, business, and government office. The project will establish an OC3 (155 megabit per second) wireless connection to the Lambda Rail (a national 10 gigabit per second IP network to support internetworking and research) from Albuquerque, New Mexico. From Crownpoint, using a network of microwave transmitters, broadband connectivity will be provided to 31 chapterhouses, or community centers/town halls. Local transmitters will allow connectivity to be radiated out from community centers to schools, medical clinics, hospitals, police departments, firehouses, and homes within a 15 to 30-mile radius of the chapterhouses. Communication, education, and business possibilities that were not possible just a few years ago are becoming a reality for thousands of Navajos, many of whom still cannot afford telephone service to their homes.

EDUCATION AND HUMAN RESOURCES

STEM Program Development

NSF's Tribal Colleges and Universities Program (TCUP) is providing significant support to Tribal Colleges in planning and implementing science, technology, engineering, and mathematics (STEM) program improvements. With support from TCUP, Tribal Colleges are able to carry out comprehensive community-based planning to identify local and regional science and engineering workforce needs and priorities, and develop or augment their STEM programs accordingly.

Salish Kootenai College is emerging as a leader in the sciences. With the assistance of NASA Goddard Space Flight Center, SKC is developing a B.S. in Computer Engineering degree program which is expected to officially open for student admissions in 2007. This new degree program builds on SKC's successful associate-level engineering transfer preparation program, and will be the first baccalaureate-level engineering degree program at a Tribal College. Currently SKC offers baccalaureate degrees in business, environmental science, forestry, information technology, nursing, and social work.

Distance Learning

Most TCUs are located in geographically isolated areas at some distance from population centers, and it is not unusual for students to travel more than a hundred miles commuting to the campus. For American Indian students living in rural and remote areas of the country, distance learning is providing access to a range and quality of educational services that had been simply unavailable before. Currently, 15 TCUs offer distance learning courses offered either asynchronously over the Internet, or synchronously through satellite, interactive television, or the Internet.

AIHEC Virtual Library

AIHEC is working to expand and solidify the AIHEC Virtual Library—a continually updated database of Web-accessible American Indian resources that was developed in partnership with the University of Michigan's School of Information. The AIHEC Virtual Library has been an important resource for TCU faculty and students, and AIHEC plans to build on its strengths, of which the most important is the collaborative effort that made it possible. The future for the AIHEC Virtual Library will be the integration of library, museum, and archival services, so that faculty, students, and community members will be able to access historical, cultural, and geographic information and data from one location. Most significantly, much of the content housed in the AIHEC VL will be generated locally, by community members for whom the information and data resources have real-life educational and economic relevance.

Partnerships: AIHEC has developed strong partnerships with national organizations, the private sector, and key federal agencies. Some examples include: the Alliance for Equity in Higher Education, IBM, Cisco, and Microsoft, NASA, NSF, DoD, USED, USDA, and EPA.

AIHEC's partnership with NASA has been particularly fruitful. Through a five-year cooperative agreement, NASA is supporting modest infrastructure and STEM program improvement efforts targeting critical areas of need, such as a climate control system for the server room at Crownpoint Institute of Technology. The NASA cooperative agreement also supports the Summer Research Experience program in which faculty and students from Tribal Colleges are spending 8–10 weeks working on research, engineering and education projects in collaboration with NASA professional staff. This partnership is a strong example of both partners furthering their respective missions through coordination and resource-sharing.

Research and Development: AIHEC is building research capacity through participation in the Minority Serving Institutions Cyberinfrastructure Empowerment Coalition (MSI-CIEC) project, a national effort to bring e-Science resources to MSIs through training, mentorships, and collaborative research opportunities. Partners in this effort include the Hispanic Association of Colleges and Universities, the National Alliance for Equity in higher Education (NAFEO), National Computational Science Alliance, the

San Diego Supercomputing Center, and Indiana University's Community Grids Laboratory.

The emerging cyberinfrastructure—a dynamic assemblage of linked computational resources, data, and instrumentation distributed throughout the world—is setting the conditions for a revolution in the way science research and education is conducted. Researchers (and students) with a connection to the Internet are able to access data from an observatory (or a tectonic sensor), ship the data to a computational facility, conduct an analysis, and visualize and publish the results, all from the comfort of their own customized research or learning portal. Teams of researchers are able to collaborate on large research projects, coordinating research tasks and sharing research resources so that no single researcher, or student, is constrained by the lack of research infrastructure at their home institution.

In an effort to accelerate the pace at which Tribal Colleges enter the world of cyberinfrastructure-faciliated e-Science, AIHEC is partnering with HACU and NAFEO on the MSI Cyberinfrastructure Empowerment Coalition project, intended to support MSI faculty in adopting cyberinfrastructure tools for STEM research and science education. Through special training events, support for participation in national conferences, and mentoring relationships with leaders in the cyberinfrastructure community, MSI-CIEC is helping to ensure that the Tribal Colleges incorporate cyberinfrastructure resources into the STEM programs and prepare their students for the world of e-Science.

An important focus of MSI-CIEC is to support colleges in acquiring their own high performance computing facilities, which can contribute to the global computing capability. In this way, TCUs can become not only recipients, but also important providers of computational resources necessary to support the national research agenda.

Culture and Community: Through our "Indigenous Digital Communities Initiative" (IDCI), AIHEC is linking with national and international Native technology initiatives, including projects with the National Museum of the American Indian. The goal of IDCI is to build capacity among native people to use emerging technologies in building partnerships, sharing resources, developing strategies for preserving and promoting indigenous cultures, developing community economies, and stimulating knowledge creation and tech transfer.

The colleges' emphasis upon culture and tribal traditions is clear. For example, as part of the National Science Foundation's Rural Systemic Initiative (RSI) and NASA programs to improve science and math in the K–12 schools, Cankdeska Cikana Community College in Fort Totten, ND, makes available to local teachers a state-of-the-art Star Lab Portable Planetarium that includes Native American Mythology curricula on the relationship between the stars and the tribal histories of the Navajo, Shoshoni, Blackfoot,

Cherokee, Hopi, and Algonquin Indian tribes. In the lab, as students learn the stories of First Man and First Woman, Spider God, and the Great Bear, they see a direct connection to the stars, astronomy, and math. Cankdeska Cikana Community College is working to adapt this curriculum to focus on the Spirit Lake Tribe's legends and stories.

In Minnesota, Fond du Lac Tribal and Community College is leading an effort to develop a multinational project that blends traditional science and technology. Focusing on indigenous sustainable development, the college is partnering with Maori Tribal Colleges in New Zealand. The goal is to build a collaborative Web-based learning environment that will enable American Indian and Maori Tribal College faculty and students to participate in both "real-time" courses and asynchronous courses that involve cross-cultural case studies. Eventually, indigenous people worldwide will be able to offer and complete educational and training programs that have been designed to address their unique cultural, social, and economic issues and opportunities.

On the Pine Ridge Indian Reservation, concern over the potential loss of tribal stories, history, and science prompted Oglala Lakota College to begin using technology to collect, store, and catalogue the lessons of their elders. Using modern music, film, and data collection strategies, a team of faculty and staff developed a standard interface, deployment platform, and secure database so that the elders' stories could be collected and stored digitally *and securely.* The team is partnering with a local company on this project, which now includes a training program so that other Tribal Colleges and tribal communities can use the lessons learned by Oglala Lakota College.

AIHEC, working with the National Museum of the American Indian, eventually could link these projects and other national and international Native technology projects through an effort called the "Indigenous Digital Communities Initiative" (IDCI). The goal of IDCI is to build capacity among Native people to use emerging technologies for preserving and promoting indigenous cultures. Emphasis is on sustainable technology applications, and on creating new opportunities for reaching a Circle of Prosperity.

Policy: AIHEC regularly testifies before Congressional committees and key NSF advisory boards on technology. The AIHEC STEM committee is drafting a model "American Indian STEM Workforce Act," and we will develop model language for a technology title within the Tribally Controlled Colleges and University Assistance Act.

Resource Development: Since the *Circle of Prosperity* was initiated, the Tribal Colleges have been very successful in receiving support for the development of both infrastructure and academic programs. Important sources of funding have included the NSF-TCUP program, NASA's TCU program, the Department of Defense Instrumentation Program for Tribal Colleges and Universities, and the Department of Education Title III Program.

AIHEC will continue working to expand these initiatives and create new opportunities through models like the American Indian Technology Workforce Development Act and new partnerships with the private sector. Always, the focus will be on sustaining technology funding and creating new opportunities for reaching a *Circle of Prosperity*.

CONCLUSION

The tribal colleges have emerged as technology leaders in Indian Country, exactly as was called for in the Tribal College Framework for Community Technology. They are creating the infrastructure and setting the stage for tribal communities to come online in the global economy as providers of goods and services, not simply consumers, and important generators of intellectual capital, not simply its beneficiaries.

Ten years ago, no one could have predicted how rapidly the tribal colleges would adopt new technologies, and thereby how much they would accomplish. Today, it is even more difficult to predict where they will be in another four years. In the face of uncertainty, and the seemingly limitless reach of the emerging "cyber-world," the tribal colleges draw on the wisdom and vision of the elders for guidance in navigating toward an evolving *Circle of Prosperity*.

CHAPTER 16

TRIBAL COLLEGES
AND UNIVERSITIES

From Where We Are
to Where We Might Go

Cheryl Crazybull

INTRODUCTION

Our future as tribal colleges and universities lies in our continued understanding of our tribal ways of living and in the continued acquisition and teaching of tribal knowledge. Remembering the vision and intentions of the founders of the tribal colleges forms this understanding. Our founders who are community elders, leaders and spiritual people intended that the way of life of each tribal nation be the foremost educational mission of each tribal college.

When the tribal colleges and universities provide education and services to students and communities, we are doing so to meet the particular goals and needs of each student. This leads us toward building tribal nations that both honor and practice traditional ways and which thrive in contemporary society. We have already demonstrated our capability to

Tradition and Culture in the Millennium: Tribal Colleges and Universities, pages 209–217
Copyright © 2009 by Information Age Publishing
All rights of reproduction in any form reserved.

provide teachers, social workers, entrepreneurs, program directors and community and elected leaders. The education and services that we provide continue to build the professional and vocational workforce in our communities. We find that our efforts also build families, communities and organizations through our commitment to cultural preservation, wellness and healthy living.

At TCUs we have to know students intimately—we have to understand who they are and where they come from. We have to help each student from where they are in order to be successful. All of the strategies that must be used to provide access and to assure retention have to be done in the context of our way of life and how we are preserving and restoring tribal language and cultural practices.

Throughout this book, prominent native educators and supporters of Indian education have shared the ways that tribal colleges have moved through western educational systems. The writers have described the successes and failures of the tribal colleges giving us examples of opportunities and best practices and advising on ways that we can continue to contribute to the pedagogy of teaching and learning and to the development of our tribal citizenry.

Tribal colleges are at a serious juncture in their development as we move toward our 40th anniversary in 2008. Economic and social conditions in our tribal communities are not improving while our population continues to grow. In many of our communities more then half of our population is under the age of 25. More and more of our tribal citizens find themselves moving away from our traditional homelands into urban settings for employment and access to services. Alcohol and drug abuse continue to take a terrible toll especially on the young as families are severely damaged by addiction and violence. Educational literacy despite the impact of our tribally controlled institutions has not universally improved. Most of our college students still come to us unprepared for the college experience.

At an institutional level, tribal colleges continue to struggle with an incredible lack of stable federal and private funding. Few institutions have the resources and access to funding that builds stable operating support through endowments or innovative entrepreneurial activities. Faculty and staff who work at the tribal colleges demonstrate a deep commitment to the education of native people because it is not the salaries and benefits that attract them.

Despite the continued barriers that in most situations would cause educational institutions to close down, tribal colleges continue to thrive. This occurs because there remains in the tribal college movement, a cadre of individuals who hold fast to the founders' intention of rebuilding tribal nations through tribal colleges—through native education.

PRESERVING AND TEACHING TRIBAL WAYS OF LIVING

Tribal colleges continue their leadership role as the places where preservation and instruction in native languages, culture and history are carried out with the active participation of community-based tribal scholars. As technology becomes increasingly available in our communities, it becomes a tool that provides native language access to a greater number of people. Increased Internet access and public access channels on cable television will serve as a means to bring language to our younger generations whose comfort level with technology is increasingly natural.

Cultural practices, in the context of understanding our history and how we evolve our practices in light of contemporary conditions, are a critical part of the evolution of the tribal college movement. TCUs must help tribal citizens preserve those characteristics and practices that make up our unique tribal identities. It is important that we continue to maintain our focus on our identity, as it existed prior to European contact and before the impact of war and treaty making. This is not to imply that our identity has not or will not continue to evolve; rather, we must make conscious decisions about our traditional practices in light of our understanding of our history. We should not allow "identity decisions" to be imposed upon us or to come about as the result of benign neglect on our part. Decisions about whom we are should be made with intention.

Two of the most important aspects of tribal identity that are deeply grounded in our languages and in our cultural practices are relationships and stewardship. Our languages and customary practices define our interactions with family members, extended family members, with other tribes and with others of different cultures and races. Our stewardship of our grandmother earth is inherently described through our language traditions. TCUs should ensure the cultural integrity of what we teach in our classrooms and through our community relationships in terms of personal and social relationships and stewardship of our natural resources.

As we move further and further away from the direct understanding of our traditional practices and our languages with the passing of elders whose ancestors lived at a time when we did not have contact with Europeans, it is critical that the leadership, faculty and students in tribal colleges become more vigilant about our instructional practices and the knowledge that we are passing on.

Tribal colleges must also find ways to recognize and support the work of tribal scholars who are often untrained in western methodologies and whose work deeply reflects our cultural and religious knowledge. As we become increasing exposed to western institutions, tribal educators and researchers become more adept at the use of western methodologies to conduct and report research. This adeptness can often come at the expenses of our traditional beliefs and practices. It is critical that TCUs actively continue to develop community-based research practices and evaluation methods that are appropriate to our cultural knowledge and experience.

EDUCATIONAL AND LAND GRANT MISSIONS

Of course, tribal colleges were founded for the purpose of providing post-secondary education to tribal citizens living in our reservation communities. In order to fulfill this post-secondary mission, TCUs have broadened their services to include developmental education, adult education, GED, community education as well as a variety of technical and vocational programs. This expansion of our mission has been necessary to serve the needs of our communities. The vast majority of our students are unprepared for a college education or for various reasons do not complete high school. In order to ensure their access to a college education, TCUs find themselves allocating resources toward the preparation of our students. We also find that ourselves serving broader community-based needs in order to build community literacy and to ensure support for education throughout our population.

TCUs will continue to expand their services in community education and college readiness. Opportunities for high quality partnerships in early childhood and K–12 education must be expanded in order for us to impact the readiness of our future students. Building a seamless educational experience from infancy to adulthood is possible in those tribal communities with early childhood programs such as tribal Headstart in partnership with K–12 tribal schools and tribal colleges. The development of model relationships inclusive of teacher training but much broader in scope and delivery is critical to the success of endeavors in this area. It will be difficult for TCUs to continue to allocate resources to GED and remedial programs without the strong support of funding agencies and expansion of partnerships with other educational entities.

More and more tribal colleges will also advance their own development by expanding into four-year degree programs and eventually graduate programs following the lead of our pioneer institutions in this area—Sinte Gleska University and Oglala Lakota College. Both of these institutions have demonstrated that commitment and willingness can lead to high quality professional degree programs despite limited resources. Our communities increasingly demand access to four-year degrees in order to ensure our own capacity to lead our organizations and to steward our resources. This is a natural evolution of our vision as post-secondary institutions. Many tribal colleges will find limitations of resources and population that might prevent such developments, making it increasingly likely that some TCUs will emerge as the providers of junior/senior level programs as well as graduate programs.

Land grant status has been in existence for the majority of the tribal colleges since 1994. This status granted us increased access to USDA programs and resources allowing us to expand the research and educational services of our institutions in natural resources, environmental science, and many other programs related to the land and the animal and plant nations. We have a long way to go to achieve parity with our sister institutions—the 1862 and 1890 land grant colleges and universities. Fiscal parity is critical to the capacity building needed in our institutions to support community-based research, leadership and resource management programs and community education through extension services. Increased opportunities for private partnerships and for access to resources from tribes who are engaged in natural resources development will open doors for tribal colleges to better serve community-based needs.

ACCREDITATION, ASSESSMENT AND FINDING OUR OWN ACCOUNTABILITY

There is a close link between our experiences with the preservation of our traditional knowledge and with the experiences of accreditation and assessment. In order for tribal nations to survive with intact resources and unique identities, we had to be accountable to each other, to ourselves and to Creator. Accreditation is a similar experience translated into contemporary terms and using contemporary methods. Native people always had standards of accountability and peer review. What has been most difficult for us have been the translations of our traditional and community-based approaches into the frameworks established to primarily serve western models of educational delivery. This has forced us to adapt our models of delivery to the western model.

TCUs have the intellectual capacity to create their own accreditation process. What has been lacking has been the financial resources and the mainstream support needed to bring this effort to fruition. It is time. Over the next few years, tribal educators with the support of AIHEC and other national Indian organizations will find themselves increasingly called upon to explain their successes and their failures. Our own accreditation process would ensure that our explanations are delivered in our voice and in the context of our understanding of accountability.

Educators at tribal colleges are the experts in the education of native students especially adult students including what is historically the non-traditional student, over the age of 24 with children. At a recent national conference on student assessment, the presentation on native student retention and cultural studies was attended by tribal college staff and a few individuals from native studies programs at mainstream institutions. Despite nearly 40 years of successfully educating Indian adults, TCUs are still not part of the mainstream discussion about student access and retention. It is critical that we promote the participation and research of our faculty and staff in order to be heard so that we may access increased resources to support our efforts.

TCUs and reservation-based education are not generally in the mainstream discussion about education even among those most committed to diversity and student access. The Department of Education, while supportive of the White House Initiative on Tribal Colleges and Universities and of AIHEC, failed to include a voice from the tribal higher education community in their study of education in the United States, this, despite that fact that more than 30,000 individuals come in contact with the tribal colleges as students in academic, vocational, community education and extension programs each year.

Through the efforts of AIHEC and the American Indian College Fund, TCUs have seen improvements in our participation and in our ability to define our own student success and our own research and evaluation methodologies. We are responsible for creating the link between those improvements and an impact on educational policy and practice in the United States.

LEADERSHIP AND MANAGEMENT OF HUMAN CAPITAL AND TRIBAL ASSETS

Throughout Indian Country many tribes are thriving economically resulting in increased access to development opportunities and a higher demand for good leaders and managers. TCUs are in a unique position to serve as providers of leadership development programs that focus on cultural competencies, human relations and organizational development. Many leadership programs in existence today focus on the framework of governance or management in areas such as federal/state/tribal relations or tribal justice systems or supervision. Helping our emerging and current leaders develop and retain their cultural practices in contemporary organizations and decision making environments is a natural fit for the tribal colleges where our access to tribal scholars and traditional knowledge is readily available every day.

TCUs can also create tribally specific decision making models that honor the teachings and practices of our traditional leadership and which bring a measure of accountability to the Creator and the expectations of our spiritual leaders and elders. Our students are a ready source of researchers and practitioners. They can gather the knowledge and information needed to develop tribally specific models, translate that knowledge for contemporary settings and help the community and elected leadership put those models into practice.

Decades of interaction with Western society and its organizations has caused us to replicate practices that are not suitable to our community life and our family relationships. TCUs can participate in policy development and organizational strategies that encourage the creation of systemic experiences that are more appropriate to the extended family-based governance of our tribal nations. We can also be models for the development of tribally specific and culturally relevant performance indicators that demonstrate to our communities, our funders and our constituents that we are good stewards of our resources and of the investments that they make in our communities.

The vast majority of reservations still have unemployment rates of 30% or higher even among those that are prospering through business development. While we have become more sophisticated as business leaders and entrepreneurs, there is still an incredible amount of work to be done. TCUs are a great place to invest resources for business development as we are among the longest standing tribal entities. TCUs have demonstrated the strength of tribally chartered, semi-independent organizations. In many ways, TCUs epitomize entrepreneurship on some of the poorest reservations in Indian Country. Tribal colleges will need to model business development through tribal-college owned businesses, through business incubators, through technology investment and through continued partnerships with national, regional and tribal enterprise organizations.

NATION BUILDING

We are already tribal nations—hundreds strong with thousands of citizens. Deep inside of each of us is our tribal identity—in some of us it emerges gradually, in others it is evident and present at all times, in still others we are still looking. Each tribe that has a tribal college has access to a particularly unique set of resources that can be used to strengthen tribal identity and to build the capacity of the tribe to govern itself. Self-governance goes beyond the decision-making of elected leadership into the realm of personal responsibility and accountability. Our tradition practices—ceremonial, social, economic, and in governance—are all about relationship and accountability to Creator.

To continue to build our tribal nations, TCUs must step into the arena of critical self-examination and analysis. We must put on our "thinking" hats and with prayer, good will and trust, we must look at our contemporary way of life within our understanding of what our traditional life would have been like. Through this informed process, we can explore creating systems that both honor and preserve our traditional teachings and which can function in a timely and thoughtful manner in today's society.

We face many challenges as tribes and as tribal colleges. With over half of our native populations living in urban and rural reservations, away from our traditional homelands, we are experiencing increasing loss of language and tribal identity. Third and fourth generations of relocated native people now live in our major cities. This makes the responsibility of our tribal governments even greater because they must use their limited resources to reach out to their citizens at many locations. We are becoming more and more of a global citizenry in our tribal nations.

WHAT THE FUTURE HOLDS FOR US?

One of the greatest challenges facing tribal nations is the decision to provide tribal education for its citizens including the decision as to whether or not to establish a tribal college. Many reservations have small populations making support of a stand-alone college financially difficult. Other reservations have competing nonnative institutions with long-standing tribal relationships. In some cases, these institutions have significant native populations. Retaining the identity of the tribal college movement will be an issue of debate among the tribal colleges, tribal governments and among educators. Historically tribal colleges possessed unique characteristics including the mission of tribal self-determination, serving a majority native student population and being located on an Indian reservation. As new institutions emerge, this definition becomes challenged. As competition for resources and students increases, the structure of a tribal college becomes an issue for consideration and debate. Distance learning can increase access but may not honor the desire of a tribe to have its own tribal college. Models of shared governance may become increasingly attractive in those circumstances. These issues will be debated and discussed for many years to come.

Our most important work lies in front of us. It is the day-to-day work of educating students who come to the tribal colleges filled with hope for a good education that will give them the skills and abilities that they need to take care of themselves and their families. It is the responsibility that we have as carriers of the vision of our ancestors to ensure that this education is solidly grounded in tribal identity. It is the responsibility that we have to be translators—to be those individuals who help bring our traditional knowledge into contemporary society for the use of our students today and for future generations.

TCUs face many financial and physical challenges. We don't have enough money or enough space. Many of our students struggle with access—with a lack of preparedness, insufficient financial resources or a lack of housing, childcare or transportation. Many of our communities despite improvements continue to struggle with unemployment and despair.

There are over hundreds of graduates of the tribal colleges. By facing the work that lies in front of us, we have already been successful. We will continue to be.

As the late Stanley Red Bird, founding Chairman of the Board of Directors of Sinte Gleska University, always said: *This is the way it must be.*

The Indian survived out open intention of wiping them out.
And since the tide has turned they have even weathered our good intentions
toward them, which can be more deadly.

—John Steinbeck

Breinigsville, PA USA
09 October 2009
225496BV00002B/1/P

9 781607 520009